BEYOND LIBERATION AND EXCELLENCE

Critical Studies in Education and Culture Series

Pedagogy and the Struggle for Voice: Issues of Language, Power, and Schooling for Puerto Ricans
Catherine E. Walsh

Learning Work: A Critical Pedagogy of Work Education
Roger I. Simon, Don Dippo, and Arleen Schenke

Cultural Pedagogy: Art/Education/Politics
David Trend

Raising Curtains on Education: Drama as a Site for Critical Pedagogy
Clar Doyle

Toward a Critical Politics of Teacher Thinking: Mapping the Postmodern
Joe L. Kincheloe

Building Communities of Difference: Higher Education in the Twenty-First Century
William G. Tierney

The Problem of Freedom in Postmodern Education
Tomasz Szkudlarek

Education Still under Siege: Second Edition
Stanley Aronowitz and Henry A. Giroux

Media Education and the (Re)Production of Culture
David Sholle and Stan Denski

Critical Pedagogy: An Introduction
Barry Kanpol

Coming Out in College: The Struggle for a Queer Identity
Robert A. Rhoads

Education and the Postmodern Condition
Michael Peters, editor

Critical Multiculturalism: Uncommon Voices in a Common Struggle
Barry Kanpol and Peter McLaren, editors

Beyond Liberation
and Excellence

Reconstructing the Public Discourse on Education

DAVID E. PURPEL and SVI SHAPIRO

Critical Studies in Education and Culture Series
Edited by Henry A. Giroux and Paulo Freire

Bergin & Garvey
Westport, Connecticut • London

Library of Congress Cataloging-in-Publication Data

Purpel, David E.
  Beyond liberation and excellence : reconstructing the public
discourse on education / David E. Purpel and Svi Shapiro.
      p.   cm.—(Critical studies in education and culture series,
  ISSN 1064–8615)
  Includes bibliographical references (p.   ) and index.
    ISBN 0–89789–416–2 (alk. paper). —ISBN 0–89789–417–0 (pbk. :
  alk. paper)
    1. Educational change—United States.   2. Education—Social
  aspects—United States.   3. Critical pedagogy—United States.
  I. Shapiro, H. Svi.   II. Title.   III. Series.
  LA210.P87   1995
  370.19′34—dc20   94–39191

British Library Cataloguing in Publication Data is available.

Library of Congress Catalog Card Number: 94–39191

ISBN: 0–89789–416–2
ISBN: 0–89789–417–0 (pbk.)
ISSN: 1064–8615

First published in 1995

Bergin & Garvey, 88 Post Road West, Westport, CT 06881
An imprint of Greenwood Publishing Group Inc.

Printed in the United States of America

∞™

The paper used in this book complies with the
Permanent Paper Standard issued by the National
Information Standards Organization (Z39.48–1984).

10 9 8 7 6 5 4 3 2 1

Copyright Acknowledgment

Grateful acknowledgment is given for permission to reprint Svi Shapiro,
"Educational Change, and the Crises of the Left: Toward a Postmodern
Educational Discourse," *Critical Multiculturalism*, edited by Barry
Kanpol and Peter McLaren (Westport, Conn.: Bergin & Garvey, 1995),
an imprint of Greenwood Publishing Group, Inc., Westport, CT.

To those engaged in making real our covenant
to create a just and loving community.

Contents

Series Foreword: Educational Reform with No Apologies

Educational reform has fallen upon hard times. The traditional assumption that schooling is fundamentally tied to the imperatives of citizenship designed to educate students to exercise leadership and public service has been eclipsed. Schooling is now the key institution for producing a professional, technically trained, credentialized worker for whom the demands of citizenship are subject to the vicissitudes of the marketplace and the commercial public sphere. During the Reagan and Bush eras, the deeper issues that frame the meaning, purpose, and use to which education might aspire were displaced by more vocational and pragmatic considerations.

The legacy of neoconservatism continues into the present in spite of the election of Bill Clinton, a moderate Democrat, to the presidency. Financial retrenchment and downsizing overshadow questions concerning social justice, equality, and community. Testing and standardization replace considerations of poverty, racial discrimination, and class inequalities and how they are reproduced by and affect the schools. Schooling and the language of educational reform have increasingly become more supportive of goals designed to train students for administrative jobs, produce new knowledge for business and the military, and reduce the art and politics of teaching to managerial and technical considerations.

In the popular press, a hysterical media points to political correctness and the violations accorded the foundations of Western culture waged by multiculturalists and academic progressives. At the same time, the guardians of Western civilization see no contradiction in their claim that public education be predicated on the virtues of a common culture rooted in the precepts of the Enlightenment while simultaneously arguing that language spoken at home by the children of immigrants, people of color, and subordinate groups is either illegal or un-American.

Of course, the war waged against the possibilities of an education wedded to the precepts of a real democracy is not merely ideological. Against the backdrop of reduced funding for public schooling, the call for privatization, vouchers, cultural uniformity, and choice, there is the often-ignored larger social reality of material power and oppression. Poverty is on the rise among children in the United States, with 20 percent of all children under the age of 18 living below the poverty line. Unemployment is growing at an alarming rate among youth, especially in the urban centers. Most disturbing about these social problems is that they have a decidedly racial overtone. Nearly half of all black children live below the poverty line, while the unemployment rate among black males is nearly double that of their white counterparts. While black bodies are policed and disciplined in and out of the nation's schools, conservative and liberal educators define education through the ethically limp discourse of achievement, standards, and global competitiveness.

In the world of policy making and talk-show politics, it has become increasingly clear that imperializing power goes hand in hand with monoculturalism, racism, class inequality, and censorship. June Jordan has argued that she sees "every root argument about public education turning upon definitions of sanity and insanity." She goes on to ask: "Shall we submit to ceaseless lies, fantastic misinformation, and fantastic omissions? Shall we agree to the erasure of our beleaguered, heterogeneous truth? Shall we embrace traditions of insanity and lose ourselves and the whole real world? . . . What does public education in a democratic state require?"[1]

While not aware of June Jordan's eloquent interrogations of public education, David E. Purpel and Svi Shapiro have framed this important book around a similar set of considerations. Attempting to address conflicting views of power, interpretation, affirmation, and critique, Purpel and Shapiro provide the theoretical signposts for a public discourse about education that is both prophetic and transformative. Eschewing traditional categories used by radicals, liberals, and conservatives, they successfully reveal the political and ethical implications of the cynicism and despair that has become endemic to the discourse of schooling. In its place, Purpel and Shapiro provide a language of hope that inextricably links the struggle over schooling to "overcoming our present social and cultural dangers." Approaching their task historically, contextually, and ethically, they provide new insights into the genesis of the language of educational reform while simultaneously offering valuable insights about how many of the current problems faced by schools, teachers, students, and parents can be addressed and transformed.

What is so refreshing about *Beyond Liberation and Excellence* is its attempt to analyze the shift to the ideological Right that public discourse has taken in the last decade and how such a discourse has contributed to a new authoritarianism and a sustained attack on both the welfare state and the foundations of democratic leadership and life. Equally important is the authors' willingness to analyze the challenges that teachers will have to face in redefining a new mission for education—one that is linked to "validating people's experiences, respecting their concerns, taking seriously our national culture's own historical commitments, reaffirming our moral responsibilities, and giving credence to the multiple forms of human oppression and injury."

What is equally significant about Purpel and Shapiro's call for educational reform is their concern with linking the new pluralism with concrete strategies for addressing the relationship between schooling and the economy; citizenship and the politics of meaning; community and the reality of the heterogeneous student bodies and identities that increasingly inhabit our multicultural, multiracial, and multilingual schools. In this instance, the politics of educational reform becomes part of a politics of pragmatic possibility attentive to both the reduction of injustices and suffering and the need for new alliances—a new politics of connectedness in which the production of knowledge, social identities, and social relations incorporates as a defining principle such categories as justice, equality, struggle, and democracy.

In part, the authors' concern for educational reform is expressed in a call for progressives and others to incorporate what they call a transformative notion of discipline. This is not a call for the production and regulation of docile bodies that Michel Foucault traces in his studies of power, but an attempt to redefine how knowledge and authority can mutually inform each other around a politics, pedagogy, and practice informed by a responsible set of ethics.

In part, such an ethics faces three major challenges that Purpel and Shapiro's reading confront.[2] First, it must provide a moral and collective vision for justifying both the institutional forms and the social practices that they legitimate and produce. Second, a transformative notion of discipline must specify in ethical terms how history, power, politics, and hope can work to contribute to the construction of public spaces whose defining principle is the decentering of power and the multiplication of democratic practices and social relations. Third, educators need to take up the challenge of developing "a conception of pedagogy that considers the relation between knowing and the production of subjectivity in a way that acknowledges the complexities of both the production of identities, competencies, and desires and the possibilities for a progressive agenda for learning within schools."[3]

Not unlike other concerned educational theorists on the left, Purpel and Shapiro reiterate the need for schools to promote forms of citizenship rooted in compassion, ethical responsibility, and social justice. For Purpel and Shapiro, the way in which educators think about schooling is crucial to the way in which we think about the construction of citizens, an ethic of care and responsibility, and that social imaginery called the future. The Critical Studies in Education and Culture Series has a long standing commitment to these concerns, and it reaffirms its position and hope with the publication of this much-needed book. *Beyond Liberation and Excellence* provides a new language for educators to link knowledge to commitment and excellence to equity. Moreover, it amplifies how educators can understand and reconstruct schooling within a broader discourse of civic responsibility and public life. This is a book that explicitly avows radical democracy as the condition and purpose for schooling and in that sense offers hope rather than mere apologies.

Henry A. Giroux

NOTES

1. June Jordan, *Technical Difficulties: African-American Notes on the State of the Union* (New York: Pantheon, 1992), pp. 198–99.

2. Henry A. Giroux, *Schooling and the Struggle for Public Life* (Minneapolis: University of Minnesota Press, 1988). For an example of how such a view of education plays itself out in other cultural spheres, see Henry A. Giroux, *Disturbing Pleasures: Learning Popular Culture* (New York: Routledge, 1994).

3. Roger I. Simon, *Teaching against the Grain* (Westport, Conn.: Bergin & Garvey, 1992), p. 6.

Preface

We have been friends and colleagues for several years, and in that time we have found our orientations to be soothingly resonant at times and at other times disturbingly dissonant. Both of us share a sense of outrage at the inexcusable injustices that inflict needless suffering and pain, and both of us see such policies reflected and legitimated in educational practice. We have differed in how we balance our concerns and responses: One has been much more focused on the political and economic structures that generate social and educational policies, while the other has focused more on a moral and spiritual critique of these institutions. To some extent, these differences reflect differences in individual experiences, histories, and backgrounds, but we are convinced that more general important social and cultural issues are also reflected in our particular set of differences and commonalities.

In our various discussions, we each came to see (however slowly) that there was value in each other's position—that is, moral critique was insufficient without a political program, and a political program perforce must be grounded in a moral vision. We made each other very much aware of the necessity as well as the limitations of critical rationality and helped each other to be mindful of both the perils and possibilities of moral critique. We both came to see that, as educators, we had to confront the problematic nature of both ignorance and sophistication, of both skepticism and cynicism, of both sentimentality and despair. This book, therefore, is the result of a dialogue directed at integrating these perspectives in the context of our current social and cultural crisis. We believed then, as we do now, that this crisis requires that our profession respond in a manner appropriate to its magnitude.

Both of us were increasingly drawn to, and disturbed by, the sharp discrepancy between the proliferating critical writing about schools and culture in the United States and the direction generally taken in our politics and public life. To us, at least, so much of the scholarship was powerful, trenchant, and incisive in what it pointed out about the nature, justice, and legitimacy of our social world and, in particular, schools. There was no shortage in it of disturbing and passionately expressed analysis about the oppressive, antidemocratic, and dehumanizing character of educational institutions and the dire effects of the whole acculturation process on the young. Yet, our nation as a whole seemed headed in directions far removed—indeed, antithetical—to anything being suggested in these analyses.

It did not need Russell Jacoby's persuasive book (*The Last Intellectuals* published in 1987) on the contemporary failure of public intellectuals (at least those who can be called politically progressive) to tell us that somehow the radical social and cultural critique of those working in the academy was not reaching a very wide audience. Our own work in the classroom told us that. Faced with, for the most part, students very different from those who write and read critical scholarship, we asked ourselves more than once if our language in the classroom and in our written scholarship was different—and, if so, in what ways.

We recognized that much of the time we were much more like public intellectuals—finding ways to translate an often dense, remote, and sometimes esoteric intellectual language into an accessible, compelling, even inspirational discourse that might—and frequently did—invite broad engagement of ideas. And this experience, as well as the grim recognition of the increasingly harsh world of the Reagan-Bush America around us, drew us increasingly into a conversation about educational reform, the prospects for deep social change, and the problematics of public and professional language.

The acuity of educational and cultural critique notwithstanding, we were dismayed at how little attempt, or even acknowledgment, there was of the need for creating a public language through which a much wider "lay" audience might find itself engaged in rethinking and reformulating the social purposes of educational institutions. The real lack in the work of educational and social critics was, we became convinced, the failure to have addressed seriously the public discourse on education—not merely to "deconstruct" what was currently spoken about, but to begin to travel the hard road toward renewal of a vibrant, resonant, and persuasive language for reenvisioning the root goals and purposes of education in America.

Of course, our turn toward the salience of language was certainly encouraged by intellectual development in the university itself—in the place that is our professional home. It should not be surprising that we made central to the focus of this book the question of discourse—the language we use, the conversations we have, and the way in which needs become defined, constructed, and communicated. Our focus was indeed spurred by the explosive interest in discourse and the social nature of language that has occurred in cultural analysis and the humanities in recent times. The subject of discourse itself has been transformed from the arcane pursuit of literary critics, aestheticians, and philosophers into the very visible, even politically contentious, stuff of public commentary and argument.

The rather esoteric writing of thinkers like Ferdinand de Saussure, Mikhail Bakhtin, Roland Barthes, and Jacques Derrida have provided resources that have fired a fundamental shift in how we think about ideas, words, the artifacts of culture (including everyday or popular culture), the meaning of self, and the way in which people are won over to particular philosophical viewpoints or political ideologies. Their work has sent shock waves through the university since it has called into question the taken-for-grantedness of academic disciplines, the legitimacy of the literary canon, and the scientific claim to know something dispassionately or objectively. The most simple claim of discourse theory is that despite what we know or think we know, there is in the end only the language that gives it form—that inscribes human consciousness through metaphors that are effective and resonant in that place and time.

Recognizing the power of language is not without its exhilaration. At a stroke, the apparent facticity of our world seems to have been reduced to a chimera. Yet, this recognition has carried with it real perils. Imprisoned in a world of language that perpetually limits any knowledge we may have of reality, it is no longer possible to talk about the real as something "out there" that the human subject can see or grasp—consequences that, to say the least, imply uncertainty about the veracity of any intellectual work and even hopelessness or despair about the real value of our efforts. The search for true understanding about the world has been replaced by the endless—and sometimes playful—process of "textual deconstruction." Reflecting the enormous influence of developments within the field of literary criticism, many have been persuaded to treat with derision all claims that human beings can really say or know what they mean—that there can be anything more than an endless series of stories told from within the historical, cultural, and linguistic perspective and horizon of the storyteller.

This erosion in our confidence about describing the real world has followed the widespread popularity of models of language associated with the work of poststructuralist writers like Derrida and Lacan. In this work, the notion that the sign—that is, the sound of a word or its inscription that represents meaning—has some nonarbitrary relation to something outside of itself is dismissed as metaphysical nonsense. From this perspective, the world that we take to be reality can be no more than the illusory world of language. Condemned to grasping or seeing reality through language, the real world eludes us and is replaced with the conventions of what is socially constructed and discursively familiar.

There can be little doubt as to the power of this kind of analysis in sweeping away claims to realistic accounts of the world. There is, in this view, an insistence that language is not a way of naming a preexisting world. It is nothing more than an arbitrary system of classification based on the creation of distinctions or differences. Language gives only the illusion of being a transparent window to a world outside of it. It is, as a consequence, not possible to actually know the world of things through some objective, empirical, scientific method. Nor can human reason somehow penetrate to the reality of things. In the "poststructural world" the claim to really know something about reality is invalidated. All we can ever know are the meanings made available through one or another discourse or language. Whether through the conventional words of every-day life, or the critical reason that claims to see through mystifying appearances, we can never *actually* move beyond the signs. We can never escape the prison-house of language.

Even more difficult, under the influence of writers like the French historian and philosopher Michel Foucault we have been forced to face the full consequences of a world where our ethical and political commit-ments have been brutally cut loose from all claims to be anchored in some Archimedean or absolute point of knowing. For Foucault, what determines "truth" is nothing but a preference about whom we wish to stand with in struggle—whose side we are on socially, politically, and morally. All the persuasive "isms" of the modern world arrogate to themselves (more particularly, to intellectuals who represent and live by them) the capacity to find what is true and actual. Their premises are almost always ones of epistemological certainty. In each there is the apparently clear distinction between truth and error, science and ideol-ogy. Each offers the promise of accurately and correctly knowing the nature of things. But from Foucault's point of view, all that we ever get—whether or not something is described as true—is a language and perspective dressed up as truth.[1]

Foucault's work brings us to what the feminist theologian Sharon Welch has described as the inevitable epistemological nihilism of the twentieth century. The events of this century, she asserts, "make it impossible to honestly assert with any assurance the likelihood of certain knowledge."[2] There is no ultimate reference point for truth outside of a history that might make something true. In a world where brutalities, injustice, and degradation demand resolute and determined human response, there is a paradox of increasing uncertainty about what we know and the ethical/political commitments consequent on this knowledge. If knowledge is always dependent on the interests of human groups, who are we to believe? And on what basis can we act? A deep—indeed infinite—suspicion settles over all our choices.

All of this strikes hard at the notion of a future in which critique, insight, and knowledge can free us from social domination. It undercuts the central plank of critical thought in which the spread of human reason makes possible a world that is fully democratic and socially just. At the root of the postmodern condition is a terrible failure of hope and possibility. The notion of transcending human oppression may be dismissed as political mythologizing. There is a deep underlying cynicism toward the possibilities of transforming society so as to bring about human liberation. Radical politics within the postmodern worldview is much more likely to be an absurd cultural spectacle or to put us on the road to some other form of domination. Strong ethical commitment is but another version of the will to power, and one must be suspicious of it. And it has been argued, as often as not, that who claimed to have released what had been "crushed" were themselves engaged in crushing elsewhere.[3]

After the degeneration and corruption of so many radical regimes and revolutionary movements with their promises of a more just and humane society, and after the recognition of impending ecological catastrophe that is the consequence of scientific reason without boundaries, the visionary dreams of radical intellectuals have been stiffled, if not extinguished. The world-transforming hopes and dreams of critical intellectuals in the twentieth century have been undermined by a deepening crisis in the systems of analysis and explanation that had been crucial to the belief that their yearnings were more than pie-in-the-sky utopias. In this sense, as Marshall Berman has argued, "the postmodern mood is the self-expression of those who have lost the sense of hope and possibility about significantly changing our world."[4] Indeed, at least in the West, it seems that widespread radical dissent becomes more and more improbable as the distinction between what things look like and what is really going on dissolve into what Jean Baudrillard calls the "hyperreality" of the media age. It is no longer possible to see through the appearance of things.

When the image is primary, so-called critique becomes nothing more than the floating of a new image—part of an all-encompassing "publicity game." Resistance is futile—destined ultimately to do no more than feed on the mindlessness of the consumer culture. Of course, such a condition vitiates any notion of a public realm in which the people, through informed debate, might discriminate between what is true and what is not. In the age of *USA Today*-style journalism and reenacted news events, the very idea of verifiable knowledge or information is discarded as meaningless and irrelevant. What is happening is not merely a recognition of the precarious and shifting nature of such information—subject, as it is, to negotiation through competition among different interest groups and ideologies—but the feeling that all attempts to ascertain what is really going on are futile. We no longer have a meaningful public space in which to struggle to define reality. Instead, the ceaseless, changing images of the media-dominated society have turned nearly everything into a public-relations event: All events have become a part of what Baudrillard called the "mega-publicity operation that is America."[5]

All of this certainly invites despair about the possibility of fundamental social change. And it is against this backdrop that our writing has taken place—one in which an affirmative moral vision and the sense of radical hope in political possibility seems improbable, if not an act of outright denial or hubris. It seems to be a time in which commitment, conviction, and hope are passé—leftovers from a more romantic or naïvely idealistic time. This mood, too, might be seen as a reflection of the absence of any social movement large enough and with sufficient identity and conviction to radically transform our society. Indeed, what we seem to be faced with now, in place of such a force, is the proliferation of interest groups, each concerned with a limited and narrow agenda. It is perhaps in response to this lack of possibility that critical intellectuals have felt compelled to consign all notions of reality to the more manageable and academic terrain of language, signs, and texts.

The sense of the improbability of radical moral and political challenges in society is mirrored not only in the increasing emphasis on aesthetic concerns and cultural analysis but also in the way the very idea of the self has become derided as a fiction (in Foucault's infamous description, a figure that would "be erased like a face drawn in the sand at the edge of the sea"). Instead, what exists is what Suzanne Moore has called a kind of cultural autism wherein the individual is emptied of any subjective center.[6]

Human subjectivity becomes nothing more than a series of social positions that together form a devastatingly contradictory and wholly elusive notion of the self. Such a view denies the existential quality of human experience and choices. It leaves us without responsibility, conscience, or hope. It fails to capture the quality of becoming, as women or men project themselves forward to address the incompleteness of their existence or to struggle for greater freedom or an expansion of justice in the world. This view of the self reflects and reinforces the separation of intellectual life from politics, academic theory from the flesh-and-blood world of commitment, sacrifice, and struggle.

Yet, it would be unfair to suggest that the postmodern mood is devoid of all subversive or critical social values. A number of writers have, for example, argued that it is necessary to distinguish between a complacent, conservative postmodernism and an emancipatory version. Certainly there is the exuberant surge of freedom that is unleashed when what is given as fixed and unalterable in the world is shown up as a human fabrication, not the immutable condition of nature. Critical intellectuals have freed us, and continue to free us, from what has appeared as a grid of meaning and value that compelled human acceptance and accommodation. In place of the overwhelming "facticity" of the world, there appears, more and more, only the "man-made" classification of what is worthwhile, valuable, beautiful, or rational—manufactured and supported by those who stand to gain most from their seeming inevitability. And around this intellectual work have crystallized powerful criticisms, concerning those who have been marginalized or shut out by the "normal" process of educational and cultural exclusion. Such work has exposed the insidious way in which the category of the "other" is constructed—silencing, trivializing, and demeaning the language, human experience, and knowledge of much of humanity. With their emancipatory energies, these insistent and intellectually acute voices have seriously challenged some of the traditional forms of higher education.

The postmodern view of the self, with its emphasis on the shifting and mobile nature of identity, does express and support a "politics of identity," with its important celebration of human difference and diversity. It has taught us to see that our words, images, ideas, and judgments are thoroughly implicated in relationships of power, whether on the basis of class, race, or gender; our homophobic sexuality; Eurocentric cultural attitudes; or the technorationality that urges us to seek control of both our inner and outer natures. In whatever form, the spread of such thinking into so many areas of intellectual life has succeeded in making the familiar increasingly strange. More than ever, it has become hard to see the world

as simply existing and given rather than socially constructed and to see
the world as historically contingent. Such consciousness invites us to see
the present reality as one possible outcome among others. And it becomes
much harder to ignore or deny the institutional and political forces that
stand behind the vast and terrible forms of material and cultural suffering
in our world.

These now ubiquitous currents of intellectual thought do not flow in
one direction—certainly not toward the avowal of some morally explicit
declaration of political aims. Their existence does, however, speak to the
gnawing and growing uncertainty of life in this culture. And we believe
it is uncertainty that is the most powerful consequence of the postmodern
intellectual era—a consequence that reverberates through the politics of
education in the 1990s. With what degree of assuredness can it now be
asserted, for example, that we know that any specific literature is
superior to another, that a particular artistic work is intrinsically more
worthwhile than another, that books are more worth looking at than
films? We know now how much our taste—and our selections—are
shaped by cultural traditions and relations of power that give preference
to some cultural products and not others. Or that our notions of scientific
rationality and progress are not judgments that are dispassionately
arrived at but contain evaluations marked by cultural or ethnic bias or
by masculine assumptions and values. Even the fruits of scientific
inquiry are given form in the context of struggles for power and recognition and are continually shaped by the metaphors that are available and
resonant at that historical moment. Scientific knowledge is never the
mirror of nature but what results when experience is refracted through
the prism of language and culture.

Yet, the freedom that comes with such insights and awareness carries
with it a paradoxical burden—"an unbearable lightness of being." Into
what are we being freed? In a world that is shown more and more to be
arbitrary—one among many possibilities, where reality is always and
only the illusory effect of images and symbols and where all such
realities are undergirded by power—emancipation seems only to offer
more of the same. Freedom becomes nothing more than the endless task
of doubting—and challenging—the veracity of whatever "regime of
truth," as Foucault calls it, we find ourselves living in. Freedom offers
little more than the never-ending opportunity of deconstructing the
beliefs, assumptions, commitments, and ideologies that structure our
world. A kind of freedom that formats what Peter McLaren calls "the
restless subjectivities" of those with "broader identities."[7] Yet, such
emancipation without grounding, freedom without anchorage, surely

offers a nightmarish specter. Endless doubt about all that we see, hear, feel, and know is surely the royal route to what the contemporary German scholar Peter Sloterdijk calls "cynical consciousness" (the dominant consciousness, he asserts, in the modern world).[8] It is a consciousness without conviction about the possibilities of a truly different and better world and without the commitment to struggle for it. Freedom brings with it only the possibility of being different from what we are today—but for what reason and to what benefit?

It is, of course, into this emancipatory cul-de-sac that conservative commentators have so effectively injected themselves. Those like William Bennett and E. D. Hirsch have responded to the collapse of certainty and the erosion of confidence in what we know or ought to know with a call to the epistemological order of yesteryear. Where there was doubt, there is the absolute assertion of cultural knowledge that is foundational to our civilization; where there appeared only the hubris of the masculine-dominated, European-oriented curriculum, there is the firm belief in what is needed to make one educated; and where there looked to be only knowledge steeped in the codes of our language and biases in our ways of seeing the world, there is the rational mind dispassionately discerning truth from untruth, value from trash, and culture from kitsch.

The demand for multicultural education (and other democratically inspired "insurgencies" against the established curriculum, such as women's studies, African-American studies, popular culture studies) must be resisted, the conservatives say, as the consequence of the postmodern zeal to demolish the traditional structures of intellectual discipline, cultural literacy, and educational values. According to conservatives, there is a conspiracy to call into question and undermine the legitimate authority of teachers, texts, intellectual traditions, and ultimately the institutions that house and reproduce them. It is, the conservatives argue, part of the insane nihilistic outcome of democratic attitudes run wild that want to subvert all forms of hierarchy and elitism. The postmodern enthusiasm for deconstruction, for multiculturalism, for the body, for the end of universal truths, for denying the foundational values of philosophy, must be understood as part of a wider set of struggles—political, cultural, and social—that have brought into contempt all those ways of being, thinking, and perceiving that support the historically tried-and-tested meanings and values of authority, community, and tradition.

We, of course, deplore the thinly veiled intolerance, elitism, and arrogance of such arguments. Yet, there is in them a kernel of truth—one that points to the limits of liberation and freedom as the overriding emphasis of the radical outlook. Such an outlook can only call into question beliefs, assumptions, and convictions. It has stripped itself of the capacity for affirmation and commitment (beyond those of the capacity to tear away all of our metaphysical illusions about meaning). It has forfeited its capacity for ethical or political leadership. Recognition of the historical contingency of all that we know is thin gruel indeed to offer a society increasingly hungry for the sustenance of a morally and spiritually compelling vision of life and community.

What we have struggled with in writing this book is the possibility of a discourse on education that goes beyond *liberation* or *excellence*; one that offers more than a radically unencumbered freedom or the seduction of a reassuring paternalism. We have found it to be no easy task: living under the shadow of postmodern intellectual uncertainty, and, at the same time, witness to the increasing brutality and degradation of life in this world. Our writing has been forged out of the twin impulses of intellectual doubt and moral outrage. How, we have found ourselves asking time and again, can these be reconciled? Each impulse nurtures its own progeny: on the one hand, existential despair, political withdrawal, and moral ambivalence; on the other hand, the unequivocal voice of human revolt, moral denunciation, and political assertiveness.

In the writing of this book, we not only had to deal with the matter of very different writing styles but also with our differing, if not sometimes conflicting, views. We decided early on that we would surely strive for clarity and cohesion in the book but not to the point of obscuring the important reality that the book had two distinctly different authors. We were warned by some colleagues that to do such a project was fraught with the possibilities of either papering over our differences and/or of straining our relationship. In reality, although we had many stimulating discussions and a few that were heated, we were able to find consensus and agreement more easily than Truth.

In retrospect "putting it all together" is probably more than we could really expect to achieve at this moment. Allowing even for our assuredly modest intellectual capabilities, we have come to believe that this is really the profound and difficult task of an epoch. We entered into the task from different starting points, and indeed we have occasionally allowed the seams in our joint work to show. No longer bound by the modernist impulse to offer a text that has a linear uniformity and coherent smoothness to it, the readers might note the sometimes awkward juxtaposition of our respective styles as authors.

Our differences, however, need to be understood as more than quirks of style or vocabulary. These differences arise out of a struggle to meld historically quite distinct, even opposed, discourses. One such discourse has evolved out of the conviction that any new social vision cannot adequately rely on the secular rational language of the enlightenment tradition. It will need to incorporate a religious language—albeit one distilled through the radical commitments to societal and ecological change of liberation- and creation-centered theologies. Another discourse is derived from a democratic socialist perspective in which change in education, as in other spheres, depends on a strategy of finding common ground and interests among the diverse social movements that now populate the political and cultural landscape of this society.

Whatever our successes in blending these perspectives and approaches, we are, together, convinced that such efforts are vital to the task that we have set ourselves in this book, and elsewhere. This task is not only to suggest an agenda for educational reform that is connected to a serious renovation of our social, cultural, and economic life, but also to offer a path to reconceive the language of educational purposes in ways that connect it to a genuine transformation of attitudes and beliefs toward nature, human life, and our shared existence. And in regard to the latter, at least, we are convinced that we will have to draw upon a very different vocabulary to express and develop this consciousness.

We know that some may perhaps find the product of our efforts disjointed. Others, perhaps will see us writing out of the continuing hubris of offering universal political prescriptions for all of humankind. Others still might see our efforts as insufficiently rigorous or, conversely, as insufficiently accessible to the wider audience we are so concerned about. For ourselves we will feel satisfied if we manage to spur wider efforts to radically challenge the public discourse in education in this country and change it, so that in some significant way it connects to the task of what the Hebrew prophets once called *tikkun olam*—the healing and repair of the world.

NOTES

1. Russell Jacoby, *The Last Intellectuals* (New York: Farrar, Straus & Giroux, 1987).

2. Sharon Welch, *Communities of Resistance and Solidarity* (New York: Orbis, 1985).

3. See H. Stuart Hughes, *Sophisticated Rebels* (Cambridge: Harvard University Press, 1980).

4. Marshall Berman, "Why Modernism Still Matters," *Tikkun* 4, no. 1 (January/February 1989), pp. 11–14, 81–86.

5. Interview with Jean Baudrillard, *Marxism Today* (January 1986), p. 54.

6. Suzanne Moore, "Gender, Post-Modern Style," *Marxism Today* (May 1990), p. 34.

7. Peter McLaren, "Critical Pedagogy, Multiculturalism, and the Politics of Risk and Resistance: A Response to Kelly and Portelli," *Journal of Education* 133, no. 3 (1991), p. 38.

8. Peter Sloterdijk, *Critique of Cynical Reason* (Minneapolis: University of Minnesota Press, 1987).

Acknowledgments

First, we want to particularly acknowledge the support of Henry A. Giroux in helping to bring this work to fruition. In acting to sustain the work of a community of resistance and hope, he continues to demonstrate what it means to be an organic intellectual, a genuine colleague, and a true friend. Sue Books and Fred Yeo provided insightful criticisms of earlier drafts of the manuscript. We wish to note with appreciation Michael Apple's suggestions, which led to our turning an earlier piece into this full-length manuscript. Jeanette Dean and Karen Stacherski both resourcefully assembled our writings into a coherent text. And, not least, unnamed classes of students challenged us to clarify our ideas and assertions about the public and professional discourse in education. We hope their contributions will be recognized in these pages.

In addition, we wish to gratefully acknowledge the contributions that our wives have made to this project. Svi Shapiro wishes to express gratitude for the loving support of his wife Sherry during the writing of this book. Her intellectual passion, respectful support, and, not least, gentle playfulness are cherished. David E. Purpel wishes to express his appreciation and gratitude to his wife Elaine for the support, hope, optimism, and energy that has helped so much to sustain him over the years.

Study for the sake of scholarship is desecration: it is a transgression of the commandment against bowing before alien gods, the idol being mere learning. The study of the Torah is a matter of the heart's devotion.

The Baal Shem Tov

We must abandon completely the naive faith that school automatically liberates the mind and serves the cause of human progress; in fact, we know that it may serve . . . tyranny as well as truth, war as well as peace, death as well as life. . . . If it is to serve the cause of human freedom, it must be explicitly designed for that purpose.

George Counts

Loss, pain, isolation: It is a tragedy that these should be the results of becoming educated, the consequences of excellence. An alternative journey . . . requires fundamental changes in both educational theory and practice . . . [that] will make it possible to diffuse throughout the population the nurturant capacities and the ethics of care that are absolutely essential to the survival of society itself, indeed, to the survival of life on earth.

Jane Roland Martin

I support efforts to empower local school districts to experiment with chartering their schools . . . or having more public school choice, or to do whatever they wish to do as long as we measure every school by one high standard: Are our children learning what they need to know to compete and win in the global economy?

President Bill Clinton

BEYOND LIBERATION AND EXCELLENCE

1

Public and Professional Discourse: Blurred Visions and Empty Dreams

This book is about education *and* society and how the public does or does not discuss education *and* society. A basic assumption of our work is that educational issues are inevitably and inextricably connected with social, cultural, moral, political, and economic issues; and, indeed, much of this book speaks not only to these relations but paradoxically to the significance of not acknowledging them. We work within the tradition that considers education part of the process by which societies and cultures develop, revise, and renew their priorities, beliefs, values, policies, and institutions. This is to echo John Dewey's notion that education is concerned with "the making of a world"; and when we speak of making a world, we inevitably raise very broad and very basic questions regarding goals, purposes, meaning, and vision.

Educational institutions, like all other social and cultural institutions, therefore both inform social policies and cultural visions and are informed by them; and it is in this sense that we say our book is also and inevitably about affirmation, that is, the process by which education is explicitly grounded in a particular social vision and moral framework. We therefore seek to avoid the dangerous isolation of educational analysis from broader contextual analysis and instead strive to relate educational matters to important social, cultural, political, and moral dimensions. Educational issues are not primarily technical but, in effect, are manifestations and reflections of social and cultural issues that are played out in educational settings.

In the research for this book, time and time again, we were struck by how often educational issues are presented in a political and moral vacuum, so that, for example, there are people who suggest major changes in social and cultural policies but recommend only trivial or technical changes in educational policy. It seems extraordinary to us that in a time when there seems to be a consensus that we require major changes in our consciousness to meet our almost overwhelming problems, the dominant proposals for educational reform are so banal, trivial, and timid. Part of the problem is that educational issues usually are presented and discussed as if they were technical (the kind that require expert knowledge) rather than cultural and social in nature (the kind that require judgment).

We therefore write this book for, among others, those educators open to the possibility of reconceptualizing education in social and cultural terms in order to inform and supplement their specialized knowledge. In the same manner, we write for social theorists open to the possibility of reconceptualizing traditional educational policies in order to become more resonant and responsive to creative and vital social theories. Perhaps, most important, we write for a more general public (or publics) who might support the need for fundamental educational and social change.

Put more concisely, this book examines public discourse on education with particular reference to the relation of educational matters to larger social, cultural, economic, political, and moral frameworks. The notion of "discourse" is itself a complex and important matter that we return to for discussion in this and other chapters (see also the preface). Suffice it for now to say that recent scholarship has enabled us to see that various analyses and discussions about issues can be represented as more or less coherent and distinct discourses or narratives.

Theoretically, there are presumably an infinite number of possible discourses on education. But in our research we found only a few such discourses, and in this book we provide a critical description and analysis of what we believe are the most influential of them. For better or worse these discourses significantly frame and influence our public and professional dialogue on educational policies and practices.

In addition to our criticism, we will present the elements of what we consider to be a more valid and compelling narrative—one that not only represents our own views but that also resonates with the hopes of a great many other people. We hope this process can help to sort out the confusing and conflicting rhetoric of educational criticism and calls for reform and will provide direction for the urgent task of remaking an agenda for social, cultural, and educational transformations.

This seems to be an unprecedented era for American education: a time of a seemingly unending series of reports, task forces, and long-range planning; of politicians competing for educational statesmanship; and of a myriad of new regulations, policies, and procedures. In spite of all the heightened concern for education, however, we believe the public is being ill served by the nature and quality of the current debate and dialogue. We believe that those who have framed the public discourse have failed to clarify the profound nature of the underlying issues and, moreover, have compounded that failure by providing a discourse that trivializes and vulgarizes those issues. It is our belief that the bulk of the public (and professional) debate on education is conducted in an appallingly naïve and simple-minded manner.

Our book attempts to go beyond the overwhelmingly technical and narrow character of contemporary discourse about education and to delve into the more vital and profound issues that underlie the current demands for educational change by directly addressing matters of ideology and affirmation. We analyze the ideologies implicit in the most significant of the discourses on education since we view them, not as inevitable distortions or hindrances, but, at least in part, as affirmations of social and cultural aspirations. We believe that educators inevitably act upon such affirmations (albeit often without full recognition and reflection) and that it is therefore incumbent upon them to involve themselves more consciously and deliberately in the process of developing and refining a social and cultural vision.

Ultimately, we believe, the responsibilities of educators include the creation of a better world—and, hence, they must struggle to both define and realize the nature of a better world as well as work to make such a world real. To educate is not only to describe the world but also to affirm and create a better one. In that spirit we will in our book not only reveal our own basic orientation and commitments but also lay out a moral and political framework for pursuing alternative educational policies and practices.

To pursue such change seems always to be appropriate, but in times of enormous crises it becomes imperative and urgent. We live in such a time, one of extraordinary danger and peril—a time of devastating poverty, hunger, and disease for untold millions and a time of potential catastrophe from the dangers of pollution, war, and hatred. The response to this worldwide crisis has ranged from dismay, anguish, and energy to cynicism, callousness, and powerlessness. As educators we believe that we must all respond to this profound crisis with hope and energy; therefore, we need to respond, not to narrowly defined "educational issues," but to the opportunities and possibilities of educational institutions in order to cope with the challenges of overcoming our present social and cultural dangers.

Sadly and regretfully, however, we believe the dominant educational discourses to be largely misleading and unresponsive to the urgent needs of our times. We find in these discourses an obsession with preserving American economic and military might and with servicing a postindustrial economy that has failed to respond adequately to the needs of developing a fair, just, and democratic society. On the other hand, our basic criticism of the professional discourse is that it seeks to avoid political, moral, and social issues, preferring the safer, less controversial realm of technical problems; in so doing the profession becomes the agent of those who shape the larger social and cultural agenda.

We believe that educators must extend their horizons by participating in the framing of a social and cultural agenda—and, in this way, assume their share of the responsibility for education *and* society. We also believe that the profession has a major responsibility to develop a discourse that is sufficiently imaginative and resonant to reach a larger public and persuade them to the relevance and viability of a different vision of educational purposes than the one now current.

We will, in succeeding chapters, provide a detailed and thorough examination and analysis of current educational discourses in both the professional and public spheres. In this chapter, we provide a brief overview of these discourses in order to provide a framework for our orientation and a point of departure not only for our criticisms but for our recommendations and proposals.

CURRENT THEMES IN PUBLIC AND PROFESSIONAL DISCOURSES IN EDUCATION

Public Discourse and Education

Education and the Economy. Much of what has been written and said about education in the 1980s and 1990s has emphasized the decline in the American economy. Indeed, it would be fair to say that public discussion about education in this period has been dominated by the perception that education has failed to contribute to the rejuvenation of an ailing economy—worse, that it is a major culprit in the decline of American productivity and international competitiveness. What has filled newspapers and television commentary on public education and has been the focus of innumerable national reports is the accusation that the declining effectiveness of American schools has contributed to the crisis conditions in the nation's industrial base. Education, say the reports, carries significant, even primary, responsibility for the steep decline in the rate of growth in the country's gross national product (a rate that in the 1980s and early 1990s was half of what it was in the decade of the 1960s) and for the growth in the nation's huge balance-of-trade deficit.

Nothing makes this emphasis in the public discourse on education clearer than these words from the most influential of the national reports on education reform—the *Nation at Risk* report:

Knowledge, learning, information and skilled intelligence are the new raw materials of international commerce and are today spreading through the world as vigorously as miracle drugs, synthetic fertilizers, and blue jeans did earlier. If only to keep and improve on the slim competitive edge we will retain in world markets, we must rededicate ourselves to the reform of our education system.

Elsewhere the same report stated:

Americans like to think of the nation as the preeminent country for generating the great ideas and material benefits for mankind. The citizen is dismayed at a steady 15-year decline in industrial productivity, as one great American industry after another falls to world competition. The citizen wants the country to act on the belief . . . that education should be at the top of the nation's agenda.[1]

Reversing the crisis of declining industrial productivity, the spread of industrial closings, lay-offs, and rising bankruptcies would require a process of educational reform that would meet this situation. American's public schools, it was argued, needed to overcome their failure to prepare adequately students for the demands of an internationally competitive high-tech and information-based economy.

Many of the educational reports of the early and mid-1980s emphasized that schools and their curricula were out of sync with the corporate needs for skilled manpower. While there were discussions of the importance of humanities and literacy in the education of young people, the emphasis was primarily on economic needs. Of course, what was especially prized was technical and computer "literacy." For some, at least, technology and international trade were transforming the "basic skills" needed in the workplace. The new electronics of computers and videodiscs, fax machines, and complex telephone systems would rank higher in the educational experience of the new generation of learners than pens and pencils.

While improvements in technical skills and scientific literacy were high on the list of educational reforms concerned with improving American productivity, it also was possible to detect slightly more "old-fashioned" means to increase industrial output. Although it was clear that such suggestions concerned the behavior of adolescents in school, not adult workers, it is probably not too fantastic to believe that there were in the recommendations of many of the educational reports such implicit statements concerning the need to ensure a less lackadaisical and more disciplined work force that was better prepared to accept long hours of labor and less prone to tardiness and absenteeism. Thus, the reports contained frequent statements regarding the need to lengthen the school day and the school year, the need to implement attendance policies with "clear sanctions and incentives" to reduce absenteeism and tardiness, and the need for increased homework assignments.

For both students and their teachers, higher economic productivity and industrial output was associated with a vision of schooling in which there would be a far greater emphasis on the competitive ranking and testing of performance. The popularity of merit pay schemes in state legislatures and in business circles spoke to a notion of teaching increasingly defined successful classroom activity in terms of efficiency and effectiveness. In attempting to tie the quest for higher economic growth to the reform of public education, the public discussion of schooling was increasingly dominated by the language and logic of industrial life—the concern with output, performance, and productivity.

Of course, while the fears concerning the American economy suffused much of the public discussion about education in the 1980s and 1990s, it would be wrong to imagine that there was clear consensus on just what this would mean for schools. The consensus about reforming education so that it would be more responsive to economic concerns was built around a diverse set of views and constituencies. Certainly there were those in business who favored an increase in the vocational content of the school curriculum, with less time spent on the traditional liberal and general curriculum. Among others in business and government, there was the view that schools should prepare students for the workplace through cultivation of more general behavioral attitudes and mental aptitudes so as to produce reliable and adaptable workers. Among some working-class parents there surely was strong support for the view that schools should provide students with basic survival skills and competencies. This certainly included the ability to look for, and hold, some kind of a job and meet its mental requirements—something that implies at least the minimum capability for reading, writing, and basic numeracy.

At another level, public debate focused on who should be responsible for adapting education to the needs of corporate America and the newly emerging forms of work. Teachers were to be monitored and evaluated much more vigorously to ensure greater classroom effectiveness. This, in reality, meant attending much more to results of students' scores on an ever-proliferating range of standardized achievement tests, as well as finding ways to rank objectively their individual performance in comparison with their peers. Implicit in many of the education reports was the understanding that our economic and educational condition required much greater leadership from government to redirect and reform public education. Contrary to the "leave it to the market" philosophy of the Reagan era, by the mid-1990s there were few states that had not struggled to implement new policies that would, it was hoped, ensure an updated, more effective school system.

Education and the State. Another major focus of public discourse in education has concerned the role of government (at all levels), particularly its obligation to respond to serious social problems such as poverty, unemployment, crime, and racism. Much of the recent discussion in this area has focused on the disenchantment or failure (real or imagined) of major government programs, especially those that constituted the Great Society initiatives of the Johnson administration. Beginning with the Carter administration, continuing through the Reagan era, and emerging again loudly in the mid-1990s, political rhetoric has been colored by vehement criticism of the size and inefficiency of government bureaucracy, the tax burden carried by middle-income Americans, and the overregulation of economic life. Under both Reagan and Bush, and the Republican "contract" of 1994, the antigovernment platform became one that called into question the state's responsibility for, and capacity to respond to, social groups that depended on it for economic, social, and legal support. Public life and discourse in the 1980s and through the 1990s has been dominated by a conservative politics that sought to dismantle or reduce in scope many of the institutions and programs that together constituted the welfare state in this country.

Central to the idea of the welfare state is the notion that government is able—and, indeed, obligated—to redress the problems or disruptions that are the consequence of the market economy. It is a recognition that, left to its own devices, the marketplace produces vast inequities in the distribution of material resources among members of the society as well as deep insecurities in the life experiences of working-class and middle-income citizens (especially among the jobless, the sick or handicapped, the elderly, and those with young children). It is a recognition that without government intervention the market alone cannot be expected to ensure *everyone* an adequate and decent standard of living (in areas like education, food and nutrition, housing or health care).

What marked public debate in the 1980s and 1990s was the charge that the state had gone too far in providing for the protection of people.[2] As a result of all the programs instituted and laws passed to achieve this, crushing burdens were said to have been imposed on working- and middle-class Americans. And in the state's zeal to cushion and ameliorate the effects of the market, free enterprise, it was argued, was regulated to the point of stifling entrepreneurial initiative and limiting the capacity of corporations to profit from their investments. The liberal politics associated with the expansion of the welfare state was charged with having been captured by the special interests of minorities, welfare recipients, and others who turned government against the interests and needs of middle-income, white America. This, it was said, contributed to the moral crisis in this country by making it possible or easier for large numbers of people to maintain themselves without working, to have and support babies out of wedlock, and to pursue deviant lifestyles protected and legitimized by the state.

Not surprisingly, the issue of education loomed large in all of this. Public education was certainly a major focus of demands by those who pushed for social policies that would support and expand the democratic promise and expectations of life in America—the possibility of decent, secure, and fulfilled lives. It has certainly and, especially in the 1960s, frequently provided a lever to groups struggling to gain from government resources and assistance that might enable their children to overcome the disadvantages that have occurred because of wealth, race, gender, physical or mental handicaps, language or other forms of inheritance. In this sense, educational policy, at least some of the time, was part of the larger "liberal" politics that aimed to expand state institutions and public programs that could compensate for the inequities of social and economic life.

Indeed, in the United States, educational opportunity has become *the* vehicle through which social, economic, and political inequities might be overcome, the means by which democratic aspirations and hopes might be reconciled with the realities of a competitive society in which the possibilities of success and achievement are available to individuals in enormously varying degrees. Student loans, Headstart, compensatory reading programs, special education, bilingual education, school busing, and so forth, all, in some way, represent efforts to overcome or redress social, cultural, and economic inequities. In this way, education helps to give a sense of legitimacy to a system that would, without such compensatory intervention by the state, call into question any claims it might make to social justice and fairness.

Despite this—or perhaps because of this—liberal philosophy of government and education, the conservative public discourse of the 1980s and 1990s challenged the egalitarian dimension of education policy.[3] This challenge was part of the larger push to dismantle or reduce in scope federal social programs, regulations, and mandates. The discourse stressed the importance of "deregulating" American society, thus freeing it from government interference and regulation. Social justice for some, it was argued, was had at the expense of others' rights and needs, especially those of the middle class. And all attempts at rectifying inequalities in this way undercut the principal tenet of American life: individual success arrived at through the capacity for competitive achievement. It upended the principles of a meritocratic society. We will return, in the next chapter, to this crisis of the economy and the state, as it has been called, and its ramifications for the shaping of the public debate about education.

Education and Culture. The Right's attack on the size of the government and the expansion of its social and educational programs was, as we have already noted, couched in more than terms of simple fiscal expedience. The size of government and the expansion of its programs were said to reflect an erosion of fundamental American values. This was the case, too, with the charge that the nation's defenses had severely weakened. This, it was said, reflected an unhealthy loss of nerve—an ambivalent attitude toward the nation's need to affect its own self-interest in the world. Not surprisingly, as with much else, conservatives traced this weakness or ambivalence back to the influence of the 1960s. That era, they said, had cast its shadow of weakness, vacillation, even a sympathy for our "natural" enemies in the world. It was a period that brought into disrepute the flag and other national insignia, that sullied the reputation of the military—indeed, that brought martial values into cynical disrepute. The nation, as a result of these "bad times," had lost its sense of will and purpose—the self-confidence to proclaim and defend its status as the preeminent nation of the world.

According to the Right, the welfare state that had developed in this period also was responsible for this decline in the traditional virtues of independence, rugged individualism, self-reliance, and competitive zeal. It was an expression and a cause of the same decline in the strength of America and the nation's commitment to excellence. Such social policies, the Right argued, had robbed Americans of the incentives to compete; tax and regulatory policies had undercut the entrepreneurial spirit of risk taking and innovation. The emphasis on equality, redistributional taxation, and welfare had produced a cultural malaise. People were supported for not working, effort or merit was not rewarded, and the striving for excellence was not recognized.

Both a national and an individual moral decline, it was argued, was traceable to the liberalism of the 1960s that had corroded time-honored American virtues of hard work, patriotism, and the commitment to self-improvement. In the dominant political language of the time, the government needed to get out of the way so that individual effort could produce its effects. The concern with equality (translated as sameness), the Right argued, had suffocated the central American value of freedom. In the Carter, Reagan, and Bush eras, and beyond, the antistate and promilitary rhetorics were joined through a discourse that bemoaned the decline of achievement, hard work, and the concern for excellence.[4]

The apparent public sympathy for a rejuvenated military and the evisceration of social programs resonated with other widespread anxieties and fears. Both in some way touched on questions of authority and hierarchy in the post-1960s era. The decline of military strength and the expansion of the welfare ethic, it was stated, were part and parcel of a morally lax and permissive culture that had encouraged a disrespect for authority in the social order. Certainly the 1960s era unleashed an unprecedented attack on traditional social relations—by minorities, women, poor people, the young, and so forth. The traditional centers of authority took a beating: teachers and school administrators, bosses, bureaucrats, government leaders, army generals, the family and parents—all were subjected to fierce criticism and questioning. Of course, this was conjoined with the regularly reported deceit of politicians and the military brass in their pursuit of the war in Vietnam and later Watergate and other political scandals. In the 1980s and into the 1990s the continuing incidence of political corruption and deceit (notable among the many were the Iran-Contra and HUD scandals, the savings-and-loan debacle, as well as questions about the role of the United States in the building of Iraq's military capacity) were swelled by the circuses of corrupt religious evangelists. All of this eroded further the legitimacy of leadership and authority and the sense of a settled and respected hierarchy. Of course, all of this represented only the surface of the moral crisis in America.

There was a larger sense in which the ordered and established notions of what is proper, right, and virtuous had been upturned in the rush of cultural and social change. The sexual and family mores of traditional small-town life (what Daniel Bell called the "Puritan temper and the Protestant ethic") had become passé in an era that sought sexual liberation and permitted, if not encouraged, a diversity of lifestyles. Elsewhere, the moral virtue of hard work had become anachronistic in a time when "making it" by any means was constantly celebrated in the mass media. Consumerism, with its insistence on never putting off until tomorrow what can be bought and enjoyed today, contested the virtues of delayed gratification. Consumer culture emphasized the centrality of pleasure, immediacy, and novelty and put into reverse traditional beliefs in thrift, impulse restraint, and duty. The celebration of alcohol pointed to the legitimacy of emotional release, escape, and social irresponsibility. Even more disturbing than the pervasiveness of alcohol in the daily round of existence was, since the 1960s, the epidemic of drug addiction. The latter was increasingly associated with the enormous expansion of violent crime in the nation's cities.

All of this contributed to the sense of a nation that was falling increasingly into decay and disorder, where daily living was accompanied by insecurity and fear. Changing sexual standards and practices also stimulated increased anxieties. Not the least of this was, of course, the wave of apprehension associated with the spread of AIDS, which to some, at least, appeared to vindicate their deep antipathy toward gay lifestyles. To a "New Right" and its supporters, it appeared that the nation was awash in perverse sexual practices and a pornographic culture. Exploitation of children for pornographic movies and magazines, increasingly visible homosexuality, the public and widespread availability of abortion, and the disintegration of lifelong monogamous relationships all fueled cultural and moral discontent among working-class and middle-class Americans. Fanned by vitriolic right-wing commentary, a moderately liberal President Clinton, became a lightening rod for much of the anxiety.

In the dominant language of the time, the moral fabric of the nation was torn in other ways, too. Notions of thrift and frugality seemed to have been jettisoned in the pursuit of immediate gratification at whatever expense (no matter whether the American economy could survive a true return to thrift—consumption geared not to credit or debt, but to one's actual capacity to pay). The general focus of this concern was less on personal forms of debt than on deficits run up by government. What was needed, argued some, was a constitutional amendment that would ensure a balanced budget. The recklessness of expenditures was matched by general indifference to long-term consequences in other areas of human activity. Unions seemed intent on driving up labor costs to the point where profit margins would be endangered and industry would no longer be competitive. American workers, it was asserted, appeared little concerned with the products of their labor, and shoddy workmanship was increasingly the rule. Speculation and merger mania provided the vehicles for get-rich-quick investments rather than investments that ensured sound, long-term growth in the economy.

All of this provided the backdrop for the moral concerns expressed in public discourse about education during the 1980s and 1990s. "Back to basics" expressed more than a concern with the need to ensure basic literacy and numeracy. It also evoked an image of earlier, more stable times when schools could be expected to teach kids a clear, unambiguous set of moral virtues centered around the importance of discipline and self-control. "Back to basics," in its moral sense, suggested a time in American life when the world was turned the right way up; when social relationships between young and old, between marital partners, between the sexes, between the races, and, not least, between students and their teachers were clearly delineated and not to be questioned or challenged. Schools, it was argued, needed to become again places where the young would learn to treat those in authority with deference and respect.[5]

Liberal or secular humanism had, it was said, fomented licentious attitudes and permissive values that needed to be staunched. The "cafeteria" image of high schools, with its presumed endless emphasis on choice and alternatives, needed to be replaced by an environment in which discipline and requirements would be the institution's touchstones. If the tide of moral disintegration and permissiveness among the young, and in society in general, were to be stemmed, then schools would have to bear down much harder on their clients. Respect and obedience needed to be learned, and very often the "old-fashioned way" was best. In the 1980s, Joe Clark was lionized. Clark was the principal of a Paterson, New Jersey, high school, with all of the problems typical of urban settings. Striding down the hallways of his building, baseball bat in hand, Clark practiced the highly disciplinarian "tough love," which cajoled kids out of the disruptive, antisocial behavior that, it was said, undermined education in such schools. Drugs, vandalism, apathy, and disruptive behavior required less psychological analysis and sympathetic understanding than uncompromising insistence, backed up by corporal punishment if needed, on the upholding of social standards and norms.

Other well-publicized voices on the Right argued, however, that moral decay and cultural disintegration required something else in addition to the emphasis on discipline. Liberal influences, it was said, had eliminated any firm set of moral commitments from public life and the process of public education in America. Schools mirrored a society in which live-and-let-live attitudes had gone too far. Tolerance for any and all beliefs and behavior had rapidly produced a world in which the fundamental Judeo-Christian values of the society were being discarded. The kind of permissive tolerance for all viewpoints taught in such educational exercises as the popular values-clarification texts encouraged children to reject the preeminence of traditional American and Christian values.

The answer to this relativity of morals and values was found in a number of proposals. Schools should be permitted to hold assemblies at which prayers would be encouraged or expected. Textbooks used in public school classrooms—especially in social studies—should be required to promote a more patriotic message and to emphasize the Christian and traditional virtues underpinning American institutions. Schools should promote premarital sexual abstinence and a veneration of monogamous and heterosexual family life. School librarians should engage in a more conscientious process to exclude literature that espouses secular humanism, sexual license, and attitudes that undermine respect for those in authority or established social institutions.

And, perhaps most visibly, the curriculum itself was an object of concern for those who argued that changes in it had contributed to the moral crisis and cultural instability of present times. Whether pointing to the erosion of instruction in the "basics" or condemning the absence of "cultural literacy" among high school graduates, the public discourse was filled with suggestions that the knowledge imparted in American public schools failed to provide the kind of essential foundation needed to work and participate effectively in this society. Indeed, educational reformers had contributed to a malaise in which the sense of there being some agreed upon and shared body of knowledge—concepts and ideas that unite all Americans in an organic culture—had been destroyed.

All of these themes will be taken up again and amplified in the next chapter. Together they provide something of a skeleton of the concerns that have structured the public debate about education in recent times. Later, we will look especially at the connections between this language of educational debate and the larger concerns that framed American life. For now, let us turn to those who, ostensibly, were the primary players in the institutional life of education and how they have responded to the political pressures for change in school policies and practices.[6]

Professional Discourse—Experts without a Cause

The professional educational community is, of course, very large and contains a great many diverse and conflicting groups, but we believe that it is fair to say that by and large it has tended either to adapt quickly to the new conventionalities or has failed in its scattered efforts to offer significantly different models of education. The recent history of professional education is largely one of co-optation and/or impotence. We as a profession tend either to get behind the current political agenda or to get left behind. There are, to be sure, small but vital progressive movements in education, and there is a great deal of lively and provocative research and analysis that goes counter to the prevailing public and professional discourse. However, these movements are mostly hidden from the public either because they are discounted or are not accessible to those in power. Jacoby's analysis of the relation between the number of public intellectuals and the increase of intellectuals in the academy can easily be applied to the field of education.[7] It is probably the case that the quality of educational analysis and research has dramatically improved over the past twenty-five years, but with the increase in erudition and sophistication has come concurrent opacity and density.

Moreover, our conclusion is that most professional educators battle to survive by treading water in the seemingly safer current of the mainstream. Although our field has perhaps more than its share of opportunists, sycophants, and poseurs, our major concern is not with them. Rather, we wish to focus on more honest problematics, those connected to the phenomenon of being caught on the horns of two separate but related paradoxes—one involving the split between short-term and long-term goals and the other involving the strategy of radical versus gradual change.

While educators, teachers, administrators, and counselors may be acutely critical of the undeniable deficiencies of our educational system, they often do not have the luxury of making such criticisms the focus of their work. Instead, these practitioners are required to expend the bulk of their energies, not on criticism and theorizing, but on day-to-day practice, that is, working with students under existing conditions and arrangements that have not only been in place for some time but also will very likely be the arrangements for some time to come.

There are educators who probably would, for example, agree that schools should not have to be responsible for feeding students, but the reality is that many of the students are hungry. Many practicing educators believe that racism is a cultural disease and that genuine social integration would preclude disruptive busing, but the reality is that neighborhoods remain segregated and so schools must take steps to avoid costly and divisive litigation. Most educators believe that social and economic conditions explain why some students are disruptive and even violent and, hence, would much prefer to be patient with and understanding and supportive of disruptive students. However, what is a teacher to do when students *are* truly disruptive and violent? When there are students who are not at all amenable to reason and persuasion?

Professional practitioners are always caught in the bind of, on the one hand, being required to have professional standards of excellence and, on the other, having the professional responsibility of working under conditions that deviate very sharply from those standards. Many educators define their major responsibilities as working with the hand that is dealt them: to respond to the particulars of the situation and to work with the students as they are, as the environment and setting is established, and within the concretized, mandated goals, objectives, expectations, requirements, roles, policies, guidelines, and so forth.

The quandary is by no means unique to educators, but it is necessary to note its place in the matter of their professional responsibility for the quality of public discourse on education. Being torn between the responsibility of dealing with the basic inadequacy of the system and the necessity of responding to students in the here and now bring frustration and resentment to many practitioners. The ongoing reality for most practitioners is that it is a major struggle just to respond to the daily obligations—never mind to provide leadership to the public. Most practitioners have significant periods when they feel overwhelmed and victimized by the system; and yet, maddeningly enough, they are severely criticized by most for not doing more and are criticized by a few for doing what they are required to do.

Teacher bashing has become yet another device to relegate educational issues to the technical realm, thereby allowing the larger culture to get off the moral and political hook. Contrary to the conventional wisdom, we believe that to a very large extent teachers are quite successful in meeting the real and concrete demands that our culture places on them. Our position is not that teachers fail social standards but rather that society has failed to establish valid educational standards. In effect we ask teachers to do things we don't really want to do (e.g., keep children occupied, disciplined, and compliant) and often project this quest on teachers. Furthermore, society has also found ways to silence the voice of teacher dissent. A very effective technique for avoiding the confronting of the vulgarity and triviality of our socially defined educational policies is to neutralize and diminish the potential power of a truly independent professional voice. An effective mode in such a technique is to overwhelm educators with large classes, impossible demands, bureaucratic molasses, and guilt induction.

A related dilemma for professionals emerges from the controversy over gradual versus radical change, which is basically an argument over tactics and human possibility. Within a context where people agree that serious change is required, people will often disagree on the possibility of rapid change. Some will argue, given a human propensity for homeostasis, that however important change may be, we as a people can only accommodate gradual change. A variation of this argument is the notion that we must be cautious in making serious change since it involves by definition moving into new realms of uncertainty.

There are, of course, difficulties with this cautious approach—one of which is that a gradual approach tends toward moderating and tempering the new approach, such that the full effect of change can be significantly truncated. This also allows the institution the time for cautious bureaucrats to indulge in one of their very few creative impulses—that of co-optation and sabotage. If the community demands that schools be accountable, for example, the schools are given procedures that actually extend central control, limit teacher autonomy, and narrow educational horizons rather than provide for significant community participation. When the school is urged to provide more experience in art, the school responds by demanding that the art teacher do more detailed planning and develop more effective testing, thus undermining the creative process. Schools have responded to demands for more freedom for gifted and talented students by raising grading standards and putting more pressure on them rather than provide a more nurturing environment for them. Such practices not only mitigate the significance of the change but also provide ways for school bureaucrats to maintain what is euphemistically called "professional autonomy."

However, the most difficult problem with the gradualist approach arises when it is linked with the belief in the myth of Progress, a notion that educational progress, while slow, is steady and continuous—if not inevitable. The historical reality we see is otherwise—an irregular and uneven course of events in which there are clearly some significant changes over time (e.g., punishment, although still plentiful, is probably significantly less cruel). However, in these times, it is increasingly difficult for practitioners to hang on to even the modest possibilities of the schools in the face of ever-increasing demands for "higher productivity and performance," code names for higher test scores. In our interpretation of recent events in the public schools, the outlook is even more bleak.

Overall, we believe the schools are significantly less pleasant, less stimulating, more joyless, more mindless, and more stultifying institutions than they were a mere twenty years ago. However, we certainly posit no golden age of education, we offer no nostalgic look backward, but only a rueful belief that school systems are mired in mediocrity and inanity, although sometimes they are interrupted by occasional brushes with joy and excitement. The schools have become increasingly desolate places having had their spirit crushed by the heavy footed, crass demands of the soulless people who direct our foreign policy and industrial engines, aided and abetted by a docile, fearful, divided profession. Educators, in any case, constantly struggle, on the one hand, with the responsibility to continue to work in the face of enormous frustration and, on the other, with the importance to work for significant improvements.

Our analysis leads us to conclude that the quality of the current discourse on education and the nature and perspective of the people and groups shaping it have combined to produce an unnecessarily shallow and genuinely unhelpful discourse. This is not only aesthetically upsetting and professionally unhealthy, it is morally and politically toxic. Our frame of reference is a culture in severe crisis, beset by enormously risky problems involving the possibilities of economic collapse, extreme poverty, massive starvation, ecological disaster, violence, and warfare. As educators we are stunned by the enormity of the crisis and the timidity of our educational response. We also have come to the conclusion that, for a variety of reasons that we shall explore, it is both unrealistic and unwise to expect the current educational leadership (lay and professional) to move us beyond our current conventionality and triviality.

We find ourselves in a time when it is appropriate to modify the traditional dictum that a vigorous educational system is required for an informed public that is central to democratic society. Our formulation is the reverse: A vigorous educational system requires an informed public—a public with a sophisticated understanding of the complex relations among social priorities, cultural values, and educational policies. We also believe very strongly that the profession can and must play an important role in this basically political responsibility.

Our indictment of the educational leadership is not, therefore, of their professional competence but of their abject failure to develop a sophisticated discourse for the public. The public requires a dialogue that goes far beyond the narrow, conventional, truncated, shallow discourse presented by most professionals. We hope both to contribute to the sophistication and profundity of public dialogue in education and to persuade our colleagues to become significantly involved in this process. Our strong belief is that the schools cannot and will not make basic changes unless and until the society and culture want to make significant changes.

Whether our society and culture are capable of making major and appropriate changes is, of course, highly questionable, but as educators we must perforce work in the faith that it is possible and, moreover, that it is imperative to participate in the process of determining the nature of such changes.

As educators we must not only share with the public our understanding and analysis of the shortsightedness of current educational policies but also show the possibilities offered by alternative educational models. Democratic policy making requires choices and the ability to predict consequences of existing policies, but we must be wary of the metaphors of corporate and military planning. Dreams and visions do not emerge from quarterly reports or from mission plans to raise SAT scores; our deepest aspirations and hopes should not be tied to the vocationalism and bottom-line mentality that are the stock and trade of those who pass for educational leaders. We believe an informed public can return to and reenergize its commitments to an education that does more than feed greed and indulge pedantry. We believe an intellectually alert, morally grounded, and professionally savvy public can, in turn, galvanize a currently dispirited profession to exercise its latent genius in designing an educational system that seeks to make real our highest hopes and deepest aspirations. This task surely is appropriate for all elements of our society, but the educational establishment has a major opportunity and responsibility here to go beyond the realms of expertise and specialized knowledge to the realm of responsibility and courageous public leadership. We surely need to be informed by the deliberate and cautious research of educational experts, but in this time of severe danger we also need the wisdom and perspective of candid educational leaders.

Forging a Moral Vision and a Political Strategy for Education

We see that our challenge as educators is to respond to the various levels of issues and problems that we face—the enormous social and cultural crisis of our era, the particular political debates of our time, and the professional responses to them. In a broad sense, this requires the employment of several perspectives—and, hence, several discourses. The challenges we face inevitably involve us in a diverse number of issues—social, cultural, political, economic, ontological, epistemological, curricular, and instructional. We deeply and profoundly affirm the importance of careful, thorough, and penetrating critical analysis in providing understanding and insight into the nature of our condition. In addition, as educators, we are necessarily concerned with policies and practices and, consequently, must directly address the question of what our policies and practices are. In other words, we must develop a set of positions that derive from basic assumptions about what constitutes a good society.

With the responsibility of developing a moral framework comes the necessity of creating a political program resonant with that framework and with the pragmatic possibilities at hand. Such a project requires the integration of varying types of discourse and consciousness—concern for detachment and passion, fairness and commitment, reason and faith, pessimism and optimism, realism and the visionary. We must also address our responsibilities in developing a discourse that is not only accessible but that offers the possibility of stimulating deeper and broader dialogue on these very serious issues, too important to be left to the professionals alone and too complex to be left to the public alone.

In our criticism of the quality of the public discourse on education, we do not want to suggest that it reflects a know-nothing public. Such a perspective would, of course, reflect enormous intellectual arrogance. It also would be wrongheaded. While we will not back off our claims as to the impoverished, frequently trivial, narrow, and mystifying character of this discourse, it does, nonetheless, many times have real and important connections to deeply felt, serious problems and concerns in the lives of the people in our society. To suggest otherwise is to fall prey to the view that ordinary citizens live in a state of utter ignorance concerning the conditions of their lives or that they are nothing but the unwitting dupes of those who hold the reins of economic and political power.

Within the broad Left tradition out of which we write, this idea of the masses'"false consciousness" has had a long and seductive appeal.[8] Acting together, it is said, the mass media, advertisers, politicians, the public relations industry, and state institutions such as schools ensure that the consciousness of such citizens is thoroughly massaged and manipulated. Working- and middle-class individuals have, as a result, little or no understanding or grasp of the real problems that confront them. Popular notions of what the real issues of our time are and the circumstances that surround them have been lost in the bamboozling images purveyed by the "captains of consciousness."

Fortunately, such a view has begun to give way to a more respectful appreciation of the way in which people apprehend and make sense of the complex social conditions that they face. In particular, the choice in favor of particular political positions or public policies is to be understood as much more than the result of ignorance and misinformation. This is true even when such choices appear to be stupefying, misguided, reactionary, or reprehensible. Our belief is that they oftentimes represent plausible, even logical, responses to the painful, oppressive, alienating, and unjust conditions that face many people in the United States.

While the goal of this book is to challenge and change the prevailing public discourse about education in the United States, we know we cannot do that without taking seriously the voices of these people. While we may not always accept or agree with what these voices say or propose, they do, we believe, reflect in some way very real concerns, anxieties, dreams, and hopes. What always impels these voices is the anguish and aspirations of people's lives. However hard it sometimes may be to decipher, we believe the public language about educational matters contains and mediates not only the often painful social realities of our time but also the individual's hopes to overcome them, if not for themselves, then for their children.

It is necessary here to do what appears, at first sight, to be paradoxical, namely, to affirm that working- and middle-class people—not just experts or intellectuals—know a good deal about their world and their lives and yet, at the same time, to call into question the way in which this understanding in matters concerning education has so often in recent years reinforced the painful and stressful conditions of our lives rather than helped to liberate us from these conditions. It follows from what we have said that the public discourse about education is always in some way connected to the larger social, cultural, moral, and economic circumstances of people's lives. Yet the actual nature of these connections often remains cloudy. It will be one of our tasks in this book to try to elucidate how issues and concerns facing the community are often displaced into, or focused around, changes in education. It is a process that is infrequently and only dimly grasped, even by those in the public proposing such changes. We believe, nonetheless, that any agenda for educational reform that would draw enthusiastic support and interest from a broad cross section of the public must address what are widely perceived and experienced as the real problems in our social, economic, and moral life.

We wish to echo what Stuart Hall, the British sociologist and an insightful commentator on the language of contemporary politics, has said. There are no right-wing issues, only right-wing discourses. That is to say, it does no good for social critics to discount what are held to be the major issues or concerns in many people's lives as the result of the mystifications produced by the dominant culture. Concern about jobs, the fear of drugs, the ubiquity of violence, the disintegration of authority, declining literacy, the absence of religious values, and so on, are *real* problems in the eyes of parents and other citizens. If it wishes to be taken seriously, an alternative agenda for change in education must acknowledge and respect these issues and be ready to address them. Trying to bring about fundamental change in education is not a matter of lining up Left versus Right issues (e.g., busing versus school prayer, multicultural education versus patriotism, critical pedagogy versus basic skills, and so on). It is, instead, a struggle over public language and meaning—over how to define and make sense of the problems and issues experienced in the daily life of working- and middle-class Americans and to relate these to what goes on, or might go on, in educational institutions.

In the 1980s we often saw how the wishes, anxieties, and hopes of people were incorporated into the language of a politics that ultimately exploited and betrayed those concerns to the advantage of elites. Michael Lerner has described eloquently the reductive character of right-wing public discourse that *appears* to speak to the deep unfulfilled emotional needs of the middle class. For example, frantic efforts, he suggests, to "protect the flag" are really about the loss of the idealized community that the flag represents and about the profound desire to find a context within which people could feel connected to a larger purpose and historical meaning that transcends their individual lives.

With the erosion of genuine community within which people can feel recognized and confirmed for who they are, people in their isolation feel drawn to seek out the imaginary community provided them through an identification with "the nation." Yet the very lack of substance in these fantasies makes people's connections to these pseudo-communities feel unstable and hence generates a frenzy and hysteria that is used to sustain a sense of a reality that might otherwise fade. In this context, the flag, the symbol of a perfect community that exists only in the imagination, becomes the venerable embodiment of all that people fear they are losing.[9]

In championing the flag or the need for community, the Right has constructed a public discourse intimately connected to the everyday concerns and anxieties of many people. Notwithstanding what we believe to be the essentially imaginary nature of its prescriptions, this language offers powerful images and a narrative that speaks to the collective experience of disintegrating personal relationships, unstable families, and eroding communal ties. It is a language that mixes *real* human desires with *fantasized* solutions that evade the important fact that it is the economic system itself that fosters an ethos of individualism and materialism that subverts stable family and communal life.

In a way similar to Lerner, Stuart Hall has identified the decade-long appeal of "Thatcherism" to the electorate in Britain. His analysis provides important clues to what it takes both to construct and to radically alter public discourse. While a fierce opponent of Margaret Thatcher's right-wing politics, Hall nonetheless emphasizes the brilliant manner in which Thatcher, like Ronald Reagan, was able to incorporate real, widely felt issues, concerns, and aspirations into political solutions that left unaddressed, or even exacerbated, the crucial social, economic, and cultural conditions faced by the majority of people. As unpleasant as it is for the Left to admit, Hall says, "We may have to acknowledge that there is often a *rational* core to Thatcherism's critique which reflects some real substantive issues which Thatcherism did not create but addresses in its own way. And since, in this sense, we both inhabit the same world the left will have to address them too."[10] Right-wing ideology, Hall insists, is not to be dismissed as a set of ideological tricks that conjure demons out of the deep. To the contrary, it emerges out of the real, if conflicting, experiences of ordinary people's lives in contemporary society.

Yet, while this ideology must be recognized as expressing the real struggles, concerns, and hopes of working-class and middle-class people, it does not, Hall emphasizes, *directly* express the conditions of people's lives. These conditions themselves must be described, defined, and given meaning. We cannot rely on the idea of appealing to the "real experience" of human beings as if experience somehow speaks for itself. The concerns, interests, and aspirations of people can become expressed in very different ways. Indeed, they can be expressed in discourses that actually oppose one another. They can just as easily be used to defend the status quo as to radically critique it. Speaking of unemployment, Hall notes: "A young unemployed person may interpret this experience to mean that you should work and vote to change the system. But it could equally be defined as a sign that you should throw your fortune in with the winner, climb on the bandwagon, earn a fast buck and look after 'number one.'"[11]

In contemporary society, there is a continuing ideological contest over how situations are to be defined and through what "discursive logic" they are to be understood. The power of the enormously successful conservative public discourse of recent years has been its ability to make sense of a whole range of human and social concerns in ideological terms that support its own economic, political, cultural, and moral logic. It has been able to harness the very real problems, concerns, and issues facing many people and to define them in the context of conservative philosophy.

To realize how successful this process has been, one only has to think of the main context in which the drug problem has been defined—namely, the personal behavior of drug abusers. As a result attention is shifted from urban neglect, corporate irresponsibility, and the alienation and despair that result when populations are thrown on the economic and social slag heap. The dominant explanation and meanings attached to the drug problem point us away from a politics of economic justice and social concern and toward further victimization of the poor.

There is no getting away from the powerful role that language and interpretation have in the pursuit of change in our public life. The struggle over how we should "name," give meaning to, and make sense of the difficulties and problems we face is central to all kinds of social change—including that of education. Our choice of images, narratives, and metaphors plays a crucial role in determining how much enthusiasm and support can be mobilized to address our crises in a given way.

Pursuit of a New Public Language

It is important to note here that the character of people's political ideas cannot be guaranteed by one's social class or economic position. Special or economic interests do not give rise to any particular kind of politics. Indeed, how we "see" our own interests is something that depends on the power of particular ideologies or "stories" to "speak" to our concerns and evoke our commitments. Commitment to a set of social, cultural, or political ideas or beliefs is not the result of a rationally determined process: It is the product of what cultural critic Peter Gabel has called "passionate understanding." It is the result of a discourse or ideology that offers people evocative images and understandings in which their lives, experiences, and identities find resonance and their hopes can be imaged.

Gary Peller has provided a startling example of this so-called passionate understanding in his essay on "creationism"—one that is worth considering for a moment.[12] The emotionally charged issue of teaching a fundamentalist theory of creation in the public schools, he argues, must not be dismissed as the consequence of ignorance and authoritarian attitudes among Southern working-class people. The debate between evolutionary theory and creationism, he says, is the symbolic face of a broader conflict over the basic terms by which social life is understood. It is one of the ways in which white working-class and poor people have experienced their rebellion against the technocrats and meritocratic values of the New South, a region in which the old personalized, local, and communal forms of social dominance have been replaced with power structures that are corporate, centralized, and managerial. The new ideology of power is derived from the rhetoric of science—rational, detached, and professional. New South leaders, says Peller, present themselves as akin to scientists: "They believe that the structure of community life is determined technocratically by neutral, objective, disinterested authorities—urban planners, lawyers, financial experts, and other university trained professionals—and thus social decision-making is presented as the result of expertise applied to objective conditions rather than the product of interest or will."[13]

In this view, power and prestige are the result of an impersonal, objective selection process that produces a "natural monitoring." In this official ideology interest, subjective bias, personality, and political will have been banished as relics of the traditional South. In public education, Peller says, the New South ideology is especially apparent. The discourse on education and its actual practice have shifted from the maternal and emotionally intimate (if harsh) climate of traditional schooling to an environment that more and more emphasizes professional efficiency and scientific methodologies. Everything in the school—from the administration specialists, to the "field-tested" centrally prescribed curriculum, to the objectively verifiable ways to measure the "performance" and "output" of students—represents the turn toward a scientific educational language of universality, impersonality, and neutrality. And, Peller says, just as the evolutionary theory is grounded in the clinical distance of the scientific method, so the general tone and feel of schools in the South today are characterized by an antiseptic, clinical distance between professionalized educators and objectified students: "the unalterable destiny of social class is communicated, not by invocation of divine order, but by computer print-outs telling working class parents their children are slow, by guidance counselors directing low-income students to training as plumbers, electricians and service workers in vocational schools."[14]

While the social structure remains rigid and unjust from the viewpoint of working-class and poor people, the composition and ideology of the ruling class has changed. And it is against this newly emergent ideology of a managerial/professional class that the creationist account is directed. It reverses the supposedly scientific norms that support the new ruling ideology's depiction of the current social hierarchy as the consequence of an impersonal, objective meritocracy. Creationism, Peller says, poses subjectivity, personality, and interest as the significant modes of understanding the world. It implicitly contends, he says, that behind the veneer of objectivity and impersonality are the motives of particular people and groups whose status and prestige are the result of historical power and will rather than a timeless adaptation of merit and function.

Of course, the form of this discourse—the way in which social injustice is articulated and expressed—is, ultimately, futile. Such "politics," in the end, does little more than reinforce the humiliation and marginality of what the rest of the world will describe as "redneck" ignorance. In the language of critical social theory, it is a cultural politics that will do little more than reincorporate subjects into their subordinate social relations. At the same time, there are important lessons to be learned here about the remaking of the public discourse about education. For one thing, such a discourse must have the courage to recognize that it needs to go well beyond the usual restrictive, rationalistic language of the Left. It needs to include a vision that speaks to questions of meaning, of community, and of the quality of our spiritual lives. While the Right's language—however much it speaks to people's everyday experience and hopes—only deepens the crisis and anxieties—the Left is unable to grasp the depths of anguish faced by people even when their material needs are to some extent addressed.

The kind of public discourse that we think is so desperately needed is one that affirms the importance of democratic renewal in our political, cultural, and economic life—and with it the quest for a more just and inclusive social order. But it is also one that can begin to address what John Berger calls the sense of homelessness that, despite all our wealth and power of communication, is the defining condition of humankind in the last decade of the twentieth century.[15] There is a necessity for a public discourse that speaks to the spiritual anguish in people's lives—the sense of pain that comes from a world that offers little in the way of meaning or significance other than the cold, calculating rationality of technological reasoning or obsessive consuming. The loss of human dignity in a world that reduces people increasingly to the status of impersonal objects, the dizzying emptiness of endless buying in the marketplace, and the erosion of a sense of something real beyond the carnival of images that surrounds us via the mass media—all demand from us a new response in public discourse and politics.

We will have to break out of the usual liberal or Left language of critique and the images that they provide. As we try to show in this book, neither Left nor Right offers the images or language needed to reconstruct the public discourse about education so that it provides a compelling and evocative vision that speaks to the needs and concerns of the majority of people. For this we need moral and spiritual language that addresses issues of meaning and purpose and that recognizes the importance of community, continuity, and a shared human vision. We need to recognize social injustice, democracy, and cultural differences, emphasized by the Left, are necessary but not sufficient components of a vital discourse about education. These must be joined to concerns that until now have been discursively monopolized by the Right, but draw from the experience of our *shared* world.

Diverse Needs, Common Agenda:
The Making of a Politics of Education

Regarding this last point, we wish to emphasize our belief that there are no groups of people who are necessarily on "our side" or "against us." Indeed, we believe it is exactly the point of this kind of ideological struggle to create social identities—to bring together a diversity of people with shared concerns who might be united by a common agenda of needs. Change depends on the way in which diverse groups—very different in their material interests, social positions, and cultural attitudes—can be brought together around what is perceived to be a unifying theme or concern. It depends on the capacity of a public discourse to construct a unity out of difference. It is, of course, what we saw happening in the politics of Reagan and Thatcher, namely, the capacity to "stitch together" into an apparently unified discourse a series of different voices and identities—the upwardly mobile young, the respectable middle class, hard-pressed blue-collar workers, the moral zealots of the evangelical right, free-wheeling entrepreneurs, corporate managers, small-business people, and cultural libertarians. All of these, and more, were brought together to form a collective personal subject, unified around a discourse that appeared and felt as if it addressed the distinct fears, anxieties, and dreams of each person or group involved.

Of course, our interest is not the creation—through the increasingly clever and familiar forms of Madison Avenue manipulation—of a discourse that *feels* as if it addresses people's concerns, but one that really does so. This means it is time to offer a far more daring and imaginative vision. We still talk as if people were incapable of responding to anything but their most immediate interests—as dwellers in a particular region; as members of a special social class, race, or ethnic group; as men or women; or some other circumscribed or particular group. While these are clearly real and important forms of identity that often do provide the measure for the policies and actions of the state, these need not impose the final limits on our thinking or concerns.

Rudolf Bahro, one of the most imaginative of the European ecosocialists, has argued that real emancipation requires that people rise above their immediate social or economic interests. The only genuine revolutionary subject now, he says, is humanity.[16] In our post-Marxist world, Bahro argues, the mental energy of very large numbers of people are no longer absorbed by the *immediate* necessities and dangers of human existence. These people are possessed of what he terms "surplus consciousness," which can orient itself to more distant and general problems. Industrial society, in other words, has sufficiently conquered scarcity to release enough mental space for the more expansive work of achieving human fulfillment. As we turn to the task of challenging how people think and talk about education, Bahro reminds us not to underestimate the capacity of growing numbers of people to break out of the conventional "tried-and-tested" modes of discourse.

Certainly, in these times, we are witness to political reform movements that break up in a matter of days or months the ossified power structures of decades; malnutrition and hunger on a global scale; growing awareness of the planetary dimensions of our ecological crisis; and telecommunications that facilitate a worldwide popular culture of the young. They are all, arguably, the leavening in the development of new and more daring forms of consciousness among a great many people. Events in the world constantly remind us that what today seems hopelessly utopian has become on the morrow part of the reform agenda. Progress, as Oscar Wilde once noted, is the realization of utopias.

While a politically effective discourse about education—that is, one that captures people's ideas and imagination—must respond to the conflicts, needs, and contradictions in our lives, it need not be narrow or parochial in its concerns. While it must offer some redress to the crisis that has emerged out of the circumstances of our economic, moral, cultural, communal, and spiritual existence, for a large number of people (particularly among the middle class), the crisis now includes the problem of the continuation of global life and planetary existence.

Our challenge is not merely to try to define, or redefine, what is the real nature of the issues that face us both individually and collectively, but to connect in a meaningful way these issues to what we do in education. We need, in other words, to extract educational talk from the morass of trivializing and conventional notions that stifle the possibility that education could, or should, boldly and directly address itself to our individual, social, and planetary wounds. To do this, we need to confront the way in which our talk about education is either so timid, so shaped by fetishistic thinking, so governed by the logic of those who are economically and culturally dominant, or, when it represents some kind of ideological challenge, so marginalized that it has little capacity to help transform our world so that we might begin to heal our wounds.

This book contains our responses to that challenge, and we seek to engage the reader in the struggles that we experienced in seeking to integrate the complex and diverse issues of public policy, moral vision, and professional practice. These struggles include the necessity of developing not only a language that deals dialectically with these various realms but also a discourse that does justice to both the necessity of the careful and deliberate process of scholarship and professionalism and the requirements of passion and outrage that are requisite to conviction and commitment.

The book is divided into two sections, the first three chapters representing our understanding of the nature of the challenges we face. In this opening chapter, we have provided an overview of those challenges that we develop more thoroughly in succeeding chapters. Chapter 2 will provide an examination of the major dominant themes of the public discourse on education, elaborating more fully on issues touched upon in this chapter. Chapter 3 discusses the nature of professional discourse with a focus on the nature of the profession's responses to current demands for educational reform.

The second half of the book represents our positive responses to these challenges and engages in the responsibility of constructing an alternative framework for public discourse on education. In chapter 4 we provide an exposition and critical examination of critical pedagogy, a major part of the basic grounding for our framework. Although we affirm much of the basic elements of this perspective, we point to a number of serious deficiencies in it, particularly its resistance to moral discourse and its relative inaccessibility.

In chapter 5 we lay out a framework for a public discourse on education that is explicitly moral in nature and, we hope, visionary and compelling in its appeal. The final chapter deals directly with how such a vision might be related to a more concrete political agenda. We set forth there a number of specific and practical possibilities for policies and practices resonant with our vision.

NOTES

1. National Commission on Excellence in Education, "A Nation at Risk," *Education Week*, April 27, 1983, pp. 12–16.

2. For an excellent and very accessible presentation of the nature and origin of this issue, see Richard A. Cloward and Francis F. Piven, *The New Class War* (New York: Pantheon, 1982). See also Chapter 7 in Svi Shapiro, *Between Capitalism and Democracy: Educational Policy and the Crisis of the Welfare State* (Westport, Conn.: Bergin & Garvey, 1990).

3. See, for example, Stanley Aronowitz and Henry Giroux, *Education under Siege* (South Hadley, Mass.: Bergin & Garvey, 1985); see also Ann Bastian et al., *Choosing Equality: The Case for Democratic Schools* (Philadelphia: Temple University Press, 1986).

4. For a very insightful and convincing description of the nature of this antiliberal rhetoric, see Kevin Phillips, *Post-Conservative America* (New York: Random House, 1982). Phillips, a one-time Nixon speech writer, writes as a "Populist Republican."

5. For a compelling and powerful account of the relation between education and wider political and cultural struggles in the 1960s, 1970s, and 1980s, see Ira Shor, *Culture Wars: Schools and Society in the Conservative Restoration* (Boston: Routledge, 1986).

6. Of course, the most visible account of this was found in the best-selling book by E. D. Hirsch, *Cultural Literacy* (Boston: Houghton Mifflin, 1987). We will return to this and other related issues in later chapters.

7. Russell Jacoby, *The Last Intellectuals* (New York: Farrar, Straus & Giroux, 1987).

8. This notion of "fake consciousness" has come under severe attack by a variety of critical intellectual voices who dislike it for its implied arrogance on the part of those apparently more enlightened souls who make such judgments. It is also seen as part of that mind-set that sustains the "binary thinking" (of truth/untruth, science/ideology, essence/appearance), which, it is claimed, is a part of the metaphysics that characterizes so much of the Western philosophical tradition.

9. Michael Lerner, editorial, *Tikkun* 4, no. 5 (September/October, 1989), p. 9.

10. Stuart Hall, "Thatcher's Lessons," *Marxism Today*, March 1989, p. 23.

11. Stuart Hall, "The Great Moving Right Show," in *The Politics of Thatcherism*, Stuart Hall and Martin Jacques (London: Lawrence and Wishart, 1983), p. 30.

12. Gary Peller, "Creation, Evolution and the New South," *Tikkun* 2, no. 5 (November/December 1987), pp. 72–76.

13. Ibid., p. 74.

14. Ibid., p. 75.

15. John Berger, *And Our Faces, My Heart, Brief as Photos* (New York: Pantheon, 1984).

16. Rudolf Bahro, *The Alternatives in Eastern Europe* (London: NLB, 1978).

2

Lost for Words: The Public Discourse in Education

As we noted in the preface to this book, we accord language enormous importance in the construction of our world. Reality itself seems more and more to consist of a fleeting and transient flow of images and symbols. Yet we take seriously the idea of human needs. Such needs—whether they are for shelter, food, health care, dignity and respect, or love—are for us real enough. Indeed, it is on this ground of the struggle for a fuller, more equitable fulfillment of our material, emotional, and spiritual needs that our work is rooted. At the same time, we understand well just how slippery such needs can become since naming them is always an interpretive process. In this sense discourse for us is quintessentially what Nancy Fraser calls "needs talk,"[1] by which she means the ways in which human needs become, through public communication and discussion, transformed into a social vision and an agenda for institutional change. Discourse and politics are closely related. It is in this mix that, as Fraser has written, "rival need interpretations are transformed into rival programmatic conceptions, rival alliances are forged around rival policy proposals, and unequally endowed groups compete to shape the formal policy agendas."[2] Public discourse is, then, that turbulent sea in which oppositional or alternative forms of needs talk arise and crystallize into new moral claims, political strategies, and the social identities that might work for and through them.

One of the most important aspects of the recent concern with discourse has been the attention paid to the development and nature of languages that pertain to medicine, sexuality, the body, psychology, and other social practices and phenomena. Each language has revealed its own peculiar form, the metaphors that underpin it, and the way in which these metaphors create and shape the practical character of a specific field. In this sense, we are moved to be more particularistic—that is, to attend to the special qualities of the diverse languages within which social life is lived. This has important relevance to education with its peculiar jargon and its specific ways of signifying meanings, purposes, and ways of evaluation.

Yet, as important as this is, we are wary of viewing things only through this particular lens. It leaves the world too fragmented, too disconnected in its meanings. The ways in which all of us see and live in our world may not be cut from a seamless, whole cloth, but neither are those ways so separated and divided. As important as is the particular nature of educational talk, it must also be looked at as infused by the wider moral, social, aesthetic, and political judgments and values—the ideology—that holds sway in society. The language of education is always deeply influenced by those ideas about human nature, the moral good, "normal" social relations, notions of cultural value, and so forth, that are ideologically dominant or significant. Educational discourse always reflects in some way cultural notions about achievement and success, the nature of intelligence, the relation between intellect and practice, what it means to become a worker and a citizen, and what it means to assume a sexual and racial identity.

We believe we must look at the distinct language of education *and* the wider, more embracing ideology that shapes it. Attending just to the former, we would see only the trees, not the forest; with only the latter, the reverse. Ideology, as we have said, is not to be seen as a set of ideas and values simply handed down by those who hold economic or political power. Ideology infers a complex combination of elements, some of which clearly serve the existing contours of wealth, power, and opportunity in society, and some of which may be found, at least on occasion, to disrupt or challenge them. With these comments in mind, let us turn to the character of the public discourse in education as it has been shaped in the last two decades in the United States.

OUT OF THE FLUX:
RETURNING TO THE BASICS

Perhaps nothing in the public language of education expressed the mood and concerns of recent years as well as the demand for an education that emphasizes what is *basic*. What notion could so effectively capture the unease about modern society, as well as the distrust of professionals and policy-makers, as the popular assertion that we needed to go back to the true, tried, tested, and readily understandable educational prescriptions of yesteryear? Something about the term *basic* evoked the feeling and image of that which is rock solid and dependable. Talk of returning to what is basic captured a widespread desire to cut through the jargon and the flimflam of the "chattering classes"—the bureaucrats and experts. In its own vague and ill-defined way, *basic* seemed to point to a reality beneath the ever-more-elusive sense of what the world is really about (and, by extension, what education should really be concerned with). Not surprisingly, the word cropped up not only in education (basic skills, basic values), but also in the language of advertisers, preachers, and politicians, all of whom touted their understanding of what was basic in America (values, beliefs, commitments, capabilities, etc.).

These frequent references to the need to "return" to what is basic articulated a common societal ambivalence about the present cultural moment in the nation, an unease about the reliability and integrity of what was currently offered by our economic, political, cultural, or educational institutions. Compared with the present, when so much seemed to lack durability or substance, the past appeared as a veritable haven of what was reliable, sure, and understandable. Talk about returning to what is basic implied a world whose daily language and meanings were not increasingly obtuse, where ordinary people did not feel disempowered by the nearly impenetrable language of the experts and professionals. It suggested a world that rested on the bedrock wisdom of enduring knowledge, instead of the fleeting attitudes of a fickle and restless public. It evoked a world in which there was something solid that did not (in Marx's vivid image) melt into air and where, beyond the dizzying and ephemeral flux of what Jean Baudrillard called the "hyperreality" of the image-oriented society, we might be able to find some sense of a reality that was experienced as firm and reliable.[3]

The wide appeal and resonance of returning to what is basic rested on the twin impulses of nostalgia for what was and resistance to what is. However disingenuous and manipulative it might have been, politicians as well as policy-makers, merchandisers, and ministers evoked, with the language of basics, an image of a time when the social, cultural, and moral order "stood the right way up"—a time when people's lives as well as social institutions, embodied what was familiar, secure and, above all, commonsensical.[4] It did not matter whether a world like this had ever really existed for the majority of Americans or whether the old world had in fact inflicted enormous injustice and oppression on whole groups of citizens; in the cultural turmoil of the 1960s, 1970s, 1980s, and 1990s, returning to such a golden age seemed very desirable.

Who, for example, knew or cared whether Pepperidge Farm cookies were really the creation of a turn-of-the-century, small-town bakery complete with horse-and-buggy home delivery? It was enough that Madison Avenue could code into their advertisements readily identifiable images of wholesome and frugal products distinct from today's all-too-frequently overpriced, chemically saturated foods.

With the marketing of President Reagan, nostalgia became the refuge of scoundrels. Whether in the television images of a sun-drenched rural idyll or in speeches that harked back to an America that was a "Jerusalem on the hill," the country was called back to its "basic" values and beliefs. Images were conjured up of neighborhoods that were unthreatening, communities that were intimate and stable, family life that was not a war zone—a time when the nation was morally and culturally united; where the bottled-up, emergent demands of racially excluded and oppressed groups did not appear to force themselves on white working-class communities. Speech writers and publicists could fill a widespread desire among ordinary people for utopian images of a world that stood in sharp contrast to the one they experienced in their place of work, on their streets, and even in their homes.[5] This readily exploited nostalgia, despite its often poignant phoniness, nonetheless reflected some deep longings for a world that was more simple, caring, dependable, and based on shared norms and values.

The nostalgic images represented one means by which the popular yearning for a more secure and dependable world could find expression and be constituted in the public discourse.[6] These images pointed to a world stripped of its overcomplexity and its disorienting characteristics—a world in which the secure, patriarchial family formed a haven of stability and reliability. This articulation of a desire to get back to values, beliefs, and forms of behavior and competence identified as basic was one way in which working-class and middle-class people could express their resistance to the modern condition. Of course, there was nothing automatic in the particular discursive form of this resistance. There were, and are, many other ways in which the distress and anxiety brought about by the conditions of life in the technocratic world of late capitalism could be articulated. In the postmodern conditions of American life where image and reality became harder to distinguish and where the frenetic and fantastical forms of MTV filled our living rooms, nostalgia for simpler times became a potent symbol of protest.[7] The eroding sense of permanence and security created fertile ground for a variety of exploitative hucksters as well as right-wing politicians.

In this context, it is easy to see how the public concern for "going back" to basics in schools (and, as we will see later, the concern for minimum competencies and the language of educational excellence) was grounded in the very real fears and concerns of ordinary people. However simplistic the assumptions behind these concerns, they nonetheless expressed anxieties about not only the schools and what kids were learning there, but also the culture in which young people were growing up. The peculiar power of the basics discourse was its capacity for uniting around a simple set of demands a variety of different publics who could see in it answers to their own hopes and fears. For example, the demand that schools teach kids reading, writing, and numeracy reflected the conviction among African-American, Latino, and other minority parents that without this there could be no hope of economic survival. For many working-class parents, the demand for schools to go back to basics reflected hostility toward barriers erected between home and school by educational managers and professionals. A;'inst an "educationalese" grown heavy with psychologistic and other technical terminology, returning to basics meant a popular reassertion of "common sense" in matters of curriculum and teaching—a reassertion of the *public* nature of schooling.

Of course, constituting a "counterhegemonic" discourse of education in this way was a double-edged sword. While it connoted a democratic claim on what goes on in the schools, the ideology of basics also carried with it a constricted and pinched notion of education. While this discourse insisted that educators talk and practice a familiar kind of teaching, it also *reinforced* the stultifying and dreary classrooms described by legions of researchers in recent years.[8] What it represented for many parents was a demand that, in at least one sphere where working-class people could exercise some kind of influence over public life, the world ought to conform to something more familiar and reassuring. At least in the classroom, if not in our streets, homes, or on our television screens, the frightening and disorienting flux of change and disruption could be resisted and traditional purposes and norms reestablished.

AUTHORITARIAN SCHOOLING AND THE MORAL PANIC

It is hard, of course, to separate the genuine public expression of resistance from the "cultural crisis" manufactured by conservative think tanks, opinion-makers in the media, and demagogic politicians in the 1970s, 1980s, and 1990s. The "moral panic," if not created by these groups after the social disruptions of the preceding decade, was certainly fueled by them. The fear and anxieties among working-class and middle-class Americans that followed the tumultuous events of that time, and whose effects continued to seep through the culture in the period that followed, were the psychic ground upon which a new, more censorious and authoritarian public discourse about schools could be created.[9] No matter that there was ample evidence that reform in the 1960s and early 1970s had not transformed schools into a licentious and permissive environment that reflected the unruly and pleasure-seeking orientation of the young.[10] Nor was it important that the claims that kids in school were less able to read or write were not unambiguously supported by the evidence. Compared with preceding groups of kids, when account was taken of the changing demographics of public school attendance, there was *no* clearly documented, significant drop in the reading or writing skills of pupils.[11]

Whether or not schools were any less successful in teaching students the basic skills of literacy and numeracy was almost beside the point. The popular crusade to "reform" education along traditional lines expressed a deep-seated anxiety about youth, public institutions, authority, the family, and the perceived liberal ideology of state-employed professionals.[12] In a broader sense, such anxiety crystallized the larger fear of a culture where the old rules and expectations no longer applied and where freedom unbounded by guilt or responsibility dictated how one lived.[13] The notion of kids not learning how to read or write evoked the images of young people who were too busy partying (or in earlier times, protesting) to knuckle down to some hard work. It suggested to ordinary people the irresponsibility and ineptitude of state institutions that were supported through the public purse. It furthered the suspicion that the ideas and language of professionals in education or social service occupations were more and more at odds with the commonsense understanding of most people. School, like much else in American society, had become too complex, too fragmented by diversity, and too indulgent of untempered desire. The result was, or so it appeared, the collapse of a clear sense of purpose—one which implied continuity with past traditions and under-girded the sense of community. In its own simple way, the notion of "returning to basics" provided a reassuring metaphor for all those who sensed a world where little could claim to be unambiguously foundational in either a cultural, moral, or institutional sense.[14]

Again, we must emphasize that there was no single direction in which all this human anxiety and concern could find expression. The fact that the unease of ordinary people latched onto the supposed decline in the ability of young people to read, write, and do arithmetic—and in such a highly charged manner—requires that we recognize the fact that the public discourse on education doesn't just fall out of the sky. It is managed and constructed especially by those with the political power to shape the official culture. In this sense, the question of basic skills—and the related anxiety about falling standards—was developed into a full-fledged crisis of education by many of the same people who led the ideological "charge" against the supposedly dissolute 1960s. The fears of people were worked up into panic over the alleged collapse of authority, and the ghost of conventional cultural norms hovers over much of the public discourse concerning education in the last two decades.[15]

Again and again the framing of educational policy from the 1970s until the present appears as the response to the decline of standards and the erosion of basic values in work, family life, and public morality. In this process the understandable fears produced by the tumult and upheaval of recent times have been incorporated by the Right's opinion-makers into a narrative of irresponsibility, violence, and indulgence. This narrative converts the real struggles for civil rights, social justice, and a less militaristic, more inclusive and participatory culture into a saga of "bad times." In this account schools are crucial beachheads in the fight to pry our institutions loose from those who have irresponsibly allowed youth to neglect the serious tasks of schooling for an unregulated and capricious classroom regime of too-easy electives.[16] In the persuasive rhetoric of the Right, the same villains who brought you the debacle of the 1960s were at work in the schools turning a once-sound and effective system into a place where kids no longer even knew how to do reading, writing, and arithmetic.[17] Working-class and middle-class parents concerned about how their offspring might make their way in a highly competitive world could only look askance at this apparent betrayal of opportunity for their children.

The Right's clever discourse managed to link the unrest and social change movements of the 1960s and beyond to a crisis of schooling that was cheating children of the possibility of gaining the basic prerequisites for security and achievement. The very real anxieties that were the consequence of cultural change and social unrest had been constructed into a public discourse about education centered on the need for schools to reemphasize the traditional concerns of curriculum and reassert the authority of the school over the educational choices of students.[18] The angry agenda of populist conservatism that emerged from this concerned itself not simply with "basic skills" but "basic values." Moments of prayer in schools, fierce and often successful battles to withdraw books from libraries or classrooms, demands to incorporate "Judeo-Christian" and "American" values in the curriculum, and curtailment of students' rights were viewed as weapons with which to fight the moral and cultural disintegration that had undercut the structure of social authority and spiritual belief in America.

The symptoms of this disintegration were not hard to find. The upheavals in social relations prompted by the civil rights struggles, the women's movement, youth unrest, and so on, have unsettled traditional forms of hierarchical relations involving blacks and whites, men and women, young and old, gays and straights, and other categories of people. Successive government scandals from Watergate to Iran-Contra repeatedly called into question the legitimacy of political authority and the ethical character of national leadership. Notions of appropriate sexual and marital behavior were irreversibly separated from a rigidly applied morality. Dependence on drugs and alcohol reached into all social strata, corroding the image of bourgeois respectability. The ethic of consumption—hedonism, immediate gratification, ever-changing novelty, ostentatious display, and infinite desire—relentlessly contradicted the message of traditional Protestant values with their emphasis on duty, persistence, sobriety, modesty, and hard work.[19]

While the most visible protagonists of a discourse concerned with moral and religious values in schools might have included blue-collar Northern Catholics and Southern white working-class evangelicals,[20] the language also found echoes within the professional classes. Robert Bellah's revealing study of middle-class life, *Habits of the Heart*,[21] showed us the decimation of the language of communal commitment among this group and threw a powerful light on the pervasively anomic underbelly of American culture, a condition that was beginning to nurture influential "green" and "New Age" cosmologies and spiritual beliefs among the well-educated classes.

For the most part, however, it was the Right that most effectively articulated the moral and spiritual crisis.[22] For a while at least (perhaps until its own contradictory and sometimes scandalous behavior caught up with it), the Right was most effective at "explaining" this crisis and offering legislative proposals to deal with it. Despite a temporary loss of influence by the early 1990s, groups such as Pat Robertson's Christian Coalition were still able to mobilize millions of voters to effect national as well as local and state politics. While the crisis was recognized as a broad social one, it was thematized in personal terms. Its causes lay in morally lax individual behavior that was the consequence of permissive lifestyles and values. The Right argued that in the 1960s and 1970s, the moral terrain was captured by the liberals and the secular humanists who fomented the culture of "anything goes." In the 1980s an authoritarian populism sought, through schools, to reinstate a moral order without the ambiguities, uncertainties, and contingencies that apparently accompanied the culture of liberalism.

MOVING RIGHT: THE "PEOPLE" VERSUS THE EDUCATIONAL ESTABLISHMENT

Real or imagined, the failures of schooling were rapidly constituted as an "us versus them" politics. The sense that school was not keeping faith with the wishes and hopes of working-class and middle-class Americans was easily converted into the angry resentment of what is effectively termed the "silent majority." The suspects were bureaucrats and social engineers, educators who had read too much psychology or sociology, and federal officials and judges who had acceded too much to the demands of minority constituencies. On the other side were the people—the ignored and abused parents who paid the taxes to support the schools that their children attended but who were excluded from influencing *their* public institutions.[23]

Here was a strange inversion of ideology and politics indeed. What had begun in the 1960s as a radical movement of community empowerment by black, Hispanic, and other minority groups to wrest control of public schools from the hands of the white bureaucratic power structure had become in the 1970s and 1980s a movement to augment local and community influence in the schools—this time on the side of a restoration of conservative educational values. A populism of the Left had become a populism of the Right.[24] Deep-seated suspicions and resentment by a white working class and middle class toward seemingly unresponsive and paternalistic state officials, policy-makers, and professional educators were readily harnessed to a conservative politics eager to further its own anti–big-government agenda.

The effect was a public discourse about education that emphasized the need for a more decentralized and publicly accountable system of schooling. The federal government and judiciary were excoriated for usurping state and local power over education. Mandated standardized testing of students was massively expanded for kindergarten through the twelfth grade, and the results were publicized to enable the lay public to judge the effectiveness of their schools. There was strong advocacy for schemes that would increase parental choice in deciding which schools their children might attend.[25]

All of these changes had a common thread: They appeared to represent a democratic movement away from the centralized and unresponsive powers of those who had held educational authority. This produced an agenda for educational reform that cast the Right in the role of empowerer of the people against a liberal establishment (whether in the teacher's unions, the courts, the federal government, or teacher-training institutions) that appeared arrogant and elitist. This was paradoxical, indeed, given the record of the Reagan and Bush administrations of supporting a massive redistribution of wealth in the direction of the topmost income holders and, more generally, of augmenting the power of the rich.[26]

Indeed, the apparently populist discourse of educational choice and accountability contained a number of less obvious but powerful anti-democratic tendencies. The first of these was the implicit racism in much of this discourse. After all, the object of working-class and middle-class rage—the federal and professional establishment—was strongly identified with programs and legislation that would open up schools to minority children. Giving more power to the state and the local communities, allowing more freedom of choice for parents, or giving tax support for private schooling could easily be interpreted as ways of easing up on the historic commitment to end racial segregation in the public schools. This language was none too subtly coded to imply an end to busing for racial integration and provided support for predominantly white parochial schools (such as the "Christian academies" that had sprung up in great numbers after busing for school integration began). Similarly, claims that too much money was being spent on the children with the least ability and not enough on other kids helped legitimate moves to decategorize federal funds so that money was no longer earmarked for disadvantaged groups, but left to the judgment of state and local officials.

These kinds of educational policies, and the public discourse within which they were framed, were both populist in the denunciation of the hierarchical insensitivity and arrogance of governmental and professional elites and regressive in its implicit racism. In this sense it traced an historically recurrent pattern in American politics, whereby deep-seated feelings of class abuse and exploitation are displaced into the ideology of racial hostility.[27]

REVOLT AGAINST THE STATE: SCHOOLING AND THE FREE MARKET

The authoritarian populism of the 1970s and 1980s also represented an explosion of anger toward the welfare state (such as it is in America). Despite its relatively threadbare nature (certainly as compared to its counterparts in Western Europe), the welfare state as an object of loathing had gradually been developing in the 1970s and reached its zenith during the early Reagan years. Within the "respectable" (mainly white) working and middle classes, the expansion of social programs and expenditures following the unrest of the 1960s and 1970s came to be interpreted as a shift in power and resources from themselves to those whose need for additional support was seen as dubious at best.[28] This army of the "undeserving poor," as it was viewed, included the perennial welfare cheats, those who were voluntarily jobless, had irresponsibly become parents, were dependent on drugs, or had dropped out of school. They were the embodiment of that well-ingrained aspect of American culture that is determined to view all those who come to depend on public support (with certain exceptions, such as Social Security) as shiftless, irresponsible, and lazy. And, preponderantly, these were perceived as black or brown.[29]

A combination of a number of factors, some real, some imagined, made it possible to construct a public discourse about the state rooted in a deep antipathy toward public institutions, especially those that served the needs of the poor and disadvantaged in American society. Such a discourse provided the justification and the fuel for the Right's savage attacks, in the early and mid-1980s, on the programs that served these most vulnerable groups. It was a political agenda that harnessed the fears and resentments of many working-class and middle-class Americans to an ideology that promoted the marketplace over the state as the vehicle for addressing social problems, on the one hand, and an ethic of private self-interest over public or collective responsibility, on the other. By the 1994 congressional election, conservatives such as Newt Gingrich were openly talking about the goal of dismantling the welfare state such as it is in America.

The effect was to produce a period unprecedented in the postwar era in its callousness and indifference to the lives and fate of poor people.[30] The anger and frustration among white workers provided an electoral mandate for policies aimed at reversing the changes and reforms of the preceding decades. The mandate was fashioned out of the frustration of an inequitable tax system that seemed to penalize middle-income earners.

In the early 1970s, this frustration boiled over into the widespread tax revolts modeled on California's Proposition 13. Aimed mainly at restricting property taxes, this movement had devastating effects on the funding of public education that continued on well into the 1990s.[31] Those who felt themselves heavily as well as unfairly taxed received relatively few social benefits from their sacrifices (indeed, compared to their peers in West European countries, the so-called social wage, of middle-class Americans is a paltry one). Their sacrifices seemed to largely support the redistribution of income to individuals (usually the poor) whose claims were frequently viewed with disbelief or suspicion—feelings that were manipulated and unashamedly exploited by some politicians able to cash in on such resentment. The economic press which made such a politics so resonant was also the consequence of an inflationary economy that propelled middle-income earners into higher and higher tax brackets (the so-called tax creep).

There were other factors at work in the anti–big-government politics of this period. The explosion in the size and scope of government made evident the enormous inefficiency, waste, and duplication of public bureaucracies.[32] Procurement scandals, kickbacks, revolving doors, and other forms of governmental corruption heightened public suspicion about the use of tax dollars that produced a hatred of politics-as-usual among increasing numbers of Americans. The apparent failures of the "wars" on drugs, poverty, illiteracy, and other social problems intensified disbelief in the capacity of public programs and interventions to effectively address such problems. All of this laid the groundwork for an unparalleled ideological crusade to drastically reduce the size and scope of government in American life.[33]

Of course the actualities of right-wing politics in the 1970s and 1980s departed dramatically from the impulse that, at least initially, gave it popular support. The crusade against big government turned out to be a crusade against only the social services side of government. Especially during the early and mid-1980s, there were unprecedented cuts in public housing, health care, nutrition, environment, Social Security, and welfare programs. Education and student loan funds also were significantly reduced.

Within a few years it became apparent that a terrible cost was being borne by the poorest and most economically vulnerable citizens. By the mid-1980s it was estimated that 20 million Americans were suffering from serious levels of hunger—two-thirds of these children. There were over half a million homeless children. Altogether over 30 million Americans were officially classified as living in poverty, including one in four children. The United States was in last place in a list of twenty industrialized countries whose infant mortality rates had been charted for the last thirty-five years. It was said that a child in Trinidad or Costa Rica had a better chance of living through their first year than a black child in Washington, D.C. The president of the Children's Defense Fund, Marian Wright Edelman, noted that "over a five-year period, more American children die from poverty than the total number of battle deaths in the Vietnam War."[34]

The result of all this was not so much a state that was smaller and less expensive, but one that had radically reshaped its spending priorities. The already meager welfare state had become even more decidedly what Herbert Marcuse called a "warfare state."[35] The attacks on government and public spending facilitated the shift toward conservative economic values—that is, a less-regulated, less-taxed business sector. Given the failures and waste in public programs, a shift toward a free market less hampered by government regulation or high corporate taxes seemed to make sense.

Within this ideological climate (of course, one that did not simply emerge but was actively fostered by the corporate interests that had most to gain), there were sharp reductions in capital gains and other business taxes as well as in the regulation of the business sector (e.g., in such things as occupational safety, consumer product standards, environmental pollution, and the rights of workers and consumers). By the end of the 1980s, for example, commercial television was free of all requirements that it allocate time or money to less profitable children's programming. The networks were without a single regularly scheduled weekday program for children (and without any, at all, of any quality).[36]

For a while it began to look as if personal interests and private space would usurp all commitment to public concerns and institutions. All that belonged to the latter was made to appear inefficient and ineffective next to the gleaming and dynamic world of the marketplace. Choice, freedom, individuality, and style were all resonant images in the rejuvenated narrative of capitalism in the Reagan era.[37] By contrast, the state and its agencies—including the schools—looked tired, monolithic, and unresponsive. In the climate of opinion constructed within this discourse, what would make better sense than to let the fresh air of the marketplace into the bureaucratically stifling world of public education?

The hold of such ideas on the public discourse was such that in the 1992 election the difference between President Bush and Governor Clinton on this matter was limited to whether the educational marketplace was restricted to public schools or should include private schools also. Not accidentally, in the early eighties a highly publicized report noted that private schools produced a significantly higher degree of academic achievement among students than did public schools.[38] Notwithstanding the questionable research validity of the report (should one, for example, compare two groups of students whose experiences differed not only in school but also at home?), the findings meshed perfectly with the prevailing climate of feeling and perception.

These findings fueled the arguments of those who wanted tax remissions for sending their offspring to private schools. More widely, it fed into the discourse of improving the quality of public education through promotion of competitive, marketlike conditions in and among school systems. For example, voucher systems, said its proponents, would subject schools to the power of consumer choice. Armed with their educational vouchers parents would be able to demonstrate their preferences among schools uncoerced by central-office bureaucrats.[39]

As in the marketplace, the logic of supply and demand would ensure a higher quality of "product." The discourse of the free market applied to schooling meant that the quality of education could be judged like any other salable commodity. It could be evaluated much like the value of a television or a refrigerator. There also was the assumption that pitting schools (and teachers) against one another would ensure an improvement in the quality of education. (In fact, other more deleterious consequences can flow from such arrangements, such as an overemphasis on test results and standardized measures of achievement. In such situations schools might be better judged by the anguish of teachers and the boredom and frustration of students.)

The discourse of the educational marketplace found its quintessential expression in former Secretary of Education William Bennett's "national score-card," which publicly ranked the educational performance of the states. This example was emulated at the state level where local school systems found themselves subject to comparisons and rank ordering. In the local school systems an invidious process of comparing the results of schools in standardized test results ensured that in the eighties more and more attention in classrooms was given to preparation for tests, and administrators were compelled to give more and more attention to the results.[40] The testing obsession in schools was the equivalent of the ratings wars among the television networks. And in neither case could it be argued with much validity that higher numbers had much to do with the enhanced quality of the experience.

CITIZENS' RIGHTS AND THE DEMAND FOR PUBLIC ACCOUNTABILITY

The discourse of the marketplace rests on a train of equivalents that can too easily be accepted. The equating of competition with choice, and choice with quality, is part of the ideological conditioning in American society, part of the self-congratulation of American capitalism relentlessly propagated through advertising and the hype of commercialism.[41] In this context it is easy to see how dissatisfaction with schools and resistance toward centralized authority can begin to find expression through the language of "free-market schooling." In this language is the assumption that the marketplace ensures popular responsiveness or accountability.[42] Of course, it is an assumption that is confirmed with every new visit to the supermarket or shopping mall—at least in the sense that the endless proliferation of new products is signified by producers and retailers as what you *really* need and want. (It is as if there are no such things as what Herbert Marcuse called "false needs"—artificially created and imposed tastes, desires, or thrills. There is only the truth as told by McDonald's: "We do it all for you.") In the marketplace, supply democratically responds to popular demand—or so it is made to seem. And in this logic of marketplace democracy the popular capacity to consume or buy in a discriminating manner ensures the quality or value of what is preferred.

When applied to education this familiar logic supports a persuasive discourse of reform. If schools can be held accountable to the public, then they will be forced to attend more to the quality of their "product." And if this product can be put in a form that is widely accessible and easily understood (i.e., a simple numerical score), then the job of comparing what is produced by one school as against another will be eased. The process of school improvement is ensured, it is argued, if schools are forced to open themselves to the scrutiny of the consuming public.

This discourse of educational accountability has had enormous public resonance in recent years, perhaps because of the significant changes in consciousness that have occurred during and since the 1960s. In this time there has developed an intensified sense of the rights of consumers.[43] Among the movements for social change born in the 1960s, the consumer movement has given organized expression to a common sense of outrage at shoddy products, deceptive advertising, and manipulative merchandising. It has legitimated the sense of moral indignation among consumers toward exploitative manufacturers and retailers and has encouraged a more critical attitude by the public toward producers and distributors.

Not surprisingly the effects of this developing consciousness have washed over into attitudes concerning the state and public services. Parents who, after all, pay taxes are more likely to take a similar "value-for-money" approach to the product of schooling as they do toward the other commodities or services they buy. In addition, this sense of economic empowerment has been paralleled by the growth in the concept of citizens' rights. Since the 1960s, there has been an explosion in the demands that ordinary citizens have felt able to make concerning the economic and social conditions of their lives. Acting in their capacity as citizens, these demands have been aimed at the state and the government.[44]

This radical change in attitude suggests that ordinary people have become less willing to leave the quality of their lives entirely to the roulette wheel of the economic marketplace. More and more people are unwilling to let the question of whether they have adequate food, shelter, health care, home heat, and so forth, depend completely on the income derived from paid employment; that is, one's good fortune to be in a decently rewarded job. Providing for human needs in this way has ensured suffering for millions of low-paid workers and single mothers as well as disabled, unemployed, and elderly people. Economic injustice has spurred the demand that political rights include economic rights; for example, the right not to go hungry, be homeless, or be excluded from quality medical care. Of course, such demands represent a fundamental departure from the dominant American ideology that historically has restricted one's rights as a citizen to a narrow band of political and civil rights (though, of course, even these have not always been afforded without sometimes fierce struggle).[45]

The demand for more social and economic rights represents a conflict between egalitarian democratic values and the values enshrined in private property and the marketplace. The central element in this conflict has to do with how much clout the ordinary citizen should have in determining the nature and material conditions of his or her life. Especially in the 1960s and 1970s, there was an enormous growth in the belief that democracy meant that people can demand that society ensure at least a minimum level of material well-being. Democratic rights, it more and more was argued, also include what some called subsistence rights. When the free market fails to ensure people's basic material needs, then people can expect—are entitled—to have their needs met through publicly supported means. The growth in the demands that ordinary people could make on government had enormous economic, social, cultural, and psychological effects that we shall return to later. For now, it is important to recognize that it altered the relation between government and citizens.

The burgeoning sense of one's rights as a citizen, spurred by the movements for economic justice and civil rights in recent decades engendered, along with the consciousness of consumers' rights, the discourse of educational accountability. Acting as both consumer and as citizen, taxpayers had come to believe as never before that schools ought to be responsive to the public's concerns and accountable for the effectiveness of their practices. Paradoxically this movement for greater parental and public accountability resulted, not in increased local control of schooling, but in more direction by state central offices. Particularly in the late 1980s after the wave of reports critical of the quality of public education, the states increasingly intervened to mandate curriculum expectations and assessments for teachers and students that undermined further local control of public education. What started off as a movement to address the inadequacies of schooling through greater popular accountability ended up concentrating more prerogatives in the hands of educational managers and bureaucrats.[46]

Indeed, by the early 1990s tribune-of-the-Right George Will was asserting that "National Testing would be a lever for moving the entire world of education."[47] It is necessary, he argued to acquire information about educational results that can "galvanize and guide reform." Contrary to the conservatives' loudly professed antistatism, Will asserted that "localism makes less and less sense in a nation of increasing mobility among regions, a nation flunking . . . the international test of competitiveness," a position he was joined in by newly elected President Clinton who also supported a system of national school tests.

By 1994 and with bipartisan support, Congress had passed "Goals 2000," the major educational bill of the Clinton administration. It authorized national performance standards across the curriculum of elementary and secondary schools. Goals 2000 was a continuation of the 1990 Bush initiative that called for the establishment of "world class" standards for what students should know and be able to do in five core subject areas. Similar policies were introduced in many states. Nothing, of course, was more likely to reinforce the uncritical and uncreative character of public education than this added emphasis on so-called "performance standards." Such an approach would, in all likelihood, exacerbate the trend toward conformist teaching in the nation's schools. It was destined to increase the concern with tests and testing among teachers and educational administrators, while further increasing the levels of boredom and alienation already so pervasive among students. The authorized content and evaluation measures often ran to hundreds of pages and elementary teachers teaching several subjects are confronted with thousands of pages of regulations and standards. The job of translating these standards into the everyday work of teaching falls to curriculum supervisors at the state or district level—a paradoxical development, given the parallel attempt in public education to shift more administrative power to classroom teachers. Talk of empowering teachers rings hollow when the very heart of the teaching process—the design and conceptualization of the curriculum—is removed from teachers' purview. Decisions about what to teach, when to teach, and how to evaluate students' work falls increasingly under the control of curriculum supervisors.

When the economic argument demanded something different from education, how easily notions of local control and empowerment could be cast aside (quite different it seems when the issue was not federal intervention to ensure more racially balanced schools).

Paradoxically such national testing was needed to combat obstruction to educational reforms posed by that hoary chestnut the "American public education establishment," which is, conservatives like Will complained, responsible for the decline in the knowledge of primary and secondary school students. Of course, in the pedagogically thin logic of this argument what was needed were ever more *measurable* standards for the classroom for assessing cognitive learning and providing criteria for pay differentials among teachers. All of this ignored the fact that by the end of the 1980s schools were veritably awash in measured tests and assessments. By the 1990s national boards had been constituted in many subject areas and were well on the way to developing a national system of examinations.

ACCOUNTABILITY AND THE NUMERICAL OBSESSION

But how to assess the effectiveness of schools? The pressure to make quick and easily understandable statements concerning the success or failure of what was happening in school classrooms meant the reduction of teaching and learning to measurable categories. The assignment of numerical values to anything of importance in the curriculum was seen as the surest way to make the kinds of comparisons that both the public and politicians were urging on the schools. A pervasive arithmetical reductionism spread throughout the educational process (from kindergarten up) as school administrators scrambled to demonstrate their progress in the acquisition of knowledge and competencies among their charges.[48]

There is, of course, a definite logic in this tendency toward numerical reduction. It is inevitable when human experience of any kind—intellectual, artistic, kinesthetic—is made the object of competitive judgements and ranking. Indeed the deep and widespread desire to engage (either directly or vicariously) in such ranking has meant that little in our national (and, indeed, global) culture will remain for long untouched by the movement to assign values to what we do so that it can be judged in competition with others. It is one of the central characteristics of modernity and a pervasive legacy of logical positivist thinking in all areas of life. All human achievements, skills, knowledge, and capability sooner or later become subject to the process of competitive judgement.[49] To subject education so drastically to this process deeply disfigures and distorts classroom life and the process of teaching.

In the 1980s and 1990s, the public discourse of accountability drove the educational process into the arms of the scholastic testers and the corporate measurers of standardized achievement. It was a match that had been long maturing in a culture that was less and less able to define its purpose and meaning in ways that were not rooted in the values and rationality of technological thinking. Understood and perceived in this way, "getting" an education meant acquiring a set of skills or competencies that could be objectified and quantified. It meant that education should be something demonstrable—about behavior and performance.[50] Classroom time, like time in the factory or office, could be evaluated as to the efficiency of its use—"time on task," as the educational managers refer to it. Classrooms were to be gauged in the same way as factories: by the degree of efficiency through which raw materials could be transformed into completed products.[51] Teachers, curriculum, texts, and administrators were only as good as their contribution to a precisely defined, discrete, and quantifiable task of learning on the part of their students.

The values of the technological culture that suffused education made teachers primarily technicians who could effectively manipulate the classroom environment to "produce" the requisite changes in students. It turned curriculum into something hideously fragmented—unrelated bits of memorizable information. It ensured that texts were bland packages of inoffensive narratives that purported to present the truth about nature or society in value-free, ideologically neutral ways, devoid of human struggle, passion, or commitment.[52] It encouraged administrators to view schools as management systems in which measurable inputs of human and material resources were to be weighed against the output of students as represented through their scores on standardized achievement tests.[53]

Of course, the effects on education of the accountability movement were not welcomed in every quarter. The increasing emphasis on test-oriented instruction appeared to empty many classrooms of creative, imaginative, or critical experiences, leaving in their place only the dry boredom of rote learning and the memorization of facts. For some in the professional middle class, education became an exasperating hunt for school environments that would provide the rich stimulation needed to ward off adolescent alienation, discontent, and sometimes hostility toward the "official" adult world.[54]

One response to the criticisms of the testing movement and its effects was the assertion that it ought not reflect the full content of the educational experience, but only an indication of what was *minimally* expected or required. Where appropriate, education should go beyond and do more than this. Wherefore the introduction in the mid-1970s of high school minimum competency examinations, which, it was argued, were not intended to reflect the breadth and depth of the high school educational experience, only the minimum capabilities assumed of a high school graduate.

The introduction of these exams into the high school graduation requirements of many states reflected the persuasiveness of such an educational policy in the light of popular experience. The notion of education as the medium for the acquisition of certain fundamental competencies that might ensure the individual a minimum degree of agency, even survival, in the pursuit of his or her livelihood formed a powerful focus for the mobilization of educational opinion, especially among working-class people.[55]

THE DISCOURSE OF "EXCELLENCE" IN AN ERA OF DECLINE

While the language of minimum standards and survival skills may have reflected the chastened, anxious period of the post-Vietnam 1970s, the language of excellence surely mirrored the more buoyant "America is back" attitudes of the early Reagan years. Of course, both kinds of discourse represented, among other things, responses to the declining economic position of the United States in the world economy—a situation that meant the decline in the competitive power of American industry vis-à-vis European or Asian economies and the prevalence of low-pay service jobs at the expense of middle-income jobs associated with manufacturing.[56] The apparently looming economic crisis created the conditions for a more aggressive, revivalistic discourse of education centered around "excellence." It was a discourse that, for a while anyway, propelled educational issues and reforms to the center of public debate and seemed to capture the concerns of a number of important, though disparate, social groups and interests.

It was indeed hard to ignore the traumatic economic conditions that have washed over this country in the last twenty years. What seemed, at the close of World War II, to be a period of economic dominance that would usher in the "American century" has all too quickly turned into a time of struggle for economic survival. Scenes familiar to us from the movies of the thirties—foreclosed farms, homeless families, loaded up automobiles headed toward more hospitable regions of the country—reappeared in the 1980s.

Things, of course, have not been as devastating for so many today as in the depression era when a quarter of the working population was unemployed. Nonetheless, the great hopes of the postwar period have certainly been dashed. The promise of the Keynesian-managed economy that could permanently deliver a rapidly increasing standard of living to working people, hold prices relatively stable, maintain low levels of unemployment, and ensure economic growth has died on the vine. Since 1968 the United States has faced the loss of its once-unchallenged position of dominance in the industrial world.

We seem to be under economic siege from Japan and the countries of the Pacific Basin in the East, and, from the West, an increasingly unified and powerful European economic community. The vast change in the economic world and the diminishing of our power as a trading nation come home to us daily. It is apparent in the size of the market for imported autos and in the ubiquity of foreign-made household appliances and consumer items. It is also evident in the rapid accumulation of real estate held by foreign individuals and corporations as well as in the extent to which the U.S. government debt is financed through the borrowing of foreign financial traders.

There was a pervasive sense that the halcyon days of the U.S. economy were behind us. The future is increasingly one in which ordinary citizens consider it less likely that their offspring will enjoy a significantly higher standard of living than their parents. Indeed, for many, children face much more difficult conditions and opportunities than did the previous generation. The classic index of middle-class status—home ownership—sharply registered the tightening conditions faced by newer generations of working-class and middle-class Americans. Across the country, the dream of owning one's own home was upset by impossibly high mortgage payments and down payments that far outstripped the average earnings of workers.

Of course, this mirrors the general phenomenon of incomes that have, for many, fallen far behind the cost of maintaining a reasonable standard of living. Over the past two decades, inflation and "tax creep" have seriously eroded the real incomes of working-class and middle-class Americans. Between 1979 and 1990 the proportion of low-wage workers dramatically increased from 12 percent to 18 percent of the work force.[57] The principal reason for this decline in earning is the effect of international competition, which has hit hardest those manufacturing industries that provide so many middle-income, male-dominated jobs. Jobs with higher-paying export- and import-competing industries have been replaced by ones with lower earnings in the rest of the economy.

In 1983, 41 percent of the entire work force had jobs that paid less than $12,500 per year. Of the 10.7 million new earners added to the economy between 1979 and 1985, nearly half were paid less than $10,000 (in 1985 dollars). Between 1979 and 1992, hourly wages (i.e., adjusted for inflation) have dropped 7.9 percent. And younger workers have suffered the most severe changes. A high school graduate with up to five years' experience in 1989 could expect to make nearly 27 percent less than his counterpart ten years earlier.[58] The relative slide in incomes and job security was greater for men only because women workers started off at a much lower point.

In addition to the squeeze on incomes through inflation and the proliferation of low-income jobs, we must also consider the significant increase in the average level of unemployment. In the 1980s, unemployment averaged 8.1 percent compared with 4.8 percent in the 1960s.[59] As startling as this increase is, the reported unemployment rate hides the true magnitude of the problem because it ignores the extent to which people are underemployed—that is, forced to accept less than full-time work or are too discouraged to even register as unemployed. The unemployment rate also obscures the catastrophic conditions of unemployment found among African Americans, Hispanics, and other minorities. In some places the jobless rate among these groups is more than 50 percent.

The inner cities today represent vast concentrations of "surplus" workers. For millions of these, the choice in providing a livelihood is frequently between minimum-income service work, welfare, or some form of hustling. The visible squalor, homelessness, street crime, and epidemic levels of drug addiction in our inner-city neighborhoods are the epicenter of an *economic crisis* that reaches its most critical conditions in these places but spreads out to touch blue-collar neighborhoods, middle-class suburbs, and the rapidly disappearing family farms in the rural areas of this country.

While deficit financing on an unparalleled scale sustained the economic expansion of the mid-1980s, by the early 1990s the chickens were coming home to roost. Lack of real investment in both the private and public sectors left an economy even more vulnerable to international competition. Industrial decline brought hardship not only among blue-collar workers but increasingly among middle management. On a scale not seen since the 1920s, the wealthy benefited from financial deregulation and tax reforms while the middle class found themselves under siege. Not surprisingly, by 1992 the Democrats had reentered the White House committed to a more rational management of the nation's resources, including education, and a politics that would more aggressively support the needs of the middle class. Yet the economic recovery following the election still left most people unsure about the future and the financially strapped. It ensured continuing volatility in the middle class's political preferences.

Within this context of economic crisis, the notion of excellence has special appeal to working-class and other groups who faced what Robert Kuttner has described as the "declining middle,"[60] the shrinking likelihood of getting a middle-income job. The restructuring of American labor identified by Kuttner, Thurow, Reich and others has provided the critical economic context that made this kind of educational discourse especially appealing. Given a sharp contradiction in the prospects for upward mobility, educational practices that appeared to embody greater selectivity were easily connected to the daily anxieties and concerns of middle-class Americans.

Excellence, in these circumstances, contains the unstated promise of school policies that will impose greater restrictions on entry into upper-level classes and programs by those who appear to have benefited disproportionately from the egalitarian educational reforms of the last two decades. Excellence and the call for improved quality in schools provided a language through which the clamor of minorities, immigrants, and other disadvantaged groups in the American underclass might be stifled. It provided a way to justify an education that in the 1980s dramatically expanded the infrastructure of educational testing and evaluation, designated and funded special elite public schools as well as programs for so-called academically gifted students, and added new graduation requirements.

In all of these ways the economic situation appeared to be addressed, but through a recipe that displaced the origins of the shrinking opportunities for economic well-being from the investment decisions of corporations and government budget priorities to what, it was argued, were the declining standards of the classroom. Such a displacement carries with it racist and nativist undertones, and shifts the blame from those who occupy the "commanding heights" of the economy to the inadequacies of teachers and students. Through a series of subtle but powerful ideological displacements the real economic problems were converted into a crisis of teaching and of educational standards that too readily rewarded and indulged those who were really not deserving of it.

It perhaps was telling that even a president who appeared less prone than his predecessors in the 1980s to a politics of division and distraction in regard to economic problems had, while governor of the State of Arkansas, fought hard for more strenuous standardized testing of public school teachers. The issue became defined, not as the product of a society that is unwilling to provide an adequate supply of decently paid, secure, and satisfying jobs, but of schools that have become too easy and too ready to indulge mediocrity. There is no doubting the appeal of such arguments to a working class and middle class concerned and resentful about diminishing future prospects for their children and prone to a politics of class and racial divisiveness as the means of struggling to attain their own well-being and security.

We noted earlier that dismissing conservative attacks on the educational reforms of the 1960s as nothing more than mystification or ideological distortion misses the very real consequences on schools brought about during this period. Notwithstanding the hysterical overreaction of critics like Allan Bloom[61] who inferred a radical transformation of the system during this time, real changes in education certainly did have an effect on working- and middle-class life. Curriculum changes, challenges to testing, opportunities for wider access by excluded and marginal groups, and so on, did indeed change some of the ideological and institutional conditions that have structured class, race, and gender relations in America.

The intense democratic and egalitarian pressures unleashed throughout the society certainly threatened, even undermined, some of the relatively privileged aspects of middle-class life and the position of portions of the working class.[62] In this sense the call for excellence and higher standards was, implicitly, a call for a return to a more socially selective set of educational practices. It was a form of resistance against the demands of excluded and marginal groups in America (women, blacks, immigrants, the handicapped, and other minorities) for more culturally responsive schools.

Conservative demands that schools raise their standards found a political resonance among those made insecure by the possibilities of a more democratic and equitable school system. These class and racial tensions found expression in insurgencies against social promotion, mainstreaming, bicultural/bilingual education, declining test scores, and affirmative action. These tensions gave rise to policies that promised to produce and enforce a greater stratification within and between schools through a more intense use of testing and greater differentiation in the curriculum.

"Standards," "excellence," and "rigor" became the rallying cry for those Americans who, embattled on the economic front and alarmed by a shutting down of the ready prospects of upward mobility for their children, chose a strategy that would increase the differentiating and hierarchical effects of schooling. The strategy gave support to methods of instruction, forms of evaluation, and curricula, that intensified the competitive aspects of education and that reasserted the culturally advantaged position of children from the middle class and of their peers from white and native working-class backgrounds. Among these groups "excellence" becomes an extension of a competitive and individualistic discourse of survival in the context of an economy whose manufacturing industry is in rapid decline and skilled work much harder to find.

EXCELLENCE AND EQUITY IN THE URBAN SCHOOL

An important variation on the discourse of excellence has emerged from the crisis of urban schooling. From this "other world" of American education—with its shocking statistics of drop-out rates, violence, absenteeism, classroom disruptions, and illiteracy—came a particular version of the discourse. In important ways it resembles the familiar kinds of conservative pedagogy. Principal Joe Clark, who we have already mentioned, received firm support from within the black community. The discourse of urban school excellence, like the discourse of excellence in general, thematized the degeneration of social life in the nation's inner cities as matters of personal immorality and poor character.

In spite of the decrepit conditions of contemporary urban life, this discourse articulated the will to improve one's life through individual resolve and commitment to rigorous and demanding standards. The puritanical component of Jesse Jackson's rhetoric, for example, decried in the harshest language the use of drugs and teenage promiscuity. The voices of black critics like Louis Farakhan acknowledge the debilitating moral and cultural consequences of ghetto life. Against idleness, passivity, dependence and psychological debility, these black critics insisted on radical personal transformation through discipline, responsibility, and commitment.[63] Ideologically inscribed in the pronouncement, "I am somebody," repeated by school kids in assemblies led by the Reverend Jackson, was the assertion of the possibilities for a better life for those able to discipline themselves (sexually, intellectually, and in relation to drugs) and dedicate themselves to the highest standards of achievement.

Yet the struggle for better education among urban minorities could never be completely divorced from the pursuit of a quite different agenda—one that distinguished it from what elsewhere resulted in a very conservative set of demands. Alongside the language of hard work, discipline, and high standards was the demand for social justice. Alongside Jackson's conservative recipe for school effectiveness and success was a radical call for political and economic empowerment. As Jackson asserted at one gathering of young people: "Three million high school seniors will graduate this May and June. You should come across that stage with a diploma in one hand symbolizing knowledge and wisdom, and a voter card in the other hand symbolizing power and responsibility."[64]

For dwellers of the inner city, the crisis of schooling (or anything else) could not be described wholly in individualistic terms. The effects of economic decline, corporate rapaciousness, inequalities of race, class and ethnicity, government indifference to poverty, collectively experienced homelessness, poor medical care, inadequate nutrition, and so forth, produced a recognition of the inseparability of a discourse of excellence from that of the need for greater social equality. In this sense, of course, the excellence movement in urban schools could never be fully absorbed into a right-wing agenda.

Equity and excellence, as the 1988 report of the Carnegie Foundation on urban education noted, *cannot* be separated.[65] The crisis of urban America that slipped from obvious view in the early and mid-1980s reemerged with the explosion of rage in Los Angeles following the acquittal of Rodney King in 1992. And about this time Jonathon Kozol's *Savage Inequalities* gained surprising public attention and interest, reminding many of the persistence of horrifying inequalities in the social conditions faced by kids in the United States. All of this spoke to the growing chasm between classes and races in the United States as it emerged from the years of conservative hegemony.

CULTURAL LITERACY AND THE EROSION OF THE AMERICAN COMMUNITY

For one other group (what has been referred to as "cultural conservatives"), the discourse of excellence and educational quality sought a "return" to an age of settled commitments, an established and certain moral order, and a culturally unified and organic community. From this perspective, curricular changes in schools play a crucial role in transmitting those "true, tried, and tested" meanings, knowledge, and values that can help reestablish the firm foundations of the moral and cultural order. In place of the uncertainty and relativism that plague the postmodern worldview, cultural conservatives proposed an education that was rooted in unquestionable moral values and an indisputable "canon" of worthwhile knowledge. The purpose of this proposed curriculum change was to reestablish the authority of what the French philosopher Michel Foucault called a "regime of truth" to replace the cacophony of voices that challenge and fragment the formerly unified and settled grammar of American life. The "cultural conservatives" blamed our present chaotic and unruly condition primarily on the 1960s, and the movements and ideas that developed in that period, with its rebellions against established values, traditional social relations, and accepted cultural behaviors.

Allan Bloom's best-seller *The Closing of the American Mind*[66] exemplified this attitude, with its furious denunciation of that period and the way in which it affected American culture as a whole, schools in particular, and the behavior and outlook of young people. In his angry attack on liberal values, Bloom castigated all those things that the Right had associated with the moral decline of America: affirmative action, equal opportunity, rock music, the 1960s, the young, and sex. Most of all, he assaulted the deleterious influence of democratic values on education. Indeed, the political scientist William Barber argued that Bloom's book qualified as one of the most profoundly antidemocratic works ever written for a popular audience.[67] Against the 1960s, which unleashed the forces of philistinism, relativism, and nihilism, Bloom yearned for the bygone era of a more civilized culture that rested securely on the bedrock of the great moral truths—truths that one could find best embodied in the Great Books of the classical curriculum.

Bloom was hostile to the moral decline of the university and its students and to most of what democrats and progressives had accomplished in the past fifty years. Philosophically, he blamed the influence of Nietzchean ideas for the undermining of American society. According to Bloom, under this Nietzchean influence, absolute Truth and a Supreme Being had become philosophically suspect: "Faced with the news of God's death and Truth's uncertainty, mass man in America has simply put his soulless self in God's place, to the peril of learning, philosophy and civilization. The demise of Authority engenders the Revolt of the Masses, whose trivialized mass culture is at war with everything noble and good."[68] American society, Bloom argued, needed protection from the "openness" that had produced relativism and nihilism. American education needed protection from democratic intrusions, affirmative action, and progressive curricular reform that undermined the authority of those who composed that special community of the intellectual elite—"the community of those who seek the truth, of the potential knowers."[69]

In a tone that is quite different, another best-seller of the late 1980s, E. D. Hirsch's *Cultural Literacy*, built its educational prescriptions on philosophical and social foundations that mirrored those of Bloom. There is something of enormous consequence missing in our national life, Hirsch said—something that reflected the failure of our schools. Young Americans were coming of age without the requisite body of shared information needed to maintain the cultural viability of the national community.[70] Schools were failing in their fundamental acculturative responsibility to ensure the conditions for the preservation of our communal life. Our shared language, beliefs, and understandings were put at risk by the educational policies promulgated during the 1960s.

Essential ingredients of a "common basis for communications" had fallen into disrepair; and without the capacity for communication that comes from a shared culture, a human group cannot function effectively. A shared culture requires above all, Hirsch argued, the transmission of specific information to children. The root cause of our political, economic, and social difficulties, Hirsch said, was the failure of our schools to provide a common discourse or langauge. The real threat to the nation came from the fragmentation of our communal life, which was the consequence of the present lack of widely shared meanings, ideas, and facts. A more effective education in these was the sine qua non for reconstructing a viable communal life.

Hirsch did not shy away from elaborating the kind of curriculum that would enable this reconstruction. He castigated those who would "carelessly allow children to hear any casual tales which may be devised by casual persons."[71] The cafeteria-style education typically found in our high schools with their wide diversity of courses diminished the possibility of sharing information between generations and between young people themselves. Such schooling was the cause of our cultural fragmentation. Reconstituting a communal culture required an approach to curriculum that was uncompromising and unapologetic about the need for a common body of knowledge, such as a reestablished "core" of worthwhile concepts, ideas, facts, and information (detailed in the sixty-three-page list at the end of his book!).

Hirsch's vision was shared by the secretary of education under Reagan, William Bennett, who in his report *James Madison High School*[72] proposed a core curriculum that stressed the acquisition of language skills and a "shared body of knowledge." Bennett argued that "there remained a common ground that virtually all our schools can reach and inhabit . . . and most Americans agree about what that common ground is." He continued: "We want our students—whatever their plans for the future—to take from high school a shared body of knowledge and skills, a common language of ideas, a common moral and intellectual discipline."[73]

As with Hirsch and Bloom, there was in this attitude a certainty about what should constitute public language and culture: an authoritative assertion of the nature and character of valuable and worthwhile knowledge. Quite clear, for example, were what the "recognized master-works of Western literature" are; the relative importance of mathematics, music, art, or physics; and the amount of time that should be allocated to any particular area of study. For Bennett and his ideological allies it was time to end the equivocation and uncertainty about what must be taught, what is important, what is to be viewed as significant or great. We know exactly where we must go and Bennett and others believed that they had provided the definitive map.

Not surprisingly, Bennett's certainty about what constitutes the canon of great or classic work resulted in his castigation of scholars who questioned the scope or legitimacy of the existing curriculum. Such questioning represented what he called a "curriculum debasement."[74] The attempt, for example, to include the voices of women, African Americans, Latinos, or other minorities in literary studies, to be less focused on European traditions and history, or to include studies in popular culture (television, movies, rock music, etc.) in our schools must be regarded, he said, as academic irresponsibility that leads to the "irreparable damage" of education and, ultimately, to the sullying of academic standards.[75]

By the beginning of the 1990s, following the lead of NEH director Lynn Cheney, newspaper editorials were calling for tough new high school examinations modeled on the European form of long and apparently erudite, essays. Such examinations would, it was assumed, compel students to become much more culturally learned and literate. Sadly, enthusiasts of the European experience forgot or ignored the class-riddled, highly selective nature of such education. Only a distinct social minority has ever been capable of writing knowledgeably and well about philosophy, history, literature, physics, or art in countries such as

England or France. Lost, too, in this enthusiasm is the question of what meaning such cognitive capability has. Such thinking, more likely harkens to the nineteenth-century mystique of the educated/cultured gentlemen on whom social progress depends—a view that a moment's reflection reveals as elitist, antidemocratic, and dependent on the self-serving prejudices of those who already wear the badges of cultural superiority.

While it seemed that much of the country recoiled from the uncensored rage exhibited by speakers at the 1992 Republican Convention, leaders of the hard Right such as Pat Robertson, Pat Buchanan, William Bennett and others served notice that a cultural war was in process. Buchanan promised to "take back the country" from those who usurped the cultural order. Presumably these involved all those who insisted upon a recognition of difference and diversity in matters of sexuality, language, identity, and ethnicity, as well as the cultural tastes, knowledge and traditions that were joined to them.

CONCLUSIONS: NOBLE IMPULSES AND DISFIGURED CONSEQUENCES

To what extent the "cultural conservatives" represented a popular point of view is open to question. The fact that Hirsch's and Bloom's books were on the best-seller list may just as easily reflect the peculiar position and circumstances of publishing in this country: which books get promoted by the publisher, which are critically reviewed, whether the media moguls decide to give airtime to some particular individual or group's concerns, and so on. Perhaps in the case of Bloom's long, repetitive, and turgid book, something as simple as its cataclysmic title might have stirred curiosity among readers. These conditions notwithstanding, we do not want to dismiss either this particular discourse or others discussed in this chapter as merely the interventions of those who hold economic, political, or cultural power. We contend in this chapter that, contrary to what some educational critics have argued, public discourse about education in the United States reflects a complex interplay between the agenda and interests of those who are socially powerful and/or intellectually influential, on the one hand, and the concerns of ordinary people on the other.

The public discourse about education is part of what critical theorists call a terrain of cultural struggle. The ways in which we think about, discuss, philosophize, and "do" education is a constant battlefield of different, often competing, visions and purposes. Such competing goals are, in some ways, rooted in the concerns and experiences of people's lives and in the greater or lesser degrees of opportunity, material resources, and recognition afforded to human beings as they deal with their own, and their children's, everyday lives. This does not mean that educational policies and practices therefore adequately or fully address the needs, hopes, or desires of the majority of people. What happens in our schools falls far short of addressing the real needs of the majority of people in this country. That is the great tragedy of education.

At the same time, the masses are not a blank sheet on which the materially powerful and the culturally dominant make their uncontested inscriptions. Despite the undeniable asymmetries of power and influence, the lives, hopes, dreams, and concerns of working- and middle-class individuals find some expression in the public discourse about education. Democratic traditions (as imperfectly realized as they are), the communal character of schools, and the simple preciousness of one's own offspring ensure the constant infusion of popular emotional and intellectual energies into the public discussion of educational matters.

Quite clearly, however, public discourse about education is always a political matter. It is a "conversation" that is always structured by power and interests. This, of course, affects not only which voices get heard the most, but, more important, whose imprint is most decisively found on the policies that shape education. Within the context of contemporary America, we must recognize the obvious fact that, to a large extent, the decisions that shape our collective life as a society and as a nation happen in conditions that fall far short of being genuinely democratic. Class, gender, racial, and other forms of inequality position us in vastly disparate conditions of access to the levers of decision making. More fundamentally, this inequality shapes the very ground upon which debate and discussion occur, limiting and organizing our assumptions about what seems possible, realistic, or reasonable to consider.

In addition, the national conversation about education is always extraordinarily mediated by the language, commitments, and assumptions of the professional educational community. The latter, as we will see in the next chapter, frequently fuse their concerns and recommendations with the larger imperatives of the nation (or at least what appears to be that of the nation). The professional community through its research agenda and focus provides crucial intellectual resources for defining the future shape, parameters, and possibilities of educational goals and practices. We will suggest the scope as well as the complexity of this process below.

Yet, in spite of this, the public discussion about education continues to be a place where the aspirations and hopes that great numbers of people have for their children find expression. Again and again these impulses infuse and shape in some way the educational agenda. There is, for example, the constant demand for the fair and equitable treatment of children as well as the wish that individuals not be withheld opportunities because of conditions and limitations that are external to the educational process itself (e.g., one's sex or race or a physical handicap). No discussion about public education can occur for long without some attention or reference to questions of social equality. In the same way, public debate about education is constantly referenced to the democratic promise of a good, secure, and dignified life for all members of society. The possibilities of economic opportunity and social well-being are forced back on to the agenda of education. Nor is it possible to separate for long the debate about education from images of appropriate social behavior and the moral basis of human relationships and from the desire to affirm human dignity, freedom, and choice as well as communal responsibilities and social connectedness.

To acknowledge that discourse about education is always, in some way, forced to confront issues of equality, democracy, freedom, community, identity, the moral basis of society, and so on, is, however, in no way to assert the adequacy or clarity of this discourse. Indeed, part of the calamity of the public discourse about education is that when we invoke the crucial moral and ideological commitments that inform education, we do so in ways that are filled with ambiguity, confusion, distortions, and silences. We have learned to confuse, for example, equality with equal opportunity, that is, to equate, in the words of William Ryan, "fair share" with "fair play." We include, sometimes in the same breath, our demand for a world in which there is universal human recognition and affirmation and our acceptance of a world that is competitive, individualistic, and resigned to the supposed inevitability of human failure.

We have come to associate education with the promise of a democratic culture, but in the very particular sense of opportunities for consumption in economic markets always brimming with new and exciting commodities. Democratic life here is reduced to the narrow materialistic terms of the consumer culture. It has little to do with a vision of citizenship wherein human beings become actual participants in the shaping of their own institutions and society or with the creation of what Hannah Arendt called a public space in which human beings engage in communicative action to determine the ethical and practical qualities of their shared life. When we talk about community, we do not easily distinguish the encouragement of loving, compassionate, and just relationships between all members of the school (or wider) community from the aggressive, parochial, and sexist ambience of the Friday night high school football game. Human dignity, which most of us have begun to consider our birthright, is, in the context of schooling, a motivational carrot dangled before children as the selective reward for those fortunate enough or smart enough to "make something of themselves."

There is a great deal to be learned from the public discourse about education as it has been formed and reformed over the past two decades. In order to make sense of the way in which we talk about education, it is necessary to distinguish sharply between the outcomes and results of this discourse, on the one hand, and the human and social impulses that fuel the educational concerns and hopes of ordinary people, on the other. We are in no doubt about the consequences of the debate about education in recent times, namely, increasingly competitive, test-oriented class-rooms; further centralization of the decision-making power in the system of schooling; a decreasing commitment to the welfare of poor and minority children; a growth in the trivialization and irrelevance of the school's curriculum in the lives of young people; and mounting pressure on the nation's teachers to prove themselves effective and efficient managers of instructional time. Yet, behind all this, however distorted and disfigured they may appear, are the impulses and concerns of human beings that, in different circumstances, might produce a discourse and a vision of education vastly more humane and inspiring than we have recently faced. We have no choice in the 1990s but to struggle for this higher ground.

NOTES

1. Nancy Fraser, *Unruly Practices* (Minneapolis: University of Minnesota Press, 1989).

2. Ibid., p. 170.

3. Jean Baudrillard, *Selected Writings*, ed. M. Poster (Stanford, Calif.: Stanford University Press, 1988).

4. There are, of course, a profusion of studies documenting the disintegration and crisis of American culture. Some examples include Daniel Yankelovitch, *New Rules* (New York: Random House, 1981); H. S. Kariel, *The Desperate Politics of Postmodernism* (Amherst: University of Massachusetts Press, 1989); Christopher Lasch, *The Culture of Narcissism* (New York: Warner Books, 1978); Daniel Bell, *The Cultural Contradictions of Capitalism* (New York: Basic Books, 1976).

5. Douglas Kellner, "Reading Images Critically Towards a Postmodern Pedagogy," *Journal of Education* 170, no. 3 (1988), pp. 31–52; Ella Taylor, *Prime-Time Families* (Berkeley: University of California Press, 1989); Neil Postman, *Amusing Ourselves to Death* (New York: Viking, 1985).

6. Marshall Berman, *All That Is Solid Melts into Air: The Experience of Modernity* (New York: Simon & Schuster, 1982); Michael Lerner, "The Pro-Flag and Anti-Abortion

Pathology," *Tikkun* 4, no. 5 (September/October 1989), pp. 8–9; Christopher Lasch, *The Minimal Self* (New York: Norton, 1984).

7. Lawrence Grossberg, "Rocking with Reagan, or the Mainstreaming of Postmodernity," *Cultural Critique* 10 (1988), pp. 123–49; Anne E. Kaplan, *Rocking Around the Clock: Music, Television, Postmodernism and Consumer Culture* (New York: Methuen, 1987).

8. Among some recent examples of this literature on education are John Goodlad, *A Place Called School* (New York: McGraw-Hill, 1986); Peter McLaren, *Life in Schools* (New York: Longman, 1989); Theodore Sizer, *Horace's Compromise* (Boston: Houghton Mifflin, 1984).

9. Stanley Aronowitz and Henry Giroux, *Education under Siege* (South Hadley, Mass.: Bergin & Garvey, 1985); Ira Shor, *Culture Wars: Schools and Society in the Conservative Restoration* (Boston: Routledge, 1986).

10. That school has not been transformed into an indulgent, pleasure-oriented institution is convincingly documented in John Goodlad's *A Place Called School* (New York: McGraw-Hill, 1984), a massive study of American schools in the 1980s; see also Larry Cuban, "Persistent Instruction: Another Look at Constancy in the Classroom," *Phi Delta Kappan* 68 (September 1986), pp. 7–11.

11. See the excellent discussion and analysis of the "literacy crisis" in Shor, *Culture Wars*, pp. 54–103; see also "NAEP Results in Reading, Writing Show Few Gains," *Education Week* 9, no. 17 (January 17, 1990), pp. 1, 21.

12. Pat Walker, ed., *Between Labor and Capital* (Boston: South End Press, 1979); Alvin W. Gouldner, *The Future of the Intellectuals and the Rise of the New Class* (New York: Seabury, 1979).

13. Of course this was a central element of the New Right's social and political critique of post-1960s America. Even on the Left there were those who shared this point of view. See, for example, Lasch, *The Culture of Narcissism*.

14. The educational implications of a society where it has become impossible to make foundational claims about our moral or cultural life is described in a number of books. Included among these are David E. Purpel, *The Moral and Spiritual Crisis in Education* (Granby, Mass.: Bergin & Garvey, 1988); Sharon Welch, *Communities of Resistance and Solidarity* (New York: Orbis, 1985); Donald W. Oliver, *Education, Modernity and Fractured Meaning* (Albany: State University of New York Press, 1989).

15. For the most incisive account of how the fear and anxieties of people over the alleged collapse of authority and conventional cultural norms was worked up into a "moral panic" that helped shape public policy, see the work of the Center for Contemporary Cultural Studies at the University of Birmingham, England entitled *Unpopular Education* (London: Hutchinson, 1981) and *Policing the Crisis: Mugging, the State, and Law and Order* (1978).

16. Theodore Sizer, *Horace's Compromise*; E. D. Hirsch, *Cultural Literacy* (Boston: Houghton Mifflin, 1987); Dave Ravitch and Chester E. Finn, Jr., *What Do Our 17-Year-Olds Know?* (New York: Harper and Row, 1987).

17. William J. Bennett, *James Madison High School: A Curriculum for American Students* (Washington, D.C.: U.S. Department of Education, 1989): Allan Bloom, *The Closing of the American Mind* (New York: Simon & Schuster, 1987); Phyllis Schlafly, "Education, the Family and Traditional Values," in *Education and the American Dream,*

ed. H. Holtz et al. (Granby, Mass.: Bergin & Garvey, 1989). Of course, in its most simplistic sense, the argument was repeated time and again by editorial writers, politicians, and other assorted commentators.

18. Stanley Aronowitz, "The New Conservative Discourse," in *Education and the American Dream*, ed. H. Holtz et al. (Granby, Mass.: Bergin & Garvey, 1989).

19. Bell, *Cultural Contradictions of Capitalism*.

20. Gary Peller, "Creation, Evolution and the New South," *Tikkun* 2, no. 5 (November/December 1987), pp. 72–76; Kevin Phillips, *Post-Conservative America* (New York: Random House, 1982).

21. Robert Bellah et al., *Habits of the Heart* (Berkeley: University of California Press, 1985).

22. Harvey Cox, *Religion in the Secular City* (New York: Simon & Schuster, 1984); Michael Lerner, "A New Paradigm for Liberals: The Primacy of Ethics and Emotions," *Tikkun* 2, no. 1 (1987), pp. 22–28, 132–38.

23. Dave Ravitch, *The Troubled Crusade* (New York: Basic Books, 1983); Jerold Starr, "The Great Textbook War," in *Education and the American Dream*, ed. H. Holtz et al. (Granby, Mass.: Bergin & Garvey, 1989), pp. 96–109.

24. Michael Apple, "The Politics of Common Sense: Schooling, Populism and the New Right," *Strategies* 2 (1989), pp. 24–44.

25. Thomas J. Sergiovanni and John H. Moore, eds., *Schooling for Tomorrow: Directing Reforms to Issues That Count* (Boston: Allyn & Bacon, 1989). In a report issued by the National Center for Fair and Open Testing, it was estimated that in the 1986–1987 school year, schools administered 100 million standardized achievement tests (*Education Week* 9, no. 19 [January 1990], p. 12).

26. See, for example, Lester Thurow, "A Surge in Inequality," *Scientific American* 256, no. 5 (May 1987), pp. 30–37; Richard A. Cloward and Francis F. Piven, *The New Class War* (New York: Pantheon, 1982); Thomas Edsall, *The New Politics of Inequality* (New York: Norton, 1984).

27. Michael Omi and Howard Winant, *Racial Formation in the United States* (New York: Routledge, 1986); Ira Katznelson and Margaret Weir, *Schooling for All* (New York: Basic Books, 1985); Cornel West, *Beyond the Fragments* (Grand Rapids, Mich.: Wm. B. Eerdsman, 1988).

28. Svi Shapiro, "The Making of Conservative Educational Policy," *Urban Education* 17, no. 2 (July 1982), pp. 233–52; Michael Harrington, *The New American Poverty* (New York: Holt, Rinehart & Winston, 1984).

29. William Ryan, *Blaming the Victim* (New York: Vintage, 1976); John V. Ogbu, *Minority Education and Caste* (New York: Academic Press, 1978).

30. Ruth Sidel, *Women and Children Last* (New York: Viking, 1986); Peter McLaren, "Broken Dreams, False Promises, and the Decline of Public Schooling," *Journal of Education* 170, no. 1 (1988), pp. 41–65.

31. Michael W. Kirst, "Who Should Control the Schools? Reassessing Current Policies," in *Schooling for Tomorrow*, ed. Thomas J. Sergiovanni and John H. Moore (Boston: Allyn & Bacon, 1989), pp. 62–88; Harold Meyerson, "Government as Gesture," *L. A. Weekly* 12, no. 16 (March 23–29, 1990), pp. 59–63.

32. See, for example, Alan Wolfe, *The Limits of Legitimacy* (New York: Free Press, 1977); also James O'Connor, *The Fiscal Crisis of the State* (New York: St. Martin's Press, 1973).

33. Perhaps the most influential example of this point of view is George Guilder, *Wealth and Poverty* (New York: Basic Books, 1981); see also David Stockman, *The Triumph of Politics* (New York: Harper & Row, 1986).

34. Reports of the Census Bureau (Washington); The Physicians Task Force on Hunger (1985); *The Health of America's Children* (n.d.); Report of the Children's Defense Fund (1989); Report of the National Coalition of the Homeless (1989).

35. Herbert Marcuse, *One-Dimensional Men* (Boston: Beacon, 1984); see also Seymore Melman, *Profits without Production* (New York: Knopf, 1983).

36. "Pressure Mounts to Improve Network Programming," *Education Week* 9, no. 6 (October 1989), pp. 1, 10.

37. Charlie Leadbetter, "Power to the People," *Marxism Today* (October 1988), pp. 14–19.

38. James Coleman, Thomas Hoffer, and Sally Kilgore, *Public and Private Schools* (Washington, D.C.: National Center for Education Statistics, 1981).

39. John E. Coons and Stephen D. Sugarman, *Education by Choice* (Berkeley: University of California Press, 1978).

40. Judith E. Lanier and May W. Sedlak, "Teacher Efficacy and Quality Schooling," in *Schooling for Tomorrow*, ed. Thomas J. Sergiovanni and John H. Moore (Boston: Allyn & Bacon, 1989), p. 314.

41. David Moberg, "Choice No Easy Remedy for American School Ills," *In These Times* 13, no. 23 (May 15–21, 1991), p. 3; and David Moberg, "For Better Education, It's a Choice Combination," *In These Times* 15, no. 24 (May 22–28, 1991), pp. 8–9.

42. For a particularly cogent analysis of this process see Stuart Hall, "Thatcher's Lessons," *Marxism Today* (March 1989), pp. 20–27.

43. See, for example, Harry Boyte, *The Backyard Revolution* (Philadelphia: Temple University Press, 1980); see also Martin Carnoy and Derek Shearer, *Economic Democracy* (New York: M. E. Sharpe, 1980).

44. Svi Shapiro, *Between Capitalism and Democracy: Educational Policy and the Crisis of the Welfare State* (Westport, Conn.: Bergin & Garvey, 1990); Jurgen Habermas, *Legitimation Crisis* (Boston: Beacon, 1975); Stuart Hall and David Held, "Lefts and Rights," *Marxism Today* (June 1989), pp. 16–23.

45. Richard A. Cloward and Francis F. Piven, *The New Class War*; Martin Carnoy and Henry Levin, *Schooling and Work in the Democratic State* (Stanford, Calif.: Stanford University Press, 1985); Michael W. Apple, *Education and Power* (Boston: Routledge, 1983).

46. Thomas P. Popkewitz, *A Political Sociology of Educational Reform* (New York: Teachers College Press, 1991).

47. George F. Will, "School Standards Keep Getting Lower," *Greensboro News and Record*, June 10, 1991, p. 12.

48. "States Turn to Student Performance as New Measures of School Quality," *Education Week* 9, no. 10 (November 1989), pp. 1, 12. *Education Week* provides a continuing record of the constant push toward "performance indicators" and behaviorally defined competencies among students in American schools.

49. See, for example, Theodore Roszack, *Where the Wasteland Ends* (Garden City, N.Y.: Doubleday, 1972); Suzy Gablik, *The End of Modernism* (New York: Thomas and Hudson, 1985).

50. John Smyth, "Teachers-as-Intellectuals in a Critical Pedagogy of Schooling," *Education and Society* 5 (1987); C. A. Bowers, "The Reproduction of Technological Consciousness," in *Teachers College Record* 83 (Summer 1982), pp. 529–57; Michael W. Apple, *Ideology and Curriculum* (London: Routledge & Kegan Paul, 1979).

51. Joel Spring, *The Sorting Machine* (New York: McKay, 1976).

52. Henry Giroux, "Schooling and the Culture of Positivism," *Educational Theory* 29, no. 4 (1979), pp. 83–97.

53. Michael W. Apple, "Systems Management and the Ideology of Control," in *Ideology and Curriculum* (London: Routledge & Kegan Paul, 1979), pp. 105–22.

54. This was evidenced, for example, in the continuing need for "open schools" within many public school systems, the development of magnet schools, and the use of programs for the "academically gifted." All of these had special appeal to professional middle-class parents who were aware of the increasingly stultifying character of the traditional classroom.

55. H. Svi Shapiro, "Curriculum Alternatives in a Survivalist Culture: Basic Skills and the 'Minimal Self,' " *New Education* 8, no. 2 (1986).

56. Mike Davis, *Prisoners of the American Dream* (London: Vergo, 1986); Manuel Castells, *The Economic Crisis of American Society* (Princeton, N.J.: Princeton University Press, 1989); Michael Harrington, *Decade of Decision* (New York: Simon & Schuster, 1980).

57. David Moberg, "Decline and Inequality after the Great U-Turn," *In These Times* (May 27–June 9, 1992), p. 6.

58. Thurrow, "A Surge in Inequality"; Moberg, "Decline and Inequality after the Great U-Turn," p. 6.

59. Thurrow, "A Surge in Inequality."

60. Robert Kuttner, "The Declining Middle," *Atlantic Monthly* 252, no. 1 (July 1983), pp. 60–72.

61. Bloom, *Closing of the American Mind.*

62. Ann Bastian et al., *Choosing Equality: The Case for Democratic Schools* (Philadelphia: Temple University Press, 1986); Ira Shor, *Critical Teaching and Everyday Life* (Chicago: University of Chicago Press, 1987).

63. In this context, as well as in Third World situations, it is often here that there is the widest gulf between middle-class radical morality with its libertarian spirit and that adopted as part of the radical ideology of a poverty-stricken underclass. The latter invariably emphasizes the need for a severe puritanical and disciplined moral regime as part of the struggle against the debilitating emotional and spiritual effects of colonial or neocolonial forms of domination.

64. Jesse Jackson, quoted in the *New York Times*, February 27, 1984, p. A18.

65. "An Imperiled Generation," the Report of the Trustees of the Carnegie Foundation for the Advancement of Teaching, 1988; see also the National Coalition of Advocates for Students, "Barriers to Excellence: Our Children at Risk" (Boston, 1985).

66. Bloom, *Closing of the American Mind.*

67. Benjamin Barber, "The Philosopher Despot," *Criticism* (Fall 1988), pp. 61–65.

68. Bloom, quoted in Barber, "Philosopher Despot," p. 63.

69. Ibid., p. 64.

70. Hirsch, *Cultural Literacy*, p. 18.

71. Quoted in ibid., p. xvi.

72. Bennett, *James Madison High School.*

73. William J. Bennett, quoted in *Education Week* 7 (January 1988), p. 27.

74. William J. Bennett, quoted in *Chronicle of Higher Education* 34, no. 23 (February 1988), p. A16.

75. Ibid.

The Profession of Education: Responsibilities, Responses, and Constraints

3

In this chapter we will examine important dimensions of the profession's response to the social and cultural movements described in chapter 2. First, we will briefly review the specific ways in which educational professionals provided the technical and operational programs designed to implement the political and social program of the Reagan and Bush era. Second, we will examine the nature of the education profession's critique of this latest round of educational reform. Third, we will deal with the broader issue of the profession's role in social and cultural leadership.

THE TECHNICAL RESPONSE

In chapter 2, we presented a picture of a revitalized conservative movement that developed an articulate and well-received critique emphasizing the need for a stronger, better disciplined, more orderly, and more competitive society. This movement puts a considerable amount of stress on formal education in the belief that a slack, permissive, and demoralized school system threatens the realization of its vision. This precipitated a great deal of high-energy activities—task-forces, commissions, and ad hoc planning groups—resulting in a plethora of recommendations, plans, and blueprints for educational reform. Out of all this emerged the fairly clear outlines of what we now think of as the educational reform movement of the 1980s and 1990s. It is important to note that its basic shape has undoubtedly been framed by political more than by professional leaders, as exemplified by the major effect of the report commissioned by the Reagan administration, titled *A Nation at Risk*. In addition, a great deal of the leadership in this educational reform movement was exercised by state governors, like Clinton in Arkansas, Riley in South Carolina, Hunt in North Carolina, and Kean in New Jersey. However, the various reforms have also required the significant involvement of the profession for expert advice and cooperative engagement. But this partnership itself between politician and professional was not without its own tension since part of the reform agenda has involved the efforts of some politicians to distance themselves from the profession. At the same time, the profession has struggled to maintain its prerogatives without seeming to sabotage the very reforms in which it was engaged.

The themes of this educational reform movement are fairly clear, as are some of its metaphors—for example, back to basics, effective schools, site-based management, and accountability. It is revealing that we can quote a politician as a good source for summarizing these themes. In a style that has come to be quite familiar, then-Governor Bill Clinton has characterized the goal of educational reform as an effort "to increase the number of courses schools have to offer and the number students must take; to reduce class size in the early grades; to increase opportunities for gifted students; to provide more computers; to test students more; to evaluate teachers more effectively."[1]

The reform movement has been often characterized as encompassing two separate phases, or "waves." According to Harry Passow, the common themes of the "first wave" focused on the quality of education: "Educational excellence needed to be promoted (the rising tide of mediocrity had to be reversed), educational standards had to be raised, and public confidence in the quality of education had to be rebuilt."[2] The so-called "second wave" of reform focused more on issues concerned with bringing about changes in teachers, teacher preparation, and teaching conditions. A crucial issue that links these two "waves" is that of centralization versus autonomy—an issue that is mirrored in two separate but related sites: the struggle between the state and the profession and the struggle within the profession between centralization and decentralization. As the profession struggles to participate in the reform movement and claim a piece of the action, much energy has been directed to maintaining significant autonomy (i.e., professional power) and at the same time providing accountability as a way of accommodating the power of the state.

In any case, none of these plans and programs could have been implemented without the help of educators, many of whom, in fact, developed the mechanisms, procedures, policies, and practices appropriate to the reform movement. Educators did, indeed develop "back to basics" curricula that stressed skill development and mastery learning. Educational administrators developed the concept of the effective school in which learning goals were quite specific; testing was frequent and their results were publicized; and energetic pressures were applied to further increase productivity, that is, higher test scores. Computers burgeoned in many schools as hardware and software became essential parts of the language and budgets of schools. Educators developed stricter, narrower promotion and graduation requirements. Specialists in mathematics and science education helped to clarify and develop higher academic standards and increased graduation requirements. Specialists in educational testing and measurement created new and more reliable tests and developed techniques for faster, more refined modes of scoring and interpreting.

New tests were also developed to test teachers and those who were interested in becoming teachers. Schools of education increased the standards for entrance into teacher education programs, and taught methods courses about competence-based education, effective discipline, and mastery learning. Professional educators presented to their school boards elaborate and detailed plans for the evaluation of schools, school administrators, and teachers. They also developed such innovations as career ladders as ways of rewarding effective teachers within a system of elaborate accountability. Educators helped to draft programs in site-based management in which teachers had considerable autonomy if they met predetermined learning goals.

In a word, a great many professionals worked very hard to put the technical flesh on the political skeleton. The profession thereby reflected its own technical skill, proficiency, and expertise, as well as its ability to adapt and respond to varying politically determined conceptions of what constitutes a valid education. This is surely not to say that there was no resistance or that professionals were not able to modify and ameliorate some proposals. In fact, many teachers have expressed irritation and resentment at the erosion of their responsibilities and the rejection of their experience and insights. Many have fought gallantly for greater genuine community involvement, for inclusion of concerns for feminine and minority representation in the curricula, and for a more sensitive and caring pedagogy. There have been organized efforts by teachers to develop alternative schools, and there is in the professional literature a considerable amount of material on more humane and sensitive instructional programs like cooperative and whole language learning. However, the harsh reality is that the major thrust of the Reagan-era education reform has not been blunted and still represents the major point of departure for educational policies and practices. It is also clear that, notwithstanding some rumblings, the profession has largely failed to publicly articulate alternative visions of education and to infuse these into the public discourse.

THE PUBLIC DISCOURSE OF THE EDUCATION PROFESSION: THE CRITICAL RESPONSE

In the next two sections of this chapter, we address the problems and dilemmas involved in professional leadership and its responsibility to the public. More particularly, we examine the nature of the professional discourse in its relationship to the public discourse on education. Although we will speak to at least some of the profession's critique of the current educational reform movement, we will also examine the broader possibilities and opportunities for the profession to provide social and cultural leadership. Such an analysis will provide a background for the recommendations that we make in the second half of the book.

An important dimension of such an analysis requires some clarification of the concept of a professional public discourse. Is "public" in this context to mean discussing the social and cultural implications of educational policies (i.e., to deal with the link between public concerns and education), or does it mean the way in which the profession addresses the public about the technical dimensions of education (i.e., clarifying and making specialized knowledge accessible to lay people)? Surely, much of the language of educators, like that of other professionals, is technical, replete with jargon and neologisms and, hence, often not readily accessible. A more basic question is whether professionals in education should engage in public education in roles other than as experts. It is one thing to say that the profession needs to make its special knowledge understandable so that others can be informed by this expertise. It is something else to say that there should be a boundary between the profession and the public. For example, we perhaps can agree that educators should take steps to make the arcana of standardized testing accessible, but it appears far less clear that educators should speak to how the public welfare is served by such tests. Put another way, do we mean by "the public discourse of educators" the way in which they talk to the public about their expertise or the way in which they integrate their specialized knowledge with broader social and cultural considerations?

What we have gleaned from our analysis of our own life-long experiences, as augmented by our recent readings, is a number of themes that suggest a profession largely working within a quite narrow range of issues and perspectives—a profession that, for the most part (either through collusion or inadvertence), has been content to put its energies into relatively narrow technical responses to issues mostly pertinent to what happens inside the schoolhouse. Even at its liveliest and most sophisticated, mainstream professional discourse is dominated by a determination to stay within bounds and not stray beyond the familiar surroundings of schools, school boards, and school systems. Equally important in the discourse is the acceptance on the part of the profession that its responsibility is to provide technical answers to the questions raised by the dominant culture. This discourse is concerned with description and detachment more than with vision and direction and, therefore, relies heavily on the social sciences for knowledge. Furthermore, the discourse has a "bottom line" quality to it. It focuses on relatively short- and middle-term indexes of performance and productivity. We will elaborate on the conclusions by an examination of several dimensions of educational discourse; scope, ideas about the relation between schools and society, and issues of social vision.

Scope of Professional Discourse

As we have said, attention to perspective is crucial to all discourse analysis; therefore, it is vital to take into account the temporal range within which the discourse is set: Are we talking about issues of immediate concern or about problems of a much larger scope, including concerns of ultimate consequences? We find many arguments futile, because the participants are operating from different temporal perspectives. Of course, there is an extremely important issue regarding *which* perspective(s) are the most crucial, but it is vital to recognize the differences in discourse that are a function of temporal perspective. It is also vital to recognize that while a response may be appropriate within one perspective, it is not necessarily appropriate within another. When, for example, a child bursts into the living room with bruised knees, tears, and pain, it would seem a time for hugs, reassurances, and Band Aid, not a time to inquire into the events that led to the injury. In a word, the short-term problem (here, easing the pain of the child) is a very important one with specific remediation. However, there likely are other important issues here, which will emerge when we learn more about the incident.

If, in our modest drama, we should find that the child's bruised knee and dignity resulted from a dispute with the neighborhood bully on the local playground, we would face a number of larger issues. Should we have allowed the child to go unattended to the playground? Have we sufficiently prepared the child to deal with bullies? For that matter, how can anyone be prepared to deal with bullies? Beyond that is the question of whether a "bully" is really a bully or a person with a problem. Why are there bullies? What is it in our culture that produces bullies, or are we dealing here with a natural and inevitable phenomenon?

Our purpose here is not to belittle any level of analysis, but, on the contrary, to stress that each is important in its own way and that each requires particular responses and qualities of thinking. It would hardly seem appropriate to respond to the crying and pained child with an analysis of original sin. By the same token, neither is it acceptable to believe that we have fully responded to the issues by providing immediate comfort and first-aid. We need also to deal not only with the child's future playground trips and relationship with the bully but also with the longer-range questions of how we and the child are to deal with adversity and oppression. These are our responsibilities not only as caregivers, parents, and members of the community but also as citizens and humans. What does this incident say, if anything, about the kind of world we have made for ourselves and about how might we respond to it? Do we regard such incidents as trivial and/or inevitable? Or do we regard them as important ones with the belief that their damage can be alleviated? Or do we regard them as urgently important with the hope that they can be eliminated through cultural transformations? Involved here is a continuum of temporal perspectives in a corresponding spectrum of appropriate responses to particular points on the continuum.

In a similar manner, one can create an ever-widening circle of educational concerns beginning with a particular student in a particular classroom in a particular time—for example, Johnny fails a test because he missed the examination question. An initial circle involves Johnny, his teachers, and perhaps the counselor, the principal, and his parents. The discourse in this circle is likely to be quite specific—for example, Johnny's reading ability, the quality of his work, his motivation, ability; the teacher's concerns, techniques, strategies, and so forth. The response to the problem is also likely to be quite specific—for example, perhaps Johnny should do some remedial work or retake the test.

We also can draw a wider circle that might include the whole school, its community, and its school district. In this circle, other questions are raised perhaps about the nature of the community, the reading program at the school, the quality of teachers, the resources they have, and so forth. In this circle, the response would be not to Johnny directly, but rather to what this case reveals about larger problems, which might involve such things as insufficient staffing, inappropriate reading materials, inadequate involvement with parents, and so forth. There surely are other circles—some smaller, some larger. Some of them overlap, yet each has unique characteristics yielding, one hopes, appropriate and varying agendas, foci, and discourses.

Our analysis of recent professional discourse reveals not only a focus on a relatively small circle of concerns but also a failure to recognize the necessarily limited discourse that emerges from such a narrow focus. In examining some of the most recent professional literature on educational reform, we did not sense that the writers whom we read were lacking in imagination, sophistication, or insight. On the contrary, much of the material was highly informative, many of the ideas were imaginative, and a great deal of the analysis was sharply incisive. Indeed, we came away impressed with the clarity, complexity, and sophistication of the education research that we read. What was disheartening was not the quality of the thinking, but its narrowness. A great deal of energy, knowledge, and understanding had been expended *in* or *on* a very small space—that of the schools and the present and immediate political context. Many educational researchers are, in this sense, caught up in a consciousness of the here and now, like newspaper and television reporters, captured by existing conceptual frameworks and by concerns for solving the problems at hand. It is not that these researchers overall are unaware of circles larger than classrooms, schools, budgets, and teachers' salaries. On the contrary, what is revealing (and frustrating) is that many of our colleagues *are* aware of the importance of considering education from the perspectives of larger circles but *choose* to focus on the narrower ones.

For example, the co-editors of *Schooling for Tomorrow*, Thomas J. Sergiovanni and John H. Moore, provide us with a particularly helpful preface in which they establish the context not only for the book, but also for the current educational reform movement. They clearly are aware of the broader perspective of education and of the more limited perspective of current reform efforts. Noting the inevitability of conflict in a democratic society, Sergiovanni and Moore say:

However, there is a fundamental distinction between disagreement related to the theme of the nation's basic values, on the one hand, and the disagreement over how these values are to be realized in policies and institutions, on the other. . . .

On the surface, the great school debates of the 1980's seem to be over ends values, and the political interests that are at stake appear to be totally at odds. However, although the differences are real and the conflicts are hard-fought, it is means values that are being contested. The issues have to do with identifying the key leverage points needed to bring about *school* improvements." (Emphasis added)

One would guess from this analysis that Sergiovanni and Moore see this as at least problematic, yet they conclude the preface with this judgment: "This book is about better means to school improvement. Much has been accomplished by early reform efforts, but the chapters of this book point future efforts in a new direction, which the contributors believe has a better chance of *changing what counts most in the day to day teaching practices and learning experience in American classrooms*" (emphasis added).[3]

This feature of the discourse—an overriding concern for the world of schools as presently constituted—is not by itself either unreasonable or irresponsible. It would be fatuous to claim that this world is only epiphenomenal and transient, since obviously the concerns of day-to-day school life are vital and compelling. However, such a concern brings with it an emphasis that serves to narrow and truncate public discourse on education. What we are witnessing in the professional discourse is the reification of the concept of education into the institution of the school. What makes this intellectually destructive process even more depressing is that it is being aided and abetted by those who know better, those who have devoted their professional lives to studying and understanding this incredibly complex process called education.

Professional educators know very well, of course, that education is not the same as schooling; that, broadly defined, the educational process permeates the culture. It goes on in many sites: the home, the workplace, the streets, in relationships—indeed, in all the events and activities of human life. We also know that our education is heavily influenced not only by schools and other educational institutions, but also by a variety of other institutions and figures—the family, the church, the media, the arts, police, industry, the military, politicians, lovers, friends, and so forth. Indeed, which institutions have the most influence on the culture is an interesting and important question, and the answer is by no means necessarily the schools. To compare the effect, for example, of films and television on the consciousness of American culture to the effects of the classroom is to invite us, at the very least, to consider important educational processes other than schooling. Clearly, the concept of "schools" cannot be interchanged with the concept of "education"; yet equally clearly, we cannot deny that the schools are an extremely important part of the educational process. However, we see time and time again, both in the public and professional discourse, the blurring of schools with education and with it the subtle, but important, implication that educational problems are to be narrowly addressed within the framework of schooling policies and practices.

The essay by the distinguished educational researcher A. Harry Passow in the Sergiovanni and Moore book is an example of the blurring of society, culture, education, and schools. He certainly displays a keen awareness of the social and cultural context of education and a skeptical sense of the relation between the magnitude of social problems and the nature of recommended educational reform. He says, "In thinking about the future directions in school reform, more attention will have to be paid to the context of education and schooling, and how reform is effected or implemented."[4] On the same page he notes "alarming statistics" on "divorce rate, venereal disease, poor voting record, alcoholism," and so forth. He goes on to raise questions about the adequacy of current reform efforts to respond to such issues, but in the end he reverts to conventional notions of school improvement. Commenting on the recent Carnegie report on teaching he says that the report is "undoubtedly the boldest and most comprehensive proposal to appear in the second wave of reform, aiming at changing the attitudes, skills, and performances of the teaching force and the conditions of teaching as essential for attaining reform."[5]

Notice how the distinction between education and schooling has now disappeared in the fulsome praise of a "bold and comprehensive proposal" directed at changing the structures of schools. In spite of clear recognition of the power of society and culture, Passow focuses all concern for reform on the schools. The closest he gets (and he comes the closest of any of the authors in the collection) to considering the role of society is in his concluding remarks where he raises some broad questions about the adequacy of the reforms to the challenge to achieve social justice and equity in the next century.

There are excellent and penetrating questions; and as important as it is, posing essential questions does not exhaust professional responsibilities. Why doesn't Passow give us *his* responses to his questions? Does Passow want to affirm or modify the values of "equity and excellence"? We want to respond to his questions by saying that the society would have to be restructured to meet both of these challenges. Should we as educators not, therefore, propose that society be restructured prior to restructuring the schools?

Perceptions of Relations between Schools and Society

Anyone who spends any time reflecting on the schools—and here we are primarily referring to public schools (kindergarten through twelfth grade)—is immediately aware of the intimate relations between the schools and their sociocultural setting. Public schools are vividly mandated, created, and governed by policies of the state, which, in turn, are presumably an expression of community will. Any kind of analysis reflects this intimate, intellectual, symbolic, and intertwined relation between the schools, the culture, and the society. Surely, it is not difficult to recognize the political, sociological, economic, and historical dimensions of education: the effect of Sputnik on curricula, the response of schools to the civil rights movement, the effect of the separation of church and state on education, the problems of financing education, and so forth. Our traditions speak loudly to the close relation between democracy and education, social class and education, economic opportunity and education, and cultural pluralism and education.

Incredibly, the mainstream discourse of professional educators reflects an almost opposite perspective, one in which schools are discussed separately and autonomously from the culture and society. In part, this denial of the significance of the sociocultural context is an inevitable consequence of professionalization, specialization, and bureaucracy. This myopic perspective results from focused and concentrated energy directed at "one" (albeit an enormously complex and perplexing one) entity—namely, the schools. This myopia seems to have intensified to the point where some educational researchers and scholars do not even bother to mention the complexities involved in examining educational issues in light of the myriad of contextual concerns.

We find a pattern among most educational researchers whereby they acknowledge the significance of social, political, and cultural forces, but then proceed to ignore them in their subsequent analyses. However, we also find authors who seem to completely ignore the larger context of education practice all together, who neither clarify the distinction between education and schools nor explore the validity of the assumption that educational reform is rooted in schools rather than in social change.

This seemingly irrational separation of the schools from the society does serve a number of important purposes and functions. As already mentioned, it is consistent with the tremendous power that our bureaucratic and professional consciousness exerts. With bureaucracy and professionalization comes the demand for specialized expertise to fill an allocation of specialized functions. However, these reasonable and sensible ideas have created vast and unmanageable bureaucracies, and with it has come a painful dependence on expertise, however bogus it may be. New specialties not only are created, but also are found to be indispensable as these specialties spawn areas of research, journals, books, professional associations, and lobbying groups. Each specialty is expected to deepen its knowledge through sharper focus and keener concentration and to establish its validity and identity through distinction from other specialties.

Educational psychology, for example, used to be a branch of psychology, which itself was a spin-off from philosophy. Today, "educational psychology" is, at best, a generic term. The field, seemingly always in flux, now is marked by a wide diversity of specialties—learning theory, developmental education, cognitive psychology, and so forth.

In part, educational research and practice with this point of view is only an extension of prevailing traditions and practices in other academic fields and professions. Here, at one level, is the politics of self-preservation, turf protection, and self-perpetuations—the seemingly unavoidable residue of bureaucracy and specialization. One way to keep any specialization going is to demonstrate its utility, and clearly it is in the interests of those who wish to preserve the specialty to claim not only utility but a monopoly of ownership of the required specialized knowledge. Educators don't have to work too hard to claim that their field is important (ironically enough, the culture has made that decision). What the field of education has to constantly strive for is to convince the society that education deserves special and unique study. It is therefore in the profession's interest to act (pretend) as if educational matters can be studied as foreground with some concern for the social and cultural context. Presumably, it might threaten existing forms of specialization (or even the notion of an education specialization) to revise background and foreground or to reconceptualize education such that it must always be studied in relational terms. In any case, part of the explanation for the extraordinary conceptual separation that educators make between society and schooling surely lies with the politics of professional and academic bureaucracies and institutions.

Educators have separated curriculum from instructional issues, elementary from secondary education, guidance from curriculum, and administration from teaching. Such distinctions as these build more and more layers of separation and deepen the energies within the divisions. One, probably unintended, consequence of this proliferation is to leave a large vacuum in what is now the taken-for-granted realms of broad social policy and of cultural direction and vision. Since the specializations have plenty of work to do within their own realms and since they do not claim to deal with broad issues, what is left outside the professional realm are the vital moral and political concerns that ought to ground all the specializations.

Issues of Vision and Direction

It is not only, however, that moral and political concerns are taken for granted or put on hold, but also that professional educators are themselves notoriously skittish about dealing with such controversial and elusive issues. Since most of the profession is dominated by social science discourse, issues of vision and direction are either not seen, seen as issues to be handled by "the public," or seen as the proper responsibility of some other specialty, for example, philosophy of education. This amounts to a division of labor in which professional educators have a virtual monopoly (expertise, technical knowledge) while others take responsibility for broad directions and purposes. In this trade-off, the profession gives up important power and responsibility in exchange for a relatively exclusive franchise to do research and teaching within a framework developed by others.

To summarize, what we have tried to establish so far has three dimensions: First, the public discourse by professional educators involves a fairly sharp separation between the schools and society. Second, we believe that this separation is intellectually unsound and politically irresponsible. Furthermore, many in the profession know better but benefit from maintaining the myth of this separation. If the matter of education were not so important we could chuckle at this situation as another example of the muddle in which universities, schools, and other institutions find themselves as they cope with modern times. However, this is no mere wry story of quirkiness that can be put aside in the way that lunacy and stupidity is transformed into whimsy in such books as *The Peter Principle*. The consequences of the reification of education are enormous given the way in which society, at least those dominant institutions that are not specifically devoted to Education, also contribute to this hoax of separation. We are once again mystified by the way in which the lay public and intelligensia are able somehow simultaneously to posit a close relation between schools and society and to put the onus for reform on the schools!

When the schools are seen as essentially separable from our society, a discourse is possible in which public leaders can shift responsibility for social ills to the "schools," the separate entity that has somehow escaped the surveillance and influence of this other entity called the "community." It also allows a discourse in which professional educators can speak in their languages of expertise and try to respond to what the community wants within narrow limits that, at the same time, protect their special prerogatives. In this way, very little has to change. The political and social leaders direct the language of change to the "schools," and the professional educators direct their language to changes within the schools, that is, technical ones. Technical changes are just that—they deal with changes in how to do things, not with what things are to be done. In the discourse that argues whether schools and society are "connected but separate," policies can be separated from the technical and, hence, can be—and are—allocated to different social segments. Typically, those in positions of social leadership are *not* calling for significant social and cultural transformation when they demand school reform, since both they *and* professional educators see the schools in technical terms. The professional educators that we have reviewed do not question the basic cultural and social structure, but engage in vigorous debate among themselves and sometimes with the public solely about *techniques*. This is seen most sharply, ironically enough, in a time when there is great public agitation over school reform and when politicians are demanding higher standards, greater control, and quantifiable results (i.e., technical issues).

The response of the mainstream professional has been *not* to challenge *at all* the social, cultural, moral, political, and economic dimensions of the various reports and political posturing that we have described in chapter 2 but only to engage in the technical debate. What does the research say about the effects of longer days or of homework? Which tests are best at determining what students have learned? Which method, which text, which test, which sequence? What might have been an extraordinary debate on our cultural and social malaise has been transformed into arguments over technical details. Instead of a debate on the nature of education and its intimate relation to cultural and social meaning, we are having a discourse over how to fine-tune schooling. Instead of asking what we should teach, we find ourselves asking which test to use; instead of wrestling with the complex and troubling issues of what human destiny is about and what constitutes an educated person, we find ourselves wrestling with the complexities and paradoxes of competency testing. This kind of discourse, of course, is greatly facilitated by the separation of society and the schools, of policy and education, and of the political and the professional.

A similar pattern has developed in the wake of the so-called second wave of educational reform—this one centering on the profession itself, particularly teachers. These criticisms focus on both the difficulties and deficiencies of teachers, which reflects an attempt to balance dissatisfaction with understanding. Blaming teachers and their working conditions for student deficiencies accomplishes several tasks: (1) it at least indirectly elevates the teaching role to one that is vital and critical, (2) it facilitates a discourse in which stronger control over students is legitimated, (3) it provides a rationale for stronger control over teachers, and (4) it takes everyone else off the hook. If the real problems are seen as improper training and supervision, insufficient salary, and limited advancement possibilities, then there is clearly no need to berate or trouble ourselves about social direction and cultural vision. Not only that, such a discourse provides tangible and achievable agendas for both the politician and professional.

Hence, state legislatures are filled with proposals for new systems of merit pay, career ladders, and changes in teacher certification. School administrators have set a full table of programs in the testing and evaluation of teachers, while schools of education have responded to the most severe cultural and social crises in history by suggesting that teacher training be extended by a year. Under the guise of significant reform is a reality of make-work projects that are visible and verifiable (although they do not deal seriously with the basic problems and issues of our time). What is more, such projects have the further advantage of not costing very much in the material or cultural sense, that is, they do not require us to give up anything of significance.

There is, however, irony and tragedy in this indictment since one of the most depressing and deceptive cultural shams is the notion that the education establishment (profession) is relatively autonomous and has parity with other powerful societal forces. This is not only ludicrous, but dissembling, if one compares the scope and depth of the profession's power with the behemoths of American society—the state, industry, banking, the media, law, medicine. The profession's power is sharply limited by the society: It is miles deep and inches wide. The profession has become, not an autonomous force that connects its expertise to a cultural vision, but a civil service paid to provide technical and administrative assistance in executing social and cultural policies decided with or without its advice and consent. This situation is seriously compounded by a tacit conspiracy to deny this reality, which provides the society with a scapegoat and the profession with gainful employment and safety. The dialectical relation between society and the schools is partly composed of a myth of significant mutuality of power and influences. In fact, the essentials of school policies and practices (as reflected in the curriculum, school ethics, relation between teachers and students and between administrators and teachers, theories of knowledge, pedagogy, etc.) are more rooted in social/cultural demands than they are in professional imperatives.

It is as if a group of gorillas decided to dance and to take as their dance partners, tall Boy or Girl Scouts. This gives the appearance of mutuality; and—as in any relation or relationship—communication, response, and sensitivity should be required and demonstrated. However, in this dance the gorillas decide on the music, the tempo, who the partners are to be, the time, the place, the style, the music—that is, basically everything. The sensible (and busy) gorillas no doubt ask (allow) the Scouts to do some research on perhaps the price, availability, and quality of various musical groups, dance floors, lighting, sound equipment, and so on. Wanting to please (and not offend) the gorillas, the Scouts are honored to be chosen as partners and are energized by having an acceptable and important role—modest but necessary. In the course of doing these chores, the Scouts become more and more knowledgeable and quite intrigued with the complexities and intricacies of these narrow but important matters. The gorillas become impatient sometimes with the time and money that the Scouts expend to prepare for the dance, but are usually mollified by the belief that excellence requires careful discipline and preparation, which the Scouts constantly reiterate. The gorillas even accept the suggestion that the Scouts, instead of being called dance partners, be appointed as creative consultants—and, indeed, the gorillas begin to accept and internalize the expertise of the Scouts.

However, every so often the gorillas get it into their heads that their dance has gone out of style and that they need to adjust the tempo, change dance partners, or perhaps learn a new dance. Often these moments reach a level of rage, frustration, and near hysteria: How could this happen to us? Other groups are making fun of us. We are lagging behind. We cannot be a land of second-rate dancers! Who is to blame for this debacle? It must be that incompetent band that the Scouts hired.

One would think that the Scouts would be outraged by this blame for the failure of the gorillas to decide on the right dance—and, privately, many are. But the gorillas are fierce and capable of severe violence, and the jobs that the Scouts get to do are fascinating. Besides, the Scouts' experience (and training) does not give them the tools they need to help decide which dance to do. To appease the gorillas, maintain their position, and avoid no-win arguments with the gorillas, the Scouts agree to do further research, hire some consultants, and trim the budget. The gorillas' rage subsides a bit, and they are relieved by the prospect of not having to learn a whole new dance.

Powerful social leaders cry, "The nation is at risk. Fix the schools!" The profession replies, "The nation is indeed at risk. We'll fix the schools!" These formulations speak to a powerful relation between the society and the schools but reflect a false and dangerously misleading picture of a world in which the schools shape society. The profession contributes to this distortion by vigorously and noisily demanding, not social and cultural reconstruction, but more autonomy and funds for attending to technical matters.

The bravest and most daring of the mainstream professional educators raise their voices high and shake their fists, not about policies of social justice, the distribution of wealth, or racial hatred, but about the importance of such matters as school decentralization; more responsibilities for teachers in choosing texts, techniques, and tests; licensing of teachers; better supervision; and increased communication with parents. The professional mainstream has responded to our crises, not with daring visions, but with technical innovations, not with a language of transformation, but with adaptation. Their recommendations tend to operate not only within the existing social/cultural/political/economic framework but also within the existing conventional model of schools. Again, it would be misleading and unfair to accuse these professionals of not being aware of broader issues and assumptions, for indeed most of these writers reflect a sophisticated understanding of the problems of existing social and educational models. But incredibly, these issues are both acknowledged and *ignored*, the implication being that ours is not to question why but to do and die. A clear demarcation relegates to professionals the technical task of researching and developing modes of executing policies developed by others.

These themes of ambivalence toward the political and social context of education can be seen in a thoughtful and insightful article on teacher education by Judith Lanier and May Sedlak in which they show an appreciation of the broader concept of education and urge that teachers be given deeper and broader preparation. They take pains to note that teachers need to know not only the content of what and how they teach, but also the nature of educational institutions and their relation to American society. However, their focus remains on the classroom, and their notion of the role of the teacher emphasizes classroom skills, not cultural leadership. Teachers should be informed and knowledgeable, but this work is to be applied in the classroom within the existing and conventional framework of the school system. Regarding the need for more effective teachers, they argue, "The weakness of pedagogical theory has been its unrelatedness to *school contexts*, the weakness of pedagogical practice has been its unrelatedness to *school subjects*, and the weakness of pedagogical practice has been its imitation of *teaching* models that reinforce the status quo"[7] (emphasis added).

Lanier and Sedlak do speak to the concern for major moral and cultural issues, but they do so as spin-offs of the school's existing curriculum. For example, in affirming the responsibility of teachers to work within a framework where justice, equality, and dignity are sought, they go on to say that such work is "an *extension* of the teacher's more traditional knowledge of their disciplines, not a replacement of this other important dimension."[8]

PROFESSIONAL RESPONSIBILITIES IN A TIME OF CRISES

The Education of the Public

Mainstream educators make quite clear what they want to do but do not speak very clearly about what they have chosen implicitly not to do—or, put another way, they do not speak to an alternative model of professional responsibility. Let us begin to reexamine some responsibilities that professionals could legitimately exercise given existing expertise and training as well as constraints. Moreover, apart from the question of whether the profession should change its role, there is the question of its ability and competence to do so. We maintain that the profession indeed needs to go considerably beyond its highly technical stance and that it could do so within its existing knowledge and power base. We have two major suggestions for this role extension: sophisticating public discourse and providing social and cultural leadership.

What we mean by sophisticating public discourse are those serious and continuing efforts by professionals to share the paradoxes, dilemmas, and problematics of formulating educational policies. It also means sharing not only the incredible if not ludicrous nature of the conditions under which teachers and students are expected to function—heavy work loads, limited resources, tremendous pressure, and so forth—but also the limitations of the profession's expertise and knowledge. The public needs not only to "know" more but also to grasp more fully the contradictions, complexities, and conflicts of what it expects of the schools. The public also needs to confront the primitive nature of the instructional framework as well as the embarrassing but real absence of professional consensus on major professional issues, such as what constitutes a valid curriculum, how students learn, and what the proper relationship should be between teachers and students.

Educating the public about education would lead to more candid and forthcoming accountability while requiring the profession to make its dialectic relationship with the public much more dynamic. Educating the public about education is, however, a necessary but not sufficient condition for the broader role of social and cultural leadership. We believe it is fair to say that the mainstream profession accepts its responsibility to provide the public with more understanding of education; our position is that it needs to do so with far more vigor, candor, and sophistication. However, when it comes to the suggestion that educators should assume leadership roles not only within the profession but also as citizen/professionals, there is a much more guarded response. Generally, the professional response again speaks to the significance of the detachment and objectivity that comes from separating policy from expertise. Certainly educators often encourage each other to participate in community/political/cultural activities—but as members of the public, not primarily in their role as professionals. What we have in mind goes beyond this modest and circumspect role.

Educators should participate along with politicians, pundits, business leaders, journalists, and other cultural leaders in public dialogue on our broad social and cultural goals, directions, and policies. Educators ought to participate vigorously in this process by virtue of *being* educators, not in spite of it. Since educators, as professionals, must perforce study and wrestle with the intimate relation between schools and society, they ought to (and often do) become quite knowledgeable and insightful about both. To withhold that insight is not only disingenuous and misleading, but also deprives the public of important insight and the professionals of the opportunity to give full expression to their expertise.

If the distinction between public and professional is inevitable, the gap in knowledge, expertise, and insight ought to be at an absolute minimum. Indeed, the profession and the public ought to move constantly to narrow whatever gap exists in all related matters—public policy, economics, plans, curricula, pedagogy, financing, teacher preparation, and so forth— and to recognize their interrelations, if not their indivisibility. The extent to which the public/professional distinction blurs without undue distortion is the extent to which the public is being served.

Our goal should be a public as well informed as the best informed professionals and a profession as well grounded as our wisest social leaders. To illustrate this point we will examine a number of issues that often are presented as "educational" problems but that are more appropriately framed as social and cultural issues that are manifested in schools. Framing such issues as "educational" rather than social/cultural enables the dominant culture to maintain the social status quo and the profession to disengage from its broader responsibilities of social leadership.

Let us begin with a brief and necessarily cursory examination of some major issues of curriculum and teaching, that is, of the intellectual heart of what goes on in classrooms. Our reading of the public (dominant) and professional (mainstream) discourse reveals a remarkable consensus on a number of profound educational questions, such as what should be taught, the nature of knowledge, and how we know when learning takes place. It is remarkable, first of all, that there is such a narrow spectrum of belief in such a diverse and enormous nation. Second, it is remarkable that such a consensus could coexist with the highly and hotly contested struggle in these areas in theoretical circles, not only in education but also in the disciplines in which education is grounded—for example, philosophy, psychology, sociology, and history. We repeatedly find an incredible reliance by the public on a taken-for-granted reality in which certain beliefs about education take on an air of certainty and inevitability. This hegemony of educational beliefs is, we believe, not as deep among the profession; but for reasons already explained the profession does little to disabuse the public of the security and smugness that comes from superficiality.

Any number of examples could illustrate this phenomenon: One of the most deeply internalized beliefs of the professional canon is the inevitability and ubiquity of individual differences that not only are real but are of enormous significance. In the face of this, there is a virtual agreement across the country on when children should begin school (age four or five), on how long school ought to last (twelve years), and on how long the school day should last (five or six hours). Some exceptions are made, of course, but they are labelled exceptions, with the implication that there are clear norms.

This issue of individual differences becomes even more complicated when we raise the deeper question of the educability of people—a question that sharply divides the profession. Some claim that any student can learn as much as anyone else given the proper environment. Others speak to inherent limitations and restrictions, unevenly distributed and of a biological or a social nature, to which the society simply cannot fully respond given the requirements of the spectrum of our population. This is because of a combination of lack of knowledge/technique and/or lack of the social commitment to provide the requirements and resources. This is clearly a situation where a "scientific" issue intersects with issues of policy and social goals and where they connect so closely that it would seem misleading to separate them, except for the moment it takes to conceptualize and clarify the situation.

The dominant culture seems to embrace the idea of equal educational opportunity, which implies policies that seek to overcome social, cultural, and physical barriers (e.g., race discrimination, physical handicaps, and poverty). There are a number of problems with this. For example, the idea stresses opportunity, not results, and assumes that in our society there inevitably will be winners and losers. The other, more technical, problem involves assumptions about intellectual differences and instructional theory. It would be difficult to sustain a policy of equal educational opportunity if we believed that the ability to learn in schools inevitably, if not naturally, varies enormously. One argument is that appropriate pedagogic interventions have the potential to overcome these differences. There is, on the other hand, the argument that while the general level of learning can be raised, no amount of instructional brilliance can produce a situation in which 70 million students will have an IQ of 130 or SAT scores of 1,200. (An important reason why this can never happen is that we would reject any test that produced such a result.)

The dilemma is not technical alone: It is a social issue with technical implications and a technical issue with enormous social implications. What should the educational psychologist who believes that individual learning differences are deeply embedded in our culture, if not our bodies, say to the political rhetoric that focuses on equal opportunity? What do the political leaders say to the educators who believe that all students are capable of high-level intellectual and artistic functioning? In our society, there presumably are rewards for those with the skills appropriate to its maintenance and growth. The converse of this, of course, is that those lacking in these skills receive far fewer, if any, rewards. This clearly resonates with the theory of individual differences—except, of course, it makes a judgment that some differences are to be valued more than others. However, if the learning theorists who claim that virtually all students can master important areas of knowledge are right, do we have a society where *all* those with the appropriate skills will be offered equivalent rewards? Or, as one writer has put it, would there be a great many more jobs if every child were able to read at grade level? Should teachers who believe that all students and their parents can be masterful tell their students that such mastery is no guarantee to social and economic advancement? Should teachers who believe in a reality of inevitable individual differences and differentiated rewards tell their students and parents that no matter what happens some students will win and others will lose?

The point here is that this bramble of social/educational complexity is one about which professionals are, at the very least, supposed to know a lot and is one about which many of them are, in fact, extremely knowledgeable. Such matters are central to professional expertise and education; but in a society in which educational issues are separated conceptually from social/cultural ones, such matters are rarely, if ever, central to public discourse on education or to the discourse that the profession uses to inform the public. Furthermore, mainstream professionals tend to brush aside the larger political and moral implications in theories of individual differences and focus their attention on more technical matters.

The overall result of this attitude and practice among mainstream professionals is our current policy of contradiction and paradox that celebrates equality and justice and meritocracy and competition. The paradox of valuing both freedom and equality is a continuing and probably permanent issue with which our society struggles. Hence, it requires continual dialogue and debate. These so-called abstract issues have very concrete manifestations and one major arena of this drama is the school. We therefore indict mainstream professionals for being aware of the relation between cultural ideas and school policies but choosing, for the most part, not to significantly integrate their understanding of the relation into their research, teaching, or dissemination efforts.

The irony of this tragic avoidance is that while it has some clear benefits for the profession (e.g., safety and security), it adds unnecessary burdens to the profession, especially to teachers. The trade-off is one in which the public can both admit serious social problems and maintain the status quo by projecting them on to an other—in this case, schools. This accommodation, as we have said, allows the profession considerable autonomy and legitimation, but it also brings unnecessarily heavy burdens of blame, shame and guilt. This is particularly true of teachers who, like a conscripted army, are asked to take the brunt of the suffering that has its origins in remote and distant quarters.

The public/profession separation hoax is the notion that the solution to our problems is more "firepower"—here, more expertise, better practices, more professional competence. As the social and cultural problems then intensify, the corollary of this hoax is a revelation of greater and greater shortcomings by teachers and administrators. When teachers and administrators buy into this sham—which, of course, however risky, is attractive since it elevates the profession to such importance—they are given the utterly impossible task of responding wisely to deep social and political issues in a technical manner. Not only that, they are asked to do so with pitiful resources and are required to assume a position of passivity, docility, and acquiescence. Thus many, many teachers lured into this trap respond with enormous frustration, pain, guilt, and, ultimately, paralysis.

Teachers as Cultural Leaders

Although we have characterized the profession's response primarily through reference to the writings of theoretically oriented academics, the single largest subgroup of the profession consists of teachers. For this reason, we want to comment on the particular role that teachers play in the determination of broad educational policies. The dilemmas and frustrations that teachers face reflect, as well as affect, the tangles and complexities of our times. There is no reason to believe that school teachers have been any less or any more wise, heroic, or imaginative than any other group of public professionals. The difficulty, of course, is that what is required from all of us to overcome our present social and cultural crisis is a great deal more wisdom, courage, and imagination than we have seen. Is it, however, reasonable to ask even more of teachers—a group clearly overworked, underpaid, and undervalued; a profession with strong traditions of passivity, gentleness, and modesty; a group that is so overshadowed by administrators, school board members, political leaders, and academics?

The plight of teachers can be compared, at least to some extent, to the frustrations and dilemmas of an army at war. We use this metaphor, not to suggest violence and destruction, but to illuminate the roles, functions, and conflicts in the definition, organization, and performance of a public task of great importance. This image suggests an army that is recruited in a burst of affirmation and idealism—for example, to defend honor, to restore democracy, to fight evil. There is great public support for this effort as articulated and crystallized by its leaders. However, while everyone is asked to make some contribution and sacrifice to the war effort, the burden inevitably falls more heavily on the shoulders of a relative few. Those few are strenuously—but, surprisingly, briefly—trained, their pay is low, and their life is difficult; but all is made endurable by the majesty of their cause. Indeed, many people volunteer to serve and yearn for the opportunity to fight for Principle, God, and Country.

The sagas and narratives of this oft-repeated story speak to the starkly unromantic dimensions of being a soldier—of boredom, loneliness, fright, and of feeling isolated, manipulated, and powerless. By the time soldiers confront their actual day-to-day tasks, the initial emotional energy will have faded. The powerful reasons for fighting are likely to have become blurred and perhaps even questioned, and there is a growing suspicion that their pain and suffering is unappreciated and that their contributions will be forgotten or unaffirmed. Some will believe that there are those back home safe from the battlefields who actually profit from the continuation of a war that seems endless and increasingly futile and that others, presumably their colleagues (e.g., officers, chaplains, support personnel), have a much more comfortable tour of duty. Some soldiers differ and quarrel among themselves—complaining can be seen as whining, and criticism of the war as lack of patriotism and cowardice—while others accept their lot fatalistically, if not heroically. One cannot but be struck by the reality that however depressed, lonely, and terrifying the task might be, virtually everyone returns to it despite the risks, frustration, and powerlessness. Since this is a very large army, responses to these tasks vary—some perform their tasks heroically (though only some are recognized), some desert, some are wounded, and some suffer psychological wounds—but probably most perform their routines remote from the action and even more remote from the larger, strategic concerns.

Like any metaphor, this one has limits and distorts as well as illumines, but there are a few parallels that we wish to stress. Society tends to have a similarly ambivalent attitude toward teachers, extolling them in a rhetoric of virtue and dedication and simultaneously affording them relatively low status and resources. Teachers tend to be seen as agents of policies determined by their professional leaders and elected officials and only vaguely understood by the public. Teachers largely see themselves as powerless, misunderstood, and undervalued, while educational theorists are apt to criticize them for an uncritical acceptance of their role and for a lack of depth, if not incompetence. One of the limitations of the metaphor lies in somewhat different traditions of autonomy. While the military stresses discipline and obedience for the soldier, there is a strong tradition in education of criticism, reflection, and dissent.

Teachers usually find themselves in an ambiguous and paradoxical situation when it comes to the issue of their professional autonomy. Teachers are, in effect, asked to be both loyal and autonomous and to be team players and stars. They are told that they will be rewarded for contributing to school goals but are rarely given a serious opportunity to determine those goals. Schools tend to be hierarchical, but school leaders often invoke the rhetoric of family and community. Theorists and administrators are apt to speak to the crucial importance of teachers but do little to change the political status of teachers. However, most central here is not so much the powerlessness of teachers but their voicelessness—that is, unlike infantrymen whose voicelessness is to some extent sanctioned, teachers have a very weak public voice even though the official rhetoric speaks otherwise. Indeed, it can easily be said that teachers have an ethical imperative to go far beyond their conventional passivity.

However, there are realms in which teachers exercise considerable influence and times when teachers' voices are clear and energetic. National and state teachers' organizations have considerable political clout in supporting candidates and social legislation at national as well as local levels, and in many communities such organizations engage in serious collective bargaining, largely over issues of salaries and working conditions. In practice, individual teachers provide valued expertise in instructional matters and often offer very helpful personal support to troubled students. However limited, these situations do indicate the potential for extending teacher influence and autonomy. At the same time, they indicate the limited range in which teachers have chosen to exercise their responsibilities.

Teachers, like other educators, tend to use a technical instructional discourse within the profession, with their clients, and with the public. Teachers, as teachers, talk about such matters as students' developmental readiness, appropriate instructional strategies, curriculum scope and sequence, and valid testing techniques. Teachers as public employees speak with their administrators about ameliorating the problems of the existing system—for example, raising wages, reducing class size, adding services. What teachers along with their colleagues in the profession tend not to do is to engage in serious moral and political discourse. To the extent that they are reflective and articulate, their criticism tends to be technical and instrumental. Like soldiers at war, no doubt many teachers sense that there are fundamental difficulties involved in their frustration—issues of a strategic rather than a tactical nature. Like foot soldiers, teachers sense a loss of their early energy that emerged out of a shining vision now blurry, if not stained. Teachers, like a forgotten army, often feel helpless and inarticulate in trying to give voice to these feelings.

Within the profession of education, teachers tend to have less prestige and autonomy than others in the field—for example, school administrators, educational researchers, and education professors. Our point, however, is that even within the constraints and limits of existing arrangements, teachers have an opportunity to go beyond their technical and subservient role, although others in the profession obviously have more freedom and different opportunities to exercise that leadership. On one level, this leadership involves the vital professional expertise that reflects a deep and sensitive understanding of how education policies and practices manifest social/cultural policies and practices. Another level of leadership that the public requires from the profession involves the reconstruction of a moral vision, or a cultural transformation.

The Profession in a Time of Crisis

Our analysis of educational issues had led us to an examination of social and cultural issues, and our conclusions on these matters resonate with those who interpret our condition to be one of crisis. A crisis does not require technical responses alone. Quite the reverse, since such responses often deepen and extend the problems. Our society, our culture, requires major structural change to respond to the magnitude of the crisis, which threatens both our largest and smallest hopes. Our largest aspirations have to do with creating a world of justice, love, peace, community, joy, and beauty for all. Our smallest hope is plain and simple survival. Both possibilities are in jeopardy.

This is certainly not the first time in history when we have been disappointed in our efforts to create a better world, but it is the first time in the modern era that we have reason to fear for any kind of world at all. The threats are not remote. Indeed, they are so familiar and frightening that their mention often engenders resistance and denial. Statistics and warnings abound, the media speak daily and vividly about the perils, and even politicians have been known to make reference to them (although to do so can put them at political risk). Here are some examples:

1. More than one billion people are chronically undernourished. Deaths related to hunger and starvation average 50,000 a day.
2. Two billion people do not have safe water to drink.
3. The twentieth century has already had 207 wars and an estimated 78 million lives lost.[9]

These issues are incredibly complex, of enormous magnitude, and involve a myriad of dimensions and perspectives. As citizens and as educators, we have come to see them both as indicators of failure in our fundamental structures and as rooted in moral confusion. Clearly, responding to these issues requires a great deal of new knowledge and intellectual acuity. However, we also have come to see that intellectual abilities have not been sufficient in preventing our crises. Indeed, we have seen genius applied to the creation of the very crises that threaten us.

We must confront certain realities—namely, that a wealthy society like ours that allows so many infants to die unnecessarily has serious flaws; that a culture that produces both a Holocaust and the concept of unconditional love is at war with itself; and that an ethic that celebrates the freedom to create both a Garden of Eden and a hole in the atmosphere represents lunacy. We must also confront two other realities—namely, that overcoming these threats will require transformation, not reform, and that, paradoxically, we seem very reluctant to own up to the severity of our crisis. We say "paradoxically" because we believe there is an emerging consensus that we do indeed face calamity—although, of course, there are many interpretations of the source and nature of the calamity and of what our response should be. We are convinced that confronting these realities requires the infusion of a vigorous moral discourse. Our task includes not only moral analysis, as crucial and vital as that is, but also the forging of a moral vision—one that can inform and energize our political will and educational strategy.

The profession must confront some of the painful dimensions of current educational practice. Educators, like the rest of us, are caught up in a system in which individual achievement, competition, success, and aggressiveness are essential elements. Formal education has become an instrument for legitimizing and defining hierarchy. Schools are sites in which people are sorted, graded, classified, and labelled, thereby giving credence to the tacit social value that dignity must be earned. Teachers are asked to prepare students differently—to give some the encourage-ment and skills to be leaders while teaching others to endure their indignities quietly and proudly. This sytem helps sustain and legitimate a society revelling in consumerism, jingoism, hedonism, greed, and hierarchy.

We urge the profession not only to reflect on its own involvement and implication in these processes but also to engage the public in a dialogue on these matters. The public has little opportunity to examine the relations between some of our culture's highest aspirations (justice, love, dignity, community), on the one hand, and educational policies and practices, on the other. Ironically, there *is* public dialogue that extends to the notion that profound social and cultural changes might be required to overcome the crises of our times. (We say "ironically" because there is very little—we could say no—parallel strong public voice that speaks to fundamental changes in the educational system. This may be an index of the public's confusion and ambivalence about the necessity for major change.) There are, for example, public voices that urge us to develop a global consciousness—or at least a bioregional, rather than a national, one. There are suggestions that we should respond to national security issues by studying peace rather than war; there are ideas about economic decentralization, alternative technologies, and new concepts of work.

These radical proposals require giving up important dimensions of the existing vision: success, the acquisition of material wealth, a sense of personal well-being, personal autonomy, national pride, and individual achievement. To move the various proposals for fundamental cultural and social changes to the educational sphere is to move from theory to practice, from fantasy to reality. Just as people from both the Right and the Left are apt to seek out conservative bankers and lawyers in their personal lives, it may be that the schools are too risky a site to deal with truly fundamental change. The schools thus offer a site of continuity, stability, and a buffer—a predictable place where newer cultural values can be filtered and modified to limit their potency.

Professionals have a profoundly important opportunity to engage the lay public in a more direct encounter with the problems of our existing educational vision. Like those soldiers fighting in the mud and jungles, teachers and other professionals need not and should not shoulder the full burden of their awe-inspiring responsibilities. Teachers and educators not only should remind the public of the ambiguity and contradictions of its expectations and of its refusal to allocate resources adequate to the magnitude of these expectations but also should urge and require the public to work with them in a common struggle. We cannot afford to continue a policy of keeping the public off the hook—a policy that keeps the profession in a continuous state of being a whipping boy.

And yet, when we examine the work and discourse of mainstream professionals, we find little to indicate that this opportunity will be taken. If anything, the profession seems to have become more entrenched in the mining of smaller and smaller nuggets of technical ore. This to us reflects a great irony, if not tragedy, for it cannot be attributed solely to shallow thinking or limited imagination since there is clearly a significant increase in the intellectual caliber of educational researchers and scholars. Indeed, when one takes a short- and middle-range perspective on educational issues, many of the responses from the mainstream professionals are imaginative and constructive, even daring. However, where leadership in education is most needed—in confronting the social and cultural crises of our times—there is abject failure.

There are, of course, important, albeit marginal, movements within the profession that advocate significant and basic changes in social and educational policy. These movements include those who seek significantly greater equity for populations marginalized because of race, gender, and class and who work energetically for significantly increased involvement of the community and of teachers in the decision-making process. There are also important and lively efforts directed at renewing the traditions of humanistic and progressive education, with a focus on imagination, self-expression, and wholeness. We are sympathetic to, and respectful of, such efforts and are optimistic about their potential to have a positive effect on the educational process. As we make clear below, although we share many of the ideas of these movements, our own orientation for the most part reflects the particular traditions of critical pedagogy. We root our responses to the present social and educational crisis in this orientation, which we examine in the next chapter.

NOTES

1. In Samuel Bachrach, *Education Reform: Making Sense of It All* (Boston: Allyn & Bacon, 1992), p. xi.

2. In Thomas J. Sergiovanni and John H. Moore, eds., *Schooling for Tomorrow: Directing Reforms to Issues That Count* (Boston: Allyn & Bacon, 1989), pp. 15–16.

3. Ibid., pp. xiv–xv.

4. Ibid., p. 29.

5. Ibid., p. 34.

6. Ibid., p. 311.

7. Quoted in ibid., p. 138.

8. Quoted in ibid., p. 142. Emphasis in original.

9. Ruth Sivard, *World Military and Social Expenditures* (New York: World Priorities, 1985), p. 27.

4

Beyond Critical Pedagogy: Affirmation and Critique

In the remaining chapters of this book, we begin the task of constructing alternatives to the mainstream educational discourse in both the public and professional realms. In doing so, we will, of course, reflect our own preferences and orientations about the directions to be taken. Such choices are, needless to say, developed within our own preexisting points of view. Especially crucial to these points of view has been the influence of critical pedagogy and critical education studies as "schools" of educational theory and practice. Although hardly a static or sharply delineated body of ideas and practices, these schools of thought do have sufficiently clear boundaries and contours that we attempt to outline below. And although we will point to some of our reservations and concerns about these critical educational perspectives, they do, nonetheless, provide us with the basic point of departure for our recommendations. Indeed, in a fundamental sense, we affirm their enormously insightful and resonant character. In attending to some of the weaknesses and failures, we also recognize our responsibilities to extend the boundaries and deepen the analysis of the existing critical work in education. For those less than familiar with the field, the historical sketch of it that follows provides not only a context for better understanding our concern and disappointments in regard to it but also a basis for our subsequent proposals (in chapters 5 and 6) for an alternative public discourse and agenda for education.

CRITICAL DISCOURSE IN EDUCATION:
THE DISTANT THUNDER OF PROTEST

Challenging the "Black Box" of Schooling

The so-called new sociology of education that emerged in Britain in the early 1970s is often regarded as an historical turning point in the development of the critical view of the nature and purpose of education. Led by Michael F. D. Young and his colleagues at the University of London Institute of Education,[1] educational theorists began to look at aspects of the educational process hitherto accepted as given and immutable. Drawing on the rather arcane intellectual traditions of phenomenological philosophy and the sociology of knowledge, they raised fundamental and disturbing questions about the process of schooling. Their work put into question much of what was simply assumed about what they referred to as the "black box" of schooling. They raised questions about how teachers come to categorize the ability of students; how success or failure were "constructed" in the classroom; the cultural prejudices built into the kinds of intelligence most valued in schools; why some kinds of curricular knowledge are distinguished in importance or, conversely, downgraded; why particular kinds of students' knowledge and information come to be validated as worthwhile and others not; and so on.

This research did more than simply raise questions about the taken-for-granted nature of the educational world. It began to show that much of what was familiar and seemingly obvious about school life was not a fact of nature but the product of social choices and the result of particular cultural and historical preferences. Most important, this research showed that what we teach kids, how we teach, and how we judge ability and achievement do not reflect universal laws but choices made in and by societies—or, more precisely, the privileged groups within those societies. The continuation of existing classroom practices depends on the common-sense beliefs of teachers and educators—assumptions and ideas that we could examine critically and, thus, if we should choose, change. The desirability of such change was not left in doubt. Classroom success, it was shown, was heavily weighted in favor of the knowledge, experience, and language of white, middle-class children. Schools actively produced social inequality and systematically discriminated against the culture of minority, working-class, and female students.

That schools passed on the inequalities of the larger society was not new to sociologists of education. But the work of the "new sociologists" put into question many of the seemingly sacrosanct traditions that shape the educational experience, especially those having to do with questions of knowledge and the curriculum.[2] Viewing the curriculum as a product of particular cultural and historical choices (rather than as something simply there or given) makes it less than obvious why, for example, algebra should be so much more valued than, say, art; or why the knowledge of nineteenth-century British literature should be more valued than contemporary rock music. The "new sociology" made problematic the strict separation and superiority accorded to school knowledge as opposed to the knowledge that kids brought into school from their homes and communities. It made clear that the kinds of knowledge and experience valued, or devalued, in the classroom had a crucial bearing on the kinds of students most likely to be successful in school. It was the classroom that made intelligent and capable human beings into apparently incapable students. The content of our curriculum, notions about what it is worthwhile to teach in school and the way in which we view intelligence—all of these create school systems that produce and maintain the forms of injustice that increasingly blight the social order.

Legitimating Social Inequality

While this work was going on in England, two radical political economists in the United States, Samuel Bowles and Herbert Gintis, were at work on another ground-breaking piece of critical analysis concerning education. Their book, *Schooling in Capitalist America,*[3] elaborated in historical and empirical detail the relation of the educational system in the United States to the structures of economic and political power. At the heart of this work was a compelling account of the way in which this system seemed to legitimate class inequalities. In an account clearer and more convincing than any other until that time, the writers showed how education prepares the young for their place in a class-divided, sexist, and racist social order. While schools have other ostensible roles (the development of rational intellect, aesthetic expression, physical health, etc.), these take a back seat to more pernicious social functions. The overriding purpose of the school is to equip students with the personality traits, ways of presenting the self, and the cognitive skills appropriate to an individual's future roles in the economic hierarchy. In so doing, schools legitimate the inequalities that permeate our society.

Central to Bowles and Gintis's description of how schools function is what they call the "correspondence principle." In essence, this referred to the way in which students from different social classes are subjected to enormously different educational experiences—how they are treated in the classroom, what is expected of them intellectually, the extent to which they may choose the kinds of school work they do, the degree to which this work demands intellectual initiative and creative autonomy, and so on. These variations are not arbitrary. There is, they say, a definite relation between the character of the classroom and future work possibilities. Simply put, the higher the social class of students, the more the school socializes them into the expectations of jobs that emphasize intellectual independence and self-evaluation, creative initiative, and control over one's time and space. The lower the social class, the more the school acts as a preparation for jobs that are routinized and mechanical and that require subordination and obedience to the authority and judgment of superiors. All this takes place through what another critical scholar, Jean Anyon, called the "hidden curriculum of work."[4] There is an unacknowledged moral dimension to the classroom curriculum—one that powerfully conveys to students a sense of their own intellectual efficacy, personal values, and the appropriate occupational and social station that, in strong likelihood, awaits them.

Of course, given the democratic commitments of American life, none of this sorting and selecting can too easily be admitted. The idea that schools are not fundamentally about enhancing the personal and social opportunities of young lives but are, instead, about regulating and channelling kids into the existing social order—perpetuating and reproducing systems of inequality—contradicts our most cherished myths concerning opportunity and freedom. Far from being the "great equalizer," schooling in America may be better characterized as what the educational historian Joel Spring called "the sorting machine."[5] Schools take and reinforce the social and economic advantages and disadvantages of students and dispatch them into a society pervaded by marked divisions of wealth, power, dignity, and opportunity. Part of the "great school legend" has been to deny the close connection that has always existed between public education and social inequality. Indeed, the mythology of schooling, with all of its emphasis on individual opportunity, "making something of yourself," and the importance of merit, has helped to sweep under the rug the dirty secrets of class privilege, sexism, and racism in American society. Something other than sheer effort and native intelligence determines who gets what in this country.

Through sometimes complex analysis, critical scholars were able to explode the notion that the social hierarchy reflects some kind of meritocracy—that is, that the social divisions between people reflect some kind of *natural* distribution of intelligence and ability. Indeed, it could be shown that intelligence had little to do with educational achieve-ment or social and economic success—a conclusion that has been ampli-fied in the work of many subsequent educational researchers.[6] The so-called objectivity of standardized intelligence and scholastic tests was shown to be little more than the way in which we rationalize or disguise how social class, race, or gender influence success or failure in the educational system. Much of this work—both historical and sociologi-cal—made clear how education's democratic purposes and goals have always been subservient to America's dominant economic interests and imperatives.[7] Concerns with industrial productivity, profits, control over labor, and the projection of military power emerge as the real guiding hands behind the American system of education—from kindergarten to graduate school. While the idea of education as the vehicle for the full realization of an individual's capabilities and talents and sometimes for the development of an aware and critical citizenry remained an ever-present demand, it has been much of the time a relatively weak presence in comparison to the imperatives set by capital and its political allies.

The Hidden Curriculum of Domination

By now the "hidden curriculum" had become, in the hands of critical scholars, a powerful concept for understanding the purpose of schools in the United States (as well as in other countries).[8] A proliferation of studies began to make clear how education socialized young people into the competitive, individualistic, and authoritarian environment of schools and society. They offered a devastating account of life in the average class-room. Schools, it became clear, are a major vehicle through which the dominant system of values, beliefs, and understanding about the self and the world are transmitted. Nor is this ultimately the consequence of badly trained teachers, administrators, or some other inadequacy of the system. Rather, argued critical theorists, schooling exists principally to "repro-duce" the existing society with its present contours of power, wealth, and opportunity and with its attendant moral and social outlook. The school environment inculcates in students an acceptance of institutional life steeped in disaffection and alienation.

From the earliest age, for example, the classroom teaches children to distinguish between "play" and "work" and to understand that work—the activity they are to spend most of their time in school engaged in—is primarily instrumental, not undertaken for its intrinsic aesthetic or intel-lectual value or satisfaction. Work was and is primarily a means to an end. In return for the psychic numbing and existential irrelevance of the classroom, schools offer grades, diplomas, and institutional honors—the major currency of achievement and success in the wider society. Knowledge provided in the classroom is, for the most part, reified or "dead" knowledge that offers students little purchase on the issues, concerns, and struggles that affect their own lives. In its delivery, such knowledge has been wrung dry of the passion and human significance that it may have had for others in another time and place.[9] Whether in the generally uncritical, unquestioning approach to classroom knowledge or in the overwhelming stress on conformity to school rules and behavior, schooling attempts to instill in the young an attitude of passivity and unthinking docility.

Drawing on the work of Continental philosophers, such as Jurgen Habermas, critical scholars of education pointed to the dehumanizing rationality that undergirded the dominant approach to the curriculum. In a series of brilliant analyses, scholars such as Michael Apple, Henry Giroux, William Pinar, James Macdonald, Maxine Greene, and others were able to show how the increasing emphasis on behavioral objectives, preset curriculum goals, and the predetermined outcome of classroom inquiry made the relationship between teacher and student increasingly manipulative.[10]

Student intelligence increasingly has come to be seen as a raw material to be shaped and processed into a standardized product. Indeed, decreasing trust in the capability of teachers to produce the desired educational ends has resulted in curriculum materials that Apple called "teacher proof"— not dependent on the ability and initiative of teachers themselves.[11] Added to this, the increasing emphasis on standardized tests and measures of "student performance" filter out of the educational experience anything that is not numerically measurable and that does not lend itself to making easy comparisons.

The consequence of all this has been a curriculum in which knowledge is broken up and flattened out—superficial, fragmented, and meaningless, except insofar as it can be memorized for the next test. Higher up, school administrators have been urged to view their institution as having measurable and discrete inputs and outputs—much like a factory. Needless to say, all of this did little to nurture in students the capacity to think critically, to act creatively, or to approach the world with a sense of justice and compassion. Indeed, quite the opposite, it did much to mutilate or deaden such capabilities.[12]

However, the concept of the hidden curriculum became useful in ways other than that of illuminating the process by which social and economic power is distributed and maintained. We have come also to see more clearly the extent and functioning of cultural and intellectual hegemony. Philosophers and social theorists began to unravel—and deconstruct— notions of truth and certainty and the epistemological foundations of mainstream rationalist thought and began to pose instead an alternative educational theory in which subjectivity and personal experience were central to the development of human understanding and knowing.

Writers such as Maxine Greene, Jane Martin, Madeline Grumet and others, helped us see that the curriculum involves a particular orientation toward knowledge and its relation to individual experience—an orientation directly challenged by their work, which sought to validate knowledge rooted in personal experiences and the particular contingencies of one's world.[13] Such work was part of a powerful feminist insurgency aimed at the heart of the male-dominated intellectual order. It became part of an emerging movement for a "feminist pedagogy" in which the abstractness and aloofness of much intellectual discourse would be replaced by classrooms oriented to the personal, sensual, and emotionally resonant narratives of students and teachers. One of the powerful consequences of this work was to make clear how classrooms function to silence the voices of women (and others)—indeed, how the complexity of human cognition and sensibility was submerged by curricula and pedagogies that refused, in any real way, to recognize cultural and human differences.

Paradoxically, while critical educational theorists drew attention to the emptiness of so much that was taught in school, they also made clear the powerful socializing effects of schooling. Indeed, it was argued, school had become the primary means through which the state shaped the ideological outlook of citizens. The notion of a value-free apolitical education is, according to this view, part of the liberal mythology about the neutrality of the state in capitalist society. Education teaches us to accept a particular ordering of the world and particular kinds of human behavior as natural and unalterable—for example, that hierarchy and competition are unavoidable, that intelligence is measurable, and that linear rationality and the separation of thought and feeling are the most socially valuable of human traits.[14]

Whether in its presentation of history or science (or of anything else), the ideological outlook transmitted through schools eliminates the process of struggle and conflict through which human beings have constantly sought to challenge and remake their worlds. Through school, one learns that social, political, or cultural change is caused by someone else—not by the committed, courageous, and conscientious efforts of ordinary people.[15]

Socialization and Resistance in the Classroom

Under the influence of neo-Marxist ideas and insights (particularly those of Antonio Gramsci, Louis Althusser, and Raymond Williams), it became clear that this shaping of human subjects depends on the constituting of selves that incorporate contradictory moral values and ideological imperatives. It became clear, for example, that schools emphasized the language of individualism *and* conformity, of egoism *and* cooperation.[16] Schools talked about the value of democracy while demanding an unquestioning obedience to authority, praised pluralism and diversity while insisting on submission to a single standard of cultural or linguistic expression, and offered a view of history and society that often obliterated the ways of life, the traditions and knowledge, of many students.[17] Perhaps most glaringly, schools claimed to offer equal educational opportunity to all students within a society deeply structured by racial, sexual, class, and other forms of inequality.

At the heart of these contradictions was the ideological and moral message conveyed by schools so relentlessly—what the philosopher C. B. Macpherson called "possessive individualism"—the idea that one could be a master of one's own destiny, the notion that every person can reach his or her goals and satisfy his or her needs if they work hard enough and have the requisite ability, the belief that the disadvantages imposed by society could be overcome through sheer effort and native ability. Public education carried with it the suggestion of a "meritocracy"—a society in which, through the purported impartial process of schooling, both winners and losers should hold only themselves responsible. This, argued critical scholars, was the ultimate mystification surrounding social injustice. It was the loser who was blamed, not the institution that persistently denied or invalidated the intelligence, knowledge, and worth of all who did not conform to the dominant middle-class, white, male, Eurocentric values of society.

Critical researchers have shown how racial, sexual, cultural, and other distinctions (such as those that sometimes result in students being classified as "special" or "exceptional") are converted into classifications that disadvantage them. Teachers prejudge—label—students on the basis of the way in which they speak, their skin color, gender, language, cultural attitudes, and so on. For many, the classroom is a place, where there is not equal opportunity, but where educators' assumptions about ability and intelligence lead to a catastrophic process of categorization and "tracking."[18] Labels, once affixed to students (e.g., in elementary school reading groups where distinctions are made between the "slow" robins and the "fast" bluebirds), become difficult to challenge or remove. Students are encouraged to accept and accommodate themselves to their now-more-limited educational options.

Classrooms, sometimes whole schools, could be turned into warehouses for those whom schools viewed as educationally handicapped, unmotivated, or unsuited to cope with more demanding intellectual tasks. Special education classes, for example, were often overloaded with black or brown children, or those whose native tongue is not English. Conversely, for some, the labeling process affirmed their more advantaged social position. Programs for the "academically gifted" fill up with the children of the white upper-middle class. For these, the language of school is a familiar and comfortable one. For many others, the classroom is a place where anything other than middle-class voices were demeaned, invalidated, and silenced.[19]

By the end of the 1970s, this picture of school life, with its image of near total domination of students' lives and values, however, was challenged by critical scholars on both sides of the Atlantic. Writers like Paul Willis, Robert Everhart, Peter McLaren, and Michelle Fine vividly described the way in which kids "resist" the stultifying and, for some groups, humiliating environment of the school.[20] Their work showed the way in which young people persistently attempt to make classroom life more pleasurable and to win some control over how they are to spend their time and energies. This means, of course, for some teachers, a constant battle over the use of classroom time and space, the manner of student interaction with their peers, and the definition of what kinds of knowledge and experience will be the focus of classroom activity.

This research reversed the usual approach to understanding disruptive classroom behavior. It was viewed, not from the standpoint of the adult authority structure, but from the "bottom up"—from the perspective of kids. The "bad" or "dysfunctional" behavior of students could now be seen as a very understandable human response to a world that thwarted the needs, interests, and concerns of young people and that provided them with little or no power over their lives during the long hours in school. Of course, such "acting out" was especially apparent with those students for whom school had historically offered the least rewards as far as opportunity for upward social mobility was concerned. In at least one study, the "subculture" formed by African-American males, with its emphasis on group loyalty, was shown to actively reject the middle-class individualistic achievement ethic associated with school.[21]

All of these studies found new ways to illustrate the alienation, boredom, and dehumanization that typically characterized life in schools—especially high school—issues that, as some critical writers observed, were nowhere to be found in the major reports on education released in the 1980s or 1990s. Indeed, as these writers argued, the reforms suggested in them would probably intensify these conditions. Greater emphasis on basic skills, longer hours in school, more homework, greater concern for test results and teacher accountability would, in all likelihood, increase the oppressive nature of the classroom experience. Nor did the turn toward computer technology in the classroom represent any kind of magical fix. Indeed, the great majority of available educational software offered little to students that was particularly creative or inventive. The skewed distribution of the new technology in schools, as Michael Apple noted, also seemed to further exacerbate class, race, and sexual inequalities among students. And it restricted further the opportunity to use the classroom as a place for dialogue—a forum where the capacity for public expression and exchange of ideas, beliefs, and concerns could be nurtured.

Critical Pedagogy and Democratic Renewal

In reflecting on all of this, critical educational theorists have charged public education with becoming further and further removed from the cultivation of those capacities that are necessary to maintain, or renew, a democratic policy.[22] Public education was doing little to combat the well-documented evisceration of democratic life in the United States by monied elites, corporate and bureaucratic interests, and the news media. Public education had largely shed even the rhetoric of concerning itself with the preparation of the younger generation for an active and critically informed role in the shaping of community life or public policy. Attention to the capacity for civic involvement and responsible citizenship that genuinely empowered individuals to affect the quality of their lives was replaced by an overwhelming concern for training a work force that could compete successfully with the Japanese or Germans in the world market. This at a time when public apathy toward, and disenchantment with, politics was at an all-time high. Among young people, even the momentous revolutionary events of 1989 did little to break through the layers of disinterest and alienation that enveloped the public world. In these circumstances, the call for a radical remaking of education in the direction of a "critical pedagogy" was a call to renew the historical connection in America between public education and a democratic culture.

The notion of a critical pedagogy represented not only a powerful indictment of the education that typically existed in American classrooms but also a morally inspiring and intellectually persuasive set of ideas about what education is for and how it might be made concrete. Inspired by the work and vision of the Brazilian educator Paulo Freire, it was augmented through the writing and teaching of a number of North American educators. At its core was an insistence that education should not be confused with schooling. The latter was about learning to conform and to accept the existing culture and way of life. Authentic education—that is, a liberating education—was about the struggle to be free in a world that constantly attempted to squash human desires and hopes and to get us to go along with a way of life that was prescribed for us by those who dominated the society. Such an existence left us culturally voiceless, politically powerless, and psychologically maimed.

In the United States, critical pedagogy meant an education that was more than memorizing information and competing with our fellow students for grades or school honors. It meant, instead, an education that was concerned with giving people an understanding of their own lives, so that they might be better able to challenge, and change, the social conditions in which their lives were lived. Critical pedagogy aimed to "problematize" the world in which we lived—that is, to set in train a process through which this world was no longer accepted as natural or given, no longer regarded as an unalterable fact of existence. Maxine Greene described critical education as one that " made the familiar strange"—that woke us up from our uncritical, passive acceptance of a world that was taken as a fact of existence.

Critical pedagogy rejected any form of education that ended up stuffing the minds of students with somebody else's knowledge or information. Such an education reinforced the zombielike role of students who were called upon merely to memorize facts, not to think or question. Of course, this demand was an arrow aimed at the heart of the school curriculum. The latter, with all of its apparently incontrovertible subject matter, true-false tests, and textbooks, presented to students knowledge about a world that appeared self-evident and factually indisputable. It was exactly this concept that critical pedagogy took issue with. From the latter's point of view, knowledge—and, therefore, what we could say about our world—was always and everywhere a human construction and interpretation. In denying the "thinglike" objectivity of knowledge, students could do more than approach the curriculum as something to be swallowed whole and ingested. What we were told, what we heard, what was presented to us in books or any other texts needed to be viewed with suspicion and opened to serious interrogation. In whose interest was it to describe the world (or history) in this way?

Critical pedagogy meant a classroom where question and dialogue, not didactic instruction, was the norm. Knowledge ought to be viewed, not as something "given" by a teacher or "found" in a text (that was the way of student passivity and of docile, unthinking acceptance), but as the outcome of students'—and teachers'—reflections on the world in which they lived. In this process not just the voice of the teacher was heard. Encouraging students' voices meant valuing *their* experience, *their* knowledge, and *their* understanding. It meant respecting the culture and values with which students grew up. Taking seriously the goal of education as that which would empower students in their relation to the world meant, in the first instance, validating the significance of the students' voices. However, this was not to be misunderstood as merely a romantic celebration of anyone's viewpoint or opinion. Quite the contrary, critical pedagogy intended that through classroom dialogue it would become possible to peel back the layers of misinformation, false understanding, and distorted notions of how we know or make sense of our world. Through this process of examination it would become possible to see how social injustice, class domination, sexism, racism, homophobia, and other forms of oppression and dehumanization act to disfigure our lives and dispower us.

Recently an important division appeared among critical educators when feminist scholars suggested that critical pedagogy was not true to its own democratic and egalitarian promises. Despite a commitment to the value of students' experiences and the integrity of the life stories told by them, some feminists claimed that the critical teacher still saw himself or herself as an arbiter of the truthfulness of these stories, a privileged judge of their correspondence with an actually existing world.[23] In this, critical pedagogy maintained its allegiance to an elitist and hierarchical tradition in which an elevated, rational few were able to see the world as it really is and not as it was seen through the distorted lenses suffered by the many. These feminist critics called for a recognition of the basic incommensurability of the stories we tell, developed as they are out of the radically different ways in which we find ourselves situated in the world. The radical teacher must give up all pretensions to truth telling and instead must act to help create a space of respect and safety within which multiple voices might emerge to describe and name the subjects' own lives, experiences, and identity.

Maxine Greene and Henry Giroux, among others, have argued, however that empowering human beings so that they might challenge the world in which they live requires more than merely acquiring the ability to question or be critical. It demands the cultivation of an imagination that can conceive of lives lived in different ways, in pursuit of different goals, in relationships of a different quality. Educators must nurture what has been called a "language of possibility." Without this, our critical minds can easily succumb to disillusion or nihilism. The sense of possibility—and hope—rests, in part, on the development of our capacity to dream, to image other kinds of lives and worlds. It also rests on recognizing the ways in which human beings in history, as well as in the present, have struggled for more justice, dignity, freedom, and control over their lives. It means to take seriously "popular culture"—what we watch on television or at the movies; how we dress, talk, dance; and so on.

In all of this imagining are expressions of people's—especially young people's—hopes, desires, dreams, and struggles in the real world (alongside, of course, escapism and status seeking). It means becoming more reflective of our bodies and their experience in the world.[24] In them are the memories of pleasure, feeling, and touch, as well as pain and hurt, that are sundered from our thinking and knowing by the world of schooling with its emphasis on the rational, the analytic, and the abstract. And it means attending very seriously and with sensitivity to the complex identities of the students in our classrooms. The latter demand a class setting that dignifies, validates, and recognizes the multiple differences, as well as the commonalities, of all students. It insists that our teaching constantly call into question words, texts, and behaviors that cast some human beings into the role of the "other." Not surprisingly, critical pedagogy argues that to take these notions seriously is to call for curricula that are multicultural and multiethnic in their orientation and emphasis and able to investigate how difference is constructed through history, and in the dynamics of social relationships.

To accomplish this, some critical educators have called for a different kind of teacher—one who might be termed a "transformative intellectual."[25] They reject the present role of the teacher in public schools as one who is more and more viewed as a technician—called upon to implement classroom objectives that are tightly controlled and defined by others higher up in the administrative chain of command. Such a role increasingly precludes the involvement of teachers from any real authority for decision making in the school. It robs them of the opportunity to think creatively about how they teach or what it is that should be taught. And it denies to them the moral and political significance of what they do. Instead, it is argued, teachers need to be allowed to reconnect to the fundamental human significance of their work. They need to be able to see how teaching is always a process that has in it the possibility for renewing our world in more just and humane ways. To do this, teachers need to be encouraged to reflect on, and understand, the broader human and social purposes of what they do and to make decisions about what and how they teach in the light of their commitments to attain these purposes. Such a view takes us very far from the increasingly visible "deskilled" teacher who is required to think little and to act robotically and who is beholden only to the masters of accountability. Such a person is required to teach with little consciousness or conscience about the fundamental values that he or she is trying to initiate in the classroom.

FAILING TO RESHAPE THE PUBLIC AGENDA: CRITICAL PEDAGOGY AND THE POLITICS OF CHANGE

There can be little doubt as to the extraordinary insights into the nature of education that critical pedagogy as well as other critical studies of education have produced in the last two decades. We have come to understand in new and sometimes startling ways exactly what it means to say that schools are social institutions—deeply and inextricably connected to the cultural, economic, moral, and political life of this society. We have come to understand, for example, the full extent of the way in which social inequality is structured into the culture and practices of school life. We have come to recognize the way in which schooling is always and everywhere implicated in the moral and ideological character of the society—that the classroom is *always* and *everywhere* a site for the transmission and inculcation of those meanings, values, beliefs, aesthetic preferences, concepts of human nature and of the "good" society that are dominant in the culture at large. We have learned to see the school as a place of political conflict where the culture of students and the school are pitted against one another in a struggle over power and where teachers struggle for meaning, dignity, and autonomy. We have come to see how we have objectified the fundamental assumptions of school life (the curriculum, notions of intelligence, teaching, etc.), as timeless and commonsensical, rather than the constructs of our culture and society. And we have come to see how little school has recognized and valued the differences of gender, ethnicity, race, and class that students bring with them into the classroom.

And yet, despite these enormous contributions to our understanding of education in the society, can there be any illusions over the widespread failure of these ideas to influence the practices of education, or to alter significantly the agenda of left or progressive politics, or to fundamentally shift the public discourse about education? Critical educational ideas remain overwhelmingly restricted to the university, and even there to that corner of it called by Bertell Ollman the "Left Academy." The promise of an educational theory that would widely reshape pedagogic practice and school policies has not materialized. Even the important debate concerning the need for a multicultural curriculum that would include the voices and language of women and other excluded or marginalized social groups has taken place in the context of colleges and universities (and even here, arguably, in a limited number of academic institutions or departments). When such concerns have arisen in kindergarten through twelfth grade, it has, for the most part, been so restricted or marginalized as to pose no significant challenge to the curriculum, the manner of teaching, or the forms of evaluation. No significant political constituency has been won over to a critical educational outlook.

Nor can this failure be explained away simply as a result of the growing rightward shift of American politics in the 1980s and 1990s. Whatever their limitations regarding policies and legislation, some aspects of a progressive political agenda *have* found their way into the popular consciousness and into the public discourse. Whatever the dissonance between promises and policies around issues like environmental protection, health care, or economic opportunities for women or minorities, the very presence of these issues does, nonetheless, reflect an important reshaping of popular expectations and public attitudes. In the language of critical social theory, it reflects a reconstituting of the "ideological settlement" that exists in American society—the accepted grammar of our moral and social outlook and way of life. A whole range of human concerns have been, and continue to be, affected by the cultural and social movements of recent years. The parameters of the public discourse and the agenda for political action have been reshaped by the demands of women, civil rights activists, public interest and citizen action groups, gays and lesbians, handicapped people, environmentalists, lobbyists for children, and others. These have shifted in sometimes deep and enduring ways the humanly acceptable, the economically and socially necessary, and the politically resonant. Such changes have produced insistent new demands on the state and community for legislative, judicial, or regulatory action.

Paradoxically, while questions about the nature of curriculum and pedagogy have been the leitmotif of the critical educational studies movement, it has most often been the political Right that has successfully made this an area of popular concern and public debate. Despite the powerful advances in understanding brought about by critical educational theory and pedagogy, it has failed to widely influence either policy or practice in any really fundamental way. It has had, as we have seen in our chapters on the public and professional discourse, only a marginal effect on popular attitudes and beliefs about schools and education. Even within the official liberal political discourse, it has failed to seriously alter the terms of the public debate about education. This debate continues to be marked, on the one hand, by its blend of meritocratic concerns for education as *the* vehicle for ensuring equal opportunity and social mobility and on the other hand, by a "human capital" focus—namely, education as the engine of a reinvigorated American technostructure that is able to compete more effectively in the world marketplace. Certainly there has been nothing comparable to the profound and widespread shifts in public attitudes and consciousness about ecology and the environment (indeed, the word *ecology* itself was virtually unknown outside of specialist circles twenty years before) that has seriously challenged economic growth as the unquestioned criterion for progress in the society or the world.

Naming the Agents of Educational Change

Central to this failure has surely been the limited conceptualization of the politics of educational change. Who, it must be asked of critical theorists, do we expect to be the agents or the primary political supporters of radical school reform? Of course, the issue has not been ignored. We have seen, for example, perspectives in which enormous responsibilities have devolved upon teachers who have the potential capacity to pursue transformative political and cultural work in schools. In the view of the "new" sociology of education (referred to earlier), school practitioners could upset, for example, the established process through which schools identify success and failure, and ability among students or the lack of it, by refusing to accept uncritically the usual assumptions, meanings, and categories of educational life. Clearly, in this process, teachers are central. If classroom reality is the product of conscious practice, then teachers can become aware of the significance of their assumptions and everyday activities and can change them in ways that benefit those typically not successful in schools, such as working-class pupils or minorities.

In a parallel, if more sophisticated, way, the recent call for teachers to become "transformative intellectuals" envisages suitably prepared, politically committed teachers able to employ a pedagogy that enables students to critically examine their own histories and experiences. This requires the development of a reconceptualized teacher education curriculum organized around a notion of "cultural politics."[26] It includes the critical study of power, language, culture, and history and assumes that the social and cultural dimensions are the primary categories for understanding contemporary schooling. The imperative of the curriculum is one that creates the conditions for students' self-empowerment and self-constitution as an active political and moral subject. It enables students to achieve some degree of critical awareness not only of their own dispowered lives but also of the disrespect and indignity rife both inside and outside of schools.

Such possibilities, however, assume more than they explain. Notions of "teacher-intellectuals" capable of engaging in a self- and socially transformative pedagogy force us to question on what basis, and in what foreseeable situation, we can expect significant support for such a radical shift in the direction of teaching and teacher training. It will surely take more than the appeal for a renewal of America's democratic values to persuade institutions of teacher preparation to move toward the kind of radical political and educational commitments that underlie these proposals.

Of course, for educators to assume the responsibility for, and become capable of, affecting progressive educational change is a necessary, though not sufficient, condition of such change. It is certainly an improvement over romanticized images of student resistance with their exaggeration of students' capacity for forming meaningful educational change. There is also, in the above, a sense of possibility absent from the more deterministic, critical theories about education. These theories have been searing in their discoveries about the relation of education to the wider structures of economic, cultural, and social life, yet they are generally unable to match their insights about how schools function with some realistic or effective notions of how flesh-and-blood human beings (whether students, teachers, parents, or citizens in general) can respond.

Indeed, such analysis by critical theorists, which turns schools into mere appendages of the system of power and control, contradicts the possibility of change through thoughtful human activity. This analysis leaves us passive and supine in the face of the overwhelming influence of those who are the beneficiaries of the existing school system with its present moral and ideological goals. Such analysis easily leads to a kind of all-or-nothing "ultraleftism." In this case, fundamental forms of educational change are tied to the prior presence of a wider and effective radical political movement. Curiously, like the more modest notion of change through redefining the goals and the practice of teaching, this analysis suffers from the same problems we have already alluded to. It, too, assumes answers to the very issues that it seeks to address. On what basis, and in what foreseeable situation, can we expect the emergence of such a significant radical movement? The answer is likely to be even less hopeful in an educational sense. Indeed, while we are open in our wish to see the emergence of such a movement (or movements) concerned with fundamental forms of social change, there is nothing to make us think that this would automatically produce the kinds of educational change that we seek. We have seen often how those who might be liberal or radical in other areas can also be quite conventional, or even conservative, in their attitudes toward education.

Critical theorists have argued that we must recognize the "relative autonomy" of education whose relation to the rest of society is far from the direct relay of influences found elsewhere. Here there is a clear sense in which schooling contributes to the reproduction of the entire social formation and does so through practices and processes quite distinctive to the particular domain of education.[27] The cultural life of the classroom and the school could not be "read off" in any straightforward or immediate way from the influence of the economy or the workplace. Education was not to be seen as simply an echo of institutions and structures that existed elsewhere in the society. Schools are partially autonomous places and possess their own distinct cultural and ideological character and social relations. What was taught in school, for example, had emerged out of the complex history of education in the United States and had been influenced by a multiplicity of traditions and ideologies.[28] (This view of education, it should be added, encouraged critical theorists to look not only at the way in which capitalism had shaped American schools but also at the way in which the classroom reflected the patriarchal culture, racial and Euro-centric attitudes, and a technorationalist view of nature.)

All of this opens up new ways of thinking about educational change. While there was little sense of who might be the agents for such change, it has become possible to contemplate a radical transformation of educational practices distinct and separate from any fundamental transformation of the rest of society. While, of course, radical change in education would, in all likelihood, have some relation to change that was occurring elsewhere, it could happen independently—in its own way and in its own time. Radical educators no longer need simply to hitch their wagons to more "important" struggles happening elsewhere in the culture. The struggle for a more just, humane, and compassionate society might, and will likely, occur in a broad range of places and institutions, not focused on one preeminent point. While we should not exaggerate the power and role of education to be a catalyst for change toward a different kind of society, we also should not be less than hopeful about its potentialities or overly pessimistic about its significance to the rest of the culture.

Surprisingly, this insight has received only a very limited response. There have been very few attempts by educational critics to formulate the kind of agenda for change that might stimulate *public* support for rethinking and redirecting the purposes of schools. And without this, no end of good ideas or insights about the work of teachers can be that effective. Without shifting the parameters of public debate about education, all talk of a widely utilized critical pedagogy is really reduced to whistling in the dark.

From Critical Pedagogy to Public Policy

The thread that runs through all this work is the failure to develop what we would like to call a *politics of educational agency*. In particular, there has been a failure, within critical educational theory, to merge the insights of cultural analysis with attention to the public discourse about education and political reform. The former's concern with matters of curriculum, pedagogy, the transmission and production of knowledge, and popular culture and its relation to students' lives has restricted the question of agency to in-house considerations. The potential protagonists of change are teachers and students.

The means of change require the transformation of pedagogy and the development of a curriculum that facilitates critical reflection on our lived experience and the examination of the culturally constituted meanings, relations, mores, norms, and values that structure that experience. All of this leads to a radical reconceptualization of what it means to teach, what is taught, and the relation of the school to other forms of cultural practice and knowledge. Yet, despite the power of such critique and the relevance of the concrete pedagogic strategies it has produced, the analysis and its effects have been inadequately connected to a *larger kind of educational politics*—one that might provide *popular* support for a transformative program of educational reform in the 1990s and beyond.

Ironically, the huge volume of critical studies dealing with politics and the state in capitalist societies in recent years has shown that real shifts in power and policies in favor of subordinate or intermediate social groups are possible—and do take place.[29] As we noted earlier, political struggles in recent years have made possible a real expansion of social, economic, and cultural rights for many kinds of citizens, including historically excluded marginalized and victimized groups. Public policy has indeed been forced to limit the free hand of capital and the socially damaging effects of the market in order to recognize new cultural needs and identities and the value of an environmental ethic. Yet, the progressive political agenda as it applied to education has remained disappointingly restricted in its definition of the problem. In its concern with the usual issues of equal opportunity, equality of access, public accountability, and so on, it has absorbed little of the ethical and pedagogic agenda of human liberation, political empowerment, social justice, and the validation of cultural differences that, as we have seen above, were associated with the critical pedagogic perspective.

What is needed, and what we shall propose later in the book, is a politics of educational change that is informed by a radically redefined notion of educational concerns and issues. In some important respects such a politics will, we believe, need to say more and say things differently from what critical educational theorists have been able to do until now. We believe that reconstructing the nature of schooling requires a strategy that speaks to those whose work and lives exist substantially outside of and removed from education. To change schools will require a language and an agenda that can mobilize and win support from a broad range of citizens. Attempts to transform education will necessitate a public discourse that relates, in some way, educational demands to the pressing concerns of people's lives. Through this, perhaps, we can find a way to integrate the powerful insights of critical educational theorists into a resonant and effective language that can develop broad sympathy and interest; one that creates a popular coalition out of the widely different social groups for whom progressive educational change might have real and meaningful appeal. It must be said, however, that the failure of the critical perspective to significantly alter the public debate in education has not been just the result of a strategic error. We believe it needs to be traced to the very nature of the critical language and perspective itself. We think it is important before turning to the development of an alternative agenda and public discourse for education, that we look briefly at some of the problematics of the critical discourse itself.

THE PROBLEMATICS OF CRITICAL PEDAGOGY AS PUBLIC DISCOURSE

Resistance to Critical Pedagogy

We must address a disturbing, but nonetheless, compelling reality, namely, that this critical discourse has not been extensively disseminated or widely accepted even in circles where it is at least known. As theorists we have the responsibility to avow and celebrate our convictions, but as educators we have the further responsibility to look for other reasons than stupidity, denial, or false consciousness to explain the failure of some to accept our ideas. The quintessential principle of pedagogy is simple but enormously important, that is, teaching begins at the point of an understanding of where students "are" in their prior understanding, their experiences, and their capacities. Our task here, then, is candidly to ask the question: If our ideas are so good, why aren't they more known, appreciated, and valued? We believe that in honestly addressing these questions much can be gained in understanding the weaknesses of these ideas, what areas need elaboration, and what processes and strategies are required to make the ideas at least more accessible, if not acceptable.

The most obvious explanation of the relative impotence of these ideas is that many thoughtful people simply do not accept the basic thrust of the orientation—one that is rooted in fundamental criticism, if not rejection, of well-accepted and deeply ingrained values and beliefs. The critical approach, by definition, goes against the grain—a process involving abrasion and discomfort. The reality is that a great many people actively and enthusiastically support the very structural elements that critical pedagogy sees as highly problematic, namely, free enterprise, competitive individualism, a stress on freedom rather than equality, and meritocracy. Indeed, a basic element of critical thought is the assumption that society is replete with conflicting, if not adversarial, interests. Critical pedagogy begins its program with an overture that trumpets a message of blaring criticism punctuated by a percussive statement of impeding doom and disaster. It is not music that soothes or reassures but that is deliberately and necessarily dissonant. How can we expect defenders of the dominant faith to respond to an analysis of this faith as rooted in oppression, distraction, and conspiracy?

There are two general groups that afford perhaps the greatest challenge to the efficacy of critical pedagogy. One is composed of those who consciously and energetically assist, affirm, and operate the present system. This group has several labels—"the power elite," "the Establishment," "the military-industrial complex," "the power structure," "the dominant class," and so forth. This group exercises a great deal of power and influence and is happy to celebrate the very values that critical pedagogy rejects. The other group, much larger and broader, is made up of people who tacitly approve, or at least do not significantly disapprove of, prevailing cultural patterns. As of yet, critical educational authorities have failed to provide an adequate explanation either of why these groups persist or of how their consciousness might be changed.

How do we explain the existence of an oppressive class, one that knowingly and deliberately pursues its own interest at the expense of others? How is it that people are prepared to design, operate, and rationalize a society in which enormous numbers of people are destined to suffer? Do people do this knowingly and deliberately or do at least some of these people delude themselves? This is a particularly crucial issue for educators because it involves the fundamental question of evil or, more precisely, the question of whether there is such a thing as "evil people." It is easy enough to believe that "evil" happens, that all of us are capable of doing evil things, or at least things that others would call evil. This is, however, the crux of the issue, for most of us will deny that what we have done is evil; or if and when we confess, it is very likely we will regret it. A truly evil person presumably deliberately strives to do evil and feels successful when what he or she accomplishes is judged to be evil. It is the difference between "that wasn't evil" or "I'm sorry to have done this evil thing" *and* "I'm delighted to know that I've done something evil for that is my general project in life."

If there are people who consciously avow evil it is difficult to know what role education can play. We have some notion of how to proceed if we consider such people "sick," "ignorant," or "deluded." However, treatment or rational persuasion are hardly serious ways to deal with truly evil persons. Politically, a more appropriate response may be to remove such people from positions of influence and from the possibility of inflicting harm on others. However, the essential constitutive element of western traditions of education—rational persuasion—is not an appropriate response to evil.

If we reject the concept of evil people (or its surrogates such as greedy, selfish, power-mad, or oppressive people), then we still must confront the question of why these people would do "evil" things. Of course, one explanation is that they know not what they do and, therefore, should be forgiven. The difficulty with this is that a great many in the power elite are extremely intelligent and knowledgeable and have high-powered analytic and creative skills. Indeed, many have had very large doses of the very kind of education that critical pedagogy involves—one with a strong emphasis on critical rationality and serious reflection. Surely, one of the lessons that we have learned from the so-called "modernist project" (to improve the world through technological, rational, scientific, and logical thinking) is that various and conflicting ideologies convince themselves that they are buttressing their positions rationally and successfully. We have all experienced the futility and frustration of seeing the skillful use of the same data, research findings, and theories to support conflicting positions.

If ideology emerges out of interests and benefits, then the role of an education based on critical rationality is severely restricted. If, on the other hand, our dominant values and beliefs emerge out of misunderstanding and misinformation, then we must confront the limitations of critical rationality to change that consciousness. In either case, we must accept the problematics of trying to change very deeply held beliefs and values through rational persuasion. Whether such beliefs are rooted in evil, ignorance, or deprivation, we need to address the role of consciousness in the educative process.

We know enough now to recognize that people do not develop their moral outlook on life inductively, that is, by coming to conclusions after careful consideration of evidence and thoughtful reflection. Surely, there are moments when this does happen, but it appears that our views and attitudes are the result of an extraordinarily complex dialectic of genetic, social, cultural, historical, personal, and particularistic circumstances. Our views and behaviors are shaped by a myriad of events and phenomena—our upbringing; our friends, parents, lovers; our health, personality, and mood; our capacities, struggles, weaknesses, dispositions—interacting with the external complexities of time, place, circumstance, and history. As educators, we surely can affirm the centrality of rational and reflective processes in the challenge of living a life of meaning. However, it also is incumbent on us as educators to be mindful of the other dimensions of consciousness and to attend most particularly to the question of *under what conditions people can most effectively rely on critical rationality.*

The courage of critical theorists to challenge deeply cherished traditions and institutions is both commendable and inspiring. Our purpose here is not to soften the critical theorists' passionate and just critique of a society so marked by unnecessary human suffering, but to deepen our understanding of the barriers and resistance to the change in consciousness that we believe is required. We cannot base a liberating education on an implied premise that those who hold conflicting views are either evil and/or will change when they agree to think very, very carefully. For example, we know that a major source of serious social conflict is nationalism, especially in its more rabid chauvinistic forms. We also know that people often reject religious discourse on the ground that religion has been used either as the rationale and/or excuse for wars of extraordinary barbarism. To think we can change such deep commitments by reading books and being critically insightful is, of course, very naive. We doubt there are many, if any, critical pedagogues who believe this can be done, but the process seems to persist in making rationality—albeit a critical one—central to the process of human change.

Here we welcome the questions raised by feminist teachers and scholars about the nature of rationality in the process of human change and liberation. This work on rationality has begun to make clear how we have denied the embodied notion of being and have left instead the intellectually deceptive claims of dispassionate and analytical knowing. This recognition that we always know or believe from "our gut" and from the place where we stand in the world means that a liberating education must recognize the complex interplay of feeling and thought, desire, and understanding, context and separation, forever at work in the human subject. This embodied way of knowing quite obviously exposes and opposes the fallacy of a rationality-centered education—critical or not— as the distorted legacy of patriarchal culture. Simply put, it suggests directions for education quite far removed from a critique-driven, text-oriented, analysis-focused form of learning. It is a direction that few of us, albeit radical pedagogues, can yet commit to.

The reality is, as critical analysis itself reveals, that as educators our constituency not only is largely composed of people who have belief systems that are very different from the ones that we believe are more conducive to creating a community of justice, love, and joy but also includes people with enormous diversity in the nature of their commitments to these beliefs. This reality of diversity itself speaks to the need to develop a more adequate critical pedagogy and perhaps to the need to explore the question of who our constituents are. Is it our task to educate *all* people? Does our constituency include oppressed *and* oppressor? Should we distinguish between redeemable and unredeemable oppressors? Should we as educators limit our responsibilities to the promotion of critical rationality in the hope that other institutions can supplement and complement this particular assignment? Should we limit our work only to those people who can respond significantly to the power of critical rationality? If critical rationality is a necessary, but not sufficient condition for the development of a morally grounded, critical consciousness, then are we as educators responsible for defining and/or developing what *would* make it sufficient?

Other Barriers to Critical Pedagogy

Critical pedagogy faces obstacles other than straightforward rejection or opposition. There is, for example, the perennial and serious problem of schismatic infighting among critical pedagogues themselves. Although these differences may seem small or opaque to other professionals or to the public, they are important to the protagonists and drain important energy from the task of making the ideas broadly accessible. The intense rivalries among critical pedagogues do not seem any better or worse than among other intellectual or professional groups, but they do emerge from the same ethos of competition and aggression and have the same damaging and debilitating effects.

There are also, of course, other significant educational critics who take more particular roads toward educational reform. These critics focus on a particular discourse such as the preservation of Western civilization as exemplified in the great books movement or base their educational program on a human development model as reflected in the early childhood movement. Within the "countercultural community," so to speak, are orientations quite at variance with critical theory—orientations that center on psychological, spiritual, religious, or learning theory discourses. These include vocal and active movements that often specifically reject almost any kind of political action and analysis, for example, New Age movements, humanistic education groups, deep ecology groups, groups focusing on experimental education, education through computers, home-based education, and so forth. For these movements, political issues are, at best, extraneous and irrelevant and, at worst, destructive of a truly valid education. As is the case with other groups, the barriers here involve the inability to accept the validity of a discourse that seriously considers the problematics of the existing social and cultural order.

A related category involves people who focus on extremely important, though particular, concerns or issues and for whom critical pedagogy does not always seem to be an especially appropriate response. There is vitally important work being done here in response to a wide variety of victimized and marginalized groups—for example, migrant workers, refugees, teenage parents, the physically and emotionally impaired, the mentally ill, and adult illiterates. This is by no means to say that some form of critical pedagogy is not relevant to these groups, although we will later speak to the necessity of making this relevance clearer and more vital.

Our point here is that our colleagues include serious and hardworking people who do not find critical pedagogy as compelling or central as we might wish because they are focusing their energies on providing other kinds of responses to the plight and suffering of particular groups and specific situations. This is especially poignant given the press of responding to the short- and middle-term needs of these victims (e.g., teenage mothers or children with AIDS have serious and immediate needs that critical pedagogy has failed or is unable to recognize sufficiently).

Nor has critical pedagogy much to say to teachers caught in the more general but still painful dilemma of practice involving the conflict between the short-range demands of accommodation and adaptation and the longer-range requirements for transformation. Teachers facing hungry or angry students who are high on drugs or depressed by poverty, in large and unmanageable classes probably do not find it easier to cope or survive by having more insight into the nature and contradictions of the emerging postindustrial society.

Challenges to Critical Pedagogy: Difficulties and Opportunities

It is customary to say that more people would come to accept the validity of critical pedagogy if the writing were better. Critical pedagogues and theorists are often accused of writing in an unnecessarily opaque, arid, tendentious, and dense manner, which promotes charges of arrogance, elitism, and hypercerebralism. This is a complex and sensitive issue, for it involves more than matters of aesthetic or linguistic style. It is surely not uncommon to witness disagreements about the boundaries between jargon and precision or about the sharing of responsibilities between readers and writers to seriously engage in a text.

Beyond these tangled and important disagreements and disputes lies an even more basic issue involving the intellectual capacities of the educational profession and the public. On one side are those who attack certain educational theorists for making their work inaccessible because of poor writing (the usual criticism refers to an overly technical and dense style), while the other side chides these critics for underestimating both the complexities of the issues and the abilities of "ordinary people" to fathom the complexities. This is not only a complicated issue but a highly emotional one since it speaks to the question of whether the problem is something over which the individual author has some control or whether it reflects inherent weaknesses in the theory. We certainly cannot criticize critical theorists for advancing complex ideas, although we can reflect on the responsibility to write clearly.

What cannot be denied is that many people who do make an effort to read critical pedagogy are put off by it, and it is imperative that we address that reality. It is also important not only to note the frustration of the readers, but also to point out the pain and hurt felt by the writers accused of being unclear and obscure. Although we are as supportive as anyone else of ever-clearer and more pleasurable writing styles, by and large we see these criticisms as symptomatic of deeper issues. The difficulty in communication, we believe, reflects more a failure of the movement to resonate significantly with other and deeper dimensions of efforts at educational reform than it does a failure in writing skills. We have indicated above a number of these dimensions; and by way of summary, we describe three broad categories of problems that the critical pedagogy movement will need to respond to creatively and substantially in order to have a more significant influence on American education and society.

1. Resistance. What we mean by resistance is parallel to the concept typically used by critical theorists to describe the refusal of students (usually from working-class and/or minority backgrounds) to be socialized and acculturated to the dominant norms and values. Here we use the term more generally to refer to a process in which people use affirmation or rejection of certain ideas as ways of identifying with other people/groups/ideologies, that is, the propensity of people to affirm particular ideas and to reject others that appear to be inconsistent with them. In this way, they develop a sense of personal definition through ownership of, and identification with, these ideas.

What is crucial here is the recognition that most people have strong and deep commitments to certain beliefs, values, ways of being, and modes of consciousness. Inevitably, then, society includes individuals and groups who will have values, beliefs, and affirmations that are at considerable variance with the essential dimensions of critical pedagogy. Some groups and individuals, for example, strongly avow meritocracy, a system of differential rewards, and the preservation of the existing order. Others may be put off on aesthetic or emotional bases because they strongly object simply to the critical, polemical, and disturbing/disruptive discourse so characteristic of critical pedagogy.

In any case, critical educational theorists have yet to address this extremely important dimension of their basic task, namely, a strategy other than opposition that recognizes the reality of resistance to criticism and that provides a model for adequately responding to it.

2. Fragmentation. Related to the phenomenon of resistance is the parallel reality of a highly complex, multilayered educational profession. What we mean here is that there are a myriad of responses in the society and professions other than support or opposition. In this realm, the problem is one of relevance, that is, the reality that many in the profession are so concerned with their own focus or speciality that critical pedagogy seems peripheral or even irrelevant. By *specialization* we mean the tendency to focus on particular educational dimensions such as (1) areas of concern (e.g., the problem of the non-English-speaking), (2) mode of analysis (e.g., cultural preservation), or (3) time perspective (e.g., immediate vs. long-range). The reality is that our efforts are expended in many different directions despite a common sympathy for the basic thrust of critical pedagogy. This is only to say the obvious, namely, that many people have sharply focused interests in education, and, as such, it is not surprising that their professional energy is absorbed in the particulars and specifics of those interests.

The problems of indifference are perhaps even more difficult and significant, for here we must deal with yet another reality, that is, that there are those who seem not to care at all about the broad and fundamental issues that are raised in the critical theory analyses. This is the reality wherein teaching is seen more as a job than as a profession, parents focus their energies on getting their children through school painlessly, and educational issues are, at best, seen as peripheral. Again, critical educators must recognize these social and educational dimensions and offer insightful analyses and appropriate responses in order to encourage broader perspectives.

3. Scope. The issue of scope integrates the questions raised in the matters of resistance and fragmentation through its concern for the breadth of critical pedagogy. We regard critical pedagogy's broad theories as immensely useful as far as they go and to the degree to which they afford insight into the sources of and solutions to our problems. We must also examine the present boundaries of critical pedagogy and the possibilities of extending them. For example, can a discourse that puts so much emphasis on critical rationality be enriched so that it can have validity for people for whom this kind of rationality—that is, a very strong emphasis on analysis, logic, and intellectual activity—is problematic (such as the mentally retarded) or aversive (such as those who are inclined to express themselves aesthetically)? In addition, although we embrace the necessity for the kind of basic and fundamental criticism that is essential to critical pedagogy there is the question of whether such a theory can adequately deal with immediate, short-, and/or middle-range problems and concerns. Furthermore, there is critical pedagogy's wariness to go beyond social, political, and economic discourses.

Critical pedagogy needs to ground itself not only in a social theory but also in considerations that speak to what it means to be human. It is clear that humans over the vastness of time and place have sought to define themselves through their capacity not only to reason and develop human relationships but also to understand themselves in relation to the mysteries of the macrocosm of the universe and the microcosm of the inner self.

One valid, albeit modest, response to such issues is to say that critical educators must not only accept the limitations of empiricism, analysis, and humanistic studies but also affirm their significance. Such a response can be justified on the grounds that the educative process inherently requires such critical rationality and that responsibility for dealing with the other important dimensions of social transformation must be borne by other institutions and processes—for example, political institutions, the arts, media, religion, and family. Critical pedagogues might also conclude that their largely intellectual orientation is basically unable to deal with many people—whether they be evil, ignorant, deluded, sick, handicapped, indifferent, or preoccupied. Indeed, critical pedagogues might focus their energy primarily on the education of those open to the possibility of a critically oriented education in the hope that there are enough such people to constitute a critical mass large enough to significantly influence the course of future possibilities.

In any event, we and our colleagues must confront these questions, dilemmas, and paradoxes and must struggle with them with humility, compassion, and faith. We surely will not facilitate the process if we are overcome by despair, blinded by romanticism, or distracted by internecine warfare. Our hope is that we can contribute to the development of this emerging educational discourse by suggesting an agenda for further work. Our intention is, of course, to respond to the challenges that critical pedagogy provides in both its strengths and weaknesses. We believe that the work of critical pedagogy can and must be continued as we incorporate its contributions and go on to the unfinished agenda.

The Postmodern Moment: Uncertainty and Commitment

Finally, it needs to be noted that the recent turn in critical educational thinking toward postmodern and poststructuralist ideas has compounded some of the issues alluded to above. This turn has added further complications to the already difficult process of galvanizing more public support for radical change in education. It has, for example, exacerbated problems of accessibility by adding new layers of complexity and difficulty to recent writings in critical pedagogy. The emerging language of analysis with its impulse toward "deconstructing" the apparently stable and unexamined assumptions of all forms of educational discourse is as forbidding and dizzying as the technical or pseudoscientific educational language it is committed to overturning.

Perhaps more consequential is the postmodern emphasis on what is called "incommensurability." This, in brief, is the assertion of the impossibility of gaining real understanding and insight into languages, cultures, and ways of life among those different from ourselves. Such claims are understandable given the way in which the voices, ways of being, and aspirations of so many have been squelched under the dominance of empires and hegemonic powers and given the growing recognition of the powerful and insidious effect of such silencing on the lives and experiences of people throughout the world. Yet this imperialism has, arguably, added new and powerful obstacles to the creation of broad-based movements concerned with social change predicated upon shared interests and goals.

The extraordinary emphasis on particularistic identities and cultural differences in what is sometimes referred to as "postmodern politics" is at odds with the expectations and possibilities of developing *common ground* among diverse groups of people. In condemning all forms of universal values, such politics sees these as little more than covert mechanisms for converting the moral standpoint and political interests of a few into the communally accepted viewpoint of the many. Such a perspective has fueled support for an uncompromising separatist outlook and has given an intellectual validity to a virulent ethnic balkanization that has become increasingly apparent in this country and in many parts of the world. It is doubtful how such intense particularism, with its inevitable tendencies toward intolerance, aggressiveness, and self-righteousness, can be harmonized with a democratic politics whose agenda is built around compromise, empathy, and civic respect.

Perhaps even more counterproductive to the development of a politics of educational change has been the devastating effect of postmodern thought on epistemological and ethical "foundationalism"—the belief in the possibility of incontrovertible knowledge and normative values. It is indeed hard to dispute that postmodern intellectual inquiry has fomented a sense of fundamental doubt about the enduring validity of everything that is known or believed. Such inquiry has produced a situation in which, as the British author Salamon Rushdie has noted, "doubt . . . is the central condition of human beings in the 20th century. One of the things that has happened to us in the 20th century as a human race is to learn how certainty crumbles in your hand, we cannot any longer have a fixed certain view of anything."

In this postmodern worldview, reality has been reduced to a "text" filled with—indeed, composed of, meanings that slip and slide in unpredictable ways, immune to any final, fixed representation of the world. Similarly, our moral commitments cannot be adduced from anything permanent or transcendent; instead they are, at best, the temporary product of normative communities and cultural conventions. Ethical standards, from this point of view, are not the product of universal imperatives but of the limited historical and social contexts in which we live our everyday lives. This unsettling view of the world outside ourselves is matched by a similar sense of the transient, unfixed nature of our inner beings.

Postmodern thinkers have assaulted the notion of there being an "essential" human nature. Human identity is, instead, a shifting, unfixed, mobile confluence of emotional and cognitive fragments. To talk of true human nature, or to go in search of our real selves, is, according to this viewpoint, a futile, purposeless quest that offers us comforting illusions of a coherent autonomous selfhood that, in fact, doesn't exist. Such a self is only an illusion—but one that has provided the basis for the exaggerated images of a stable and integrated being so crucial to notions of modern, rational man and that has given credence to the supposedly immutable characteristics of a gender-differentiated humanity.

It goes without saying that such assertions about our external and internal world, with all of their notions of uncertainty and instability, contradict human yearnings for a life that offers a sense of security and permanence. The unfixity of knowledge, values, and identity spells for many increased anxiety about a world that is morally adrift and culturally disintegrating. Intellectual revelry at the postmodern condition, with its recognition of the unboundedness of reality and personal identity, is not easily reconciled with the desire for a world of communal responsibility and human commitment. What frames the latter is a sense of obligation to compelling moral principles and a self-impelled, clear sense of its own needs and possibilities.

Clearly, we respond with ambivalence to the postmodern analysis of our world and our subjecthood. There is a price to be paid for such intellectual insights—one that conditions the usefulness of a critical pedagogy influenced by it to the making of an alternative public discourse on education. Yet, we know too that it cannot easily be disregarded or ignored. It is simply too cogent and telling for that. Indeed, in the remaining chapters, our debt to this entire critical tradition will not be in doubt, though our attempt to speak to its inadequacies and shortcomings will also be clear. What we intend is that our proposals for an educational discourse and agenda will be shaped by the concerns and intellectual vitality of critical pedagogy but will not be completely limited by the latter's implicit moral and political vision.

NOTES

1. Michael F. D. Young, ed., *Knowledge and Control: New Directions for the Sociology of Education* (London: Collier-Macmillan, 1985). For a full discussion of the "new sociology of education" see Geoff Whitty, *Sociology and School Knowledge* (London: Methuen, 1985).

2. See, for example, Geoff Whitty and Michael F. D. Young, *Explorations in the Politics of School Knowledge* (Driffield, England: Nefferton Books, 1976).

3. Samuel Bowles and Herbert Gintis, *Schooling in Capitalist America* (New York: Basic Books, 1976). This work was echoed in a number of other studies. See, for example, Martin Carnoy and Henry M. Levin, *Schooling and Work in the Democratic State* (Stanford, Calif.: Stanford University Press, 1985).

4. See Jean Anyon, "Social Class and the Hidden Curriculum of Work," *Journal of Education* 162, no. 1 (Winter 1980), pp. 67–92.

5. Joel Spring, *American Education: An Introduction to Social and Political Aspects* (New York: Longman, 1985).

6. See, for example, Michael W. Apple, *Ideology and Curriculum* (Boston: Routledge, 1979), and Michael W. Apple, *Education and Power* (Boston: Routledge, 1982). See also Svi Shapiro and David E. Purpel, eds., *Critical Social Issues in American Education* (New York: Longman, 1993).

7. See, for example, Stanley Aronowitz and Henry Giroux, *Education under Siege* (South Hadley, Mass.: Bergin & Garvey, 1985). See also H. Svi Shapiro, *Between Capitalism and Democracy: Educational Policy and the Crisis of the Welfare State* (Westport, Conn.: Bergin & Garvey, 1990).

8. See Henry Giroux and David Purpel, *The Hidden Curriculum and Moral Education* (Berkeley, Calif.: McCutchan, 1983).

9. See, for example, Ira Shor, *Critical Teaching and Everyday Life* (Chicago: University of Chicago Press, 1987). See also Maxine Greene, *The Dialectic of Freedom* (New York: Teachers College Press, 1988).

10. William Pinar, ed., *Curriculum Theorizing: The Reconceptualists* (Berkeley, Calif.: McCutchan, 1975).

11. Michael W. Apple, *Teachers and Texts* (New York: Routledge, 1988).

12. Henry Giroux, *Theory and Resistance: A Pedagogy for the Opposition* (South Hadley, Mass.: Bergin & Garvey, 1983).

13. See, for example, Madeline Grumet, *Bitter Milk: Women and Teaching* (Amherst: University of Massachusetts Press, 1988). See also Mary F. Belenky et al., *Women's Ways of Knowing* (New York: Basic Books, 1986).

14. C. A. Bowers, *Elements of a Post-Liberal Theory of Education* (New York: Teachers College Press, 1987).

15. Jonathan Kozol, *The Night Is Dark and I Am Far from Home* (Boston: Houghton Mifflin, 1975).

16. David E. Purpel, *The Moral and Spiritual Crisis of Education: A Curriculum for Social Justice* (Granby, Mass.: Bergin & Garvey 1988).

17. Maxine Greene, *Landscapes of Learning* (New York: Teachers College Press, 1978).

18. Michelle Fine, *Framing Dropouts* (Albany: State University of New York, 1991).

19. Peter McLaren, *Life in Schools* (New York: Longman, 1989).

20. Paul Willis, *Learning to Labor* (Lexington, Mass.: Heath, 1977); Robert Everhart, *Reading, Writing and Resistance* (Boston: Routledge, 1983).

21. Signithia Fordham, "Racelessness and Facts in Black Students' School Success: Pragmatic Strategy or Pyrrhic Victory," *Harvard Educational Review* 58, no. 1 (February 1988), pp. 54–84.

22. Ann Bastian et al., *Choosing Equality: The Case for Democratic Schools* (Philadelphia: Temple University Press, 1986); Henry Giroux, *Schooling and the Struggle for Public Life* (Minneapolis: University of Minnesota, 1991).

23. See, for example, Elizabeth Ellsworth, "Why Doesn't This Feel Empowering? Working Through Repressive Myths of Critical Pedagogy," *Harvard Educational Review* 59, no. 3 (1989); see also Carmen Luke and Jennifer Core, *Feminism and Critical Pedagogy* (New York: Routledge, 1983).

24. See, for example, Henry Giroux and Roger Simon, eds., *Popular Culture: Schooling and Everyday Life* (Westport, Conn.: Greenwood Press, 1989); Sherry Taylor, "Skinned Alive: Towards a Postmodern Pedagogy of the Body," *Education and Society* 9, no. 1 (1991).

25. Henry Giroux, *Teachers as Intellectuals* (Granby, Mass.: Bergin & Garvey, 1988).

26. See Henry A. Giroux and Peter McLaren, "Teacher Education and the Politics of Engagement: The Case for Democratic Schooling," *Harvard Educational Review* 56, no. 3 (August 1986), pp. 213–38.

27. L. Athusser, "Ideology and the Ideological State Approaches," in *Lenin and Philosophy and Other Essays*, ed. L. Athusser (New York: Monthly Review Press, 1971).

28. Herbert M. Kliebard, *The Struggle for the American Curriculum, 1893–1958* (Boston: Routledge, 1986).

29. See, for example, Jurgen Habermas, *Legitimation Crisis* (Boston: Beacon, 1975); see also Richard A. Cloward and Francis F. Piven, *The New Class War* (New York: Pantheon, 1982).

5

Beyond Liberation and Excellence: A Discourse for Education as Transformation

THE CHALLENGE OF THE POSTMODERN: COHESION IN A WORLD OF DIFFERENCE

Although much of our own social and educational orientation has been reflected in the first four chapters of this book, most of what we have said has been in the nature of criticism and analysis of existing public and professional discourse. It is now time for us to be more direct and explicit about our own point of view, fundamental assumptions, and particular recommendations. In this chapter, we set out a broad framework—or, if you will, a credo—in which we provide a framework for an education directed at a morally grounded social vision. The book concludes with a chapter that deals with a political agenda that reflects that framework.

As we have indicated, our starting point is the critical pedagogy tradition; however we intend to respond to a number of our criticisms of this movement, particularly to its failure to articulate a political program, its failure to respond to important psychological dimensions, its diffidence and wariness about dealing with moral and spiritual issues, and its inability to extricate itself from conflictual discourse. In writing this chapter, we have also had to directly confront our own differing perspectives and to develop positions that were truly integrative rather than merely complementary. We wanted to (and did) experience the creative as well as the conflictful tensions between points of view that differed in emphasis between the political and the moral, between short- and long-range perspectives, between essentialist and pragmatic tendencies, between optimism and despair, and between existential and historical outlooks. We believed that we accomplished more than most people thought we could and yet less than we had hoped for.

There is something that must be confessed at the outset of writing this chapter. Call it masculine hubris or intellectual arrogance perhaps. Our intention was to find and offer a language or vision for education that would express all aspects of our hopes and commitments for educational renewal and change. This discourse would tie together all of our concerns with a *single* thread. We felt capable of finding that one powerful, resonant image or representation of educational purpose and goals that could claim the allegiance, and capture the imagination, of the broad mass of citizens in this country. Indeed, we felt impelled to discern that unitary overarching demand for education that might unleash the political will and drive for educational reform—one that would connect changes in education to the impulse for changing our society in directions that are more socially just, democratic, and compassionate. It seemed to us that our combined visionary power and perspicacity would allow us to unlock the discursive secret for mobilizing wide public support and sympathy for transforming the nature and goals of education in the United States. As will become clear, our response to this challenge is more complex and rests less on a simple formula or clear-cut notions than perhaps we may have liked.

Perhaps our desire or our confidence in the possibility of finding such a language was the legacy of what has been called "totalizing" political thinking that, especially in the twentieth century, has promised to provide us with some key to social change.[1] This kind of thinking rests on a self-confident assumption that there is always an historically correct strategy that a group of committed political individuals can discern. On the political Left (with which we identify ourselves), this has meant, very often, the belief that there is a single, preeminent motive that, when galvanized, can bring a society toward its own transformation. Left intellectuals, in particular, have long operated under the assumption that, with the acquisition of a critical level of cultural, economic, and political understanding, it is possible to uncover the secret of social transformation; that, armed with their often prodigious knowledge of a society's nature and development, the mechanism of social change can be ignited and the quest for human emancipation will roar to life.[2] This belief has been one component of the often frantic intellectuality of Left intellectuals who are convinced that a final or complete grasp of the whole social situation is within their reach. The failures, losses, and unpredictability of events in this century—not the least of which have been the revolutionary changes in Europe at the end of the 1980s—have surely challenged this faith. These events have, or should have, tempered our belief in our capacity to know and steer the hearts and minds of the *masses* (a term itself that reeks of the separation between that privileged group who provide intellectual and moral guidance and the rest who may receive it).

Yet, and despite our own admission here, the difficulty of keeping faith with the promise of this book to provide some straightforward, clear, and evocative language by which to stir educational revolt or insurgency is a disappointment, even a bitter pill. Of course, this recognition is not ours alone. We are quite aware that it is no more than what a number of our thoughtful colleagues and comrades in struggles have also found. The pages of some of the most creative Left publications, such as *Tikkun* magazine, Z magazine, *In These Times*, and the *Utne Reader*, give testimony to this. The world is too complex, the range of views too wide, the diversity of concerns too differentiated, to imagine that there can, any more, be simple unanimity of goals or interests that unites all of us who desire deep political, social, economic, cultural, and educational change. Nor can we hold fast to the belief that all of those who are now apathetic, cynical, detached, or even hostile to social change can be mobilized around some all-embracing hope or that they can be won over to some transcendent image, representation, or vision of the future. Of course, as we have already noted, it is also possible to conclude, as some critical scholars have, that there is nothing left to unify us, no common human goal or vision, nothing for those of us who seek fundamental social change to attend to and support but the endless proliferation of different voices, each trying to find some justified place in the sun after imprisonment in silence, or exclusion. We in no way wish to diminish the recognition of the multiplicity of ways in which human beings have been oppressed, their dignity undermined, and the full realization of their humanity thwarted. For we have, at last, begun to enter a world where the multiple ways in which human beings suffer and are dehumanized is achieving its proper recognition.

Yet—and we will return to this later—something is lost in this radical discourse of difference. Where are the bridges that connect the suffering of one group of human beings to another? Where is the sense of commonality among different people—not just within the *particular* oppressed group itself?[3] If we all speak only from within our specific situations and identities (the sexually oppressed, native people, the old, the mentally disabled, women, and so forth), who speaks for humanity? While the socialist tradition of emphasizing working-class struggles may have arrogantly ignored or dismissed so many other forms of human pain and struggle, it did, at least, maintain some kind of universal human vision.

We will need to decide whether such universal visions are part of man's megalomaniacal desire for power and uniformity or part of the deep failure of political nerve that now afflicts so many of those concerned with social transformation. The catastrophic failures of revolutionary social experiments in the twentieth century certainly can be seen as giving credence to either argument or position.

Such has indeed been the case with articulating an alternative radical discourse about education among what is undoubtedly a fragmented, divergent public. In this sense, we have come to accept the implication of what might be called our postmodern reality.[4] Our identities in the world are so complexly shaped that the "call to arms" to fight a clearly focused, unique opponent has become an outmoded discourse inapplicable to the particular social, cultural, political, and economic conditions that we now encounter in the United States.

More and more we have come to understand ourselves as "positioned" in the world in complex and contradictory ways with allegiances, concerns, and needs that are anything but given, static, or singular. Identities are not fixed by one or another sociological category, and people do not have predetermined ways of looking at or making sense of their world. Neither those whom we envisage as our "natural" allies in the struggle for our own survival nor those whom we come to see as our necessary nemesis or opponents is foretold by history. One only has to consider, for example, Elie Wiesel's assertion that today "all of us have become Jews."

Today all of humanity can be seen as victims living under the Damoclean sword of a world in the process of destroying its delicate web of life-giving resources. The carcinogenic effect of the pollution of water and food, the erosion of the ozone layer, and so forth, places even the wealthiest and most powerful among us at risk. In this sense, at least, much of humanity faces the death-dealing prospects of its own making. If it is self-interest that motivates collective action, then the spectrum of people who may be attracted to a socially transformative political—or educational—agenda could be very much wider than we often assume.

The sometimes surprising and unexpected nature of political commitment in the contemporary world is surely demonstrated in what is now frequently referred to as "green" politics. We have seen how such politics, as well as the closely related antinuclear and peace movements, have received their major support from the professional middle classes.[5] These relatively well-educated groups have what the German political thinker and activist, Rudolf Bahro, has termed "surplus consciousness," which allows them to consider, and be attentive to, far more than the immediate needs and imperatives of their existence.[6]

Such groups can be concerned about the destruction of the Brazilian or African rain forests because their consciousness (and conscience) radically expands the time and space coordinates that locate what is experienced as threatening or endangering to them. Humanity itself—not just a nation, a class, a race, or some other relatively circumscribed social entity—is under the gun, facing not just exploitation but global annihilation. The focus of struggle becomes the future of the earth itself; what is at stake is the continuity of our species. In this sense, there is a common human struggle—one which posits a common and shared human identity.

Bahro's analysis has taken on particular significance in the light of the successful uprisings against Stalinism and bureaucratic socialism in Eastern and Central Europe. The role of professional and white-collar middle-class groups, artists and intellectuals and their concern with issues of ecological deterioration, and peace and cultural freedom was obviously an important, even crucial, element in the transformation of the states in these countries. These concerns obviously were conjoined with working-class concerns for a poor and deteriorating standard of living and oppressive working conditions. In Western capitalist societies, the enormous growth of the state is both the product of, and the catalyst for, a vast expansion and proliferation of social struggles.

Traditional Marxist notions of class struggle at the point of production have been supplemented (if not replaced) with a multiplicity of popular movements that demand from government an expansion of their social, economic, political, and cultural rights.[7] AIDS, questions of abortion rights for women, consumer protection, the needs of senior citizens, financial support for students, and health care for those who cannot afford to buy it in the marketplace are among many such areas of struggle. Each organizes and mobilizes a distinct and different social entity; each need constitutes a different identity of want or deprivation.

However, while the range of political struggles expands to embrace more and more of our complex lives, the potential social fragmentation, divisiveness, and competition grows apace. Politics is paradoxically more pervasive and more insinuated in our lives and more particularistic, limited in its immediate concerns and mean-spirited as each constituency defines its objectives in highly parochial ways.

MORAL IMAGINATION AND EDUCATIONAL DISCOURSE

As we come to perceive our place among other human beings, we develop what Douglas Kellner has called our "political imaginary."[8] This, he says, is the cognitive and moral mapping that gives individuals a vision of the existing state of their world and what it should or could become and that provides the sense of identification as to who does or does not share our needs and concerns in the world. The imaginary offers specific ways of seeing and interpreting the events and issues that people must deal with in their everyday lives. On the basis of what we have said, it is clear that the imaginary can be shaped and constituted in many diverse ways, though it is not infinitely elastic. It must, in some way, speak to people's needs, anxieties, tensions, feelings of insecurity, and so forth (though quite obviously these can be understood and made sense of in many different ways). Thus, for example, to see the world as threatened, and humanity itself as victims, makes it possible to see ourselves in a fundamentally different way and in a new kind of connection to others (and perhaps to nature itself). With the emergence of alternative ways of imaging our situation, different concerns are articulated, unrecognized or unfulfilled desires come to the fore, new voices are heard, and new forms of outrage and indignation are expressed.

The question of what kinds of discourse govern how citizens think of and define education belongs to this larger question of what kind of political imaginary—what kind of cognitive and moral map—governs our understanding of the existing state of our world and of what it should or could become. The question of the public discourse about education is then nothing less than the question of what kind of world we live in, what we wish it to become, and who are the innovators who may favor or obstruct such possibilities. Of course, as we have argued throughout this book, the relation of the public discourse about education to the larger questions of culture and society have typically been treated with varying degrees of obfuscation, denial, and mystification. Its dominant tendencies have ranged from the assertion by some of the need for education's moral and political neutrality (obviously something that we think is impossible) to the overwhelming centrality of an economic rationale for education (the "human capital" view of the purpose of schools), to the Right's demand that education act as a brake on the moral and cultural disintegration of the nation.[9]

While we disagree with the prescriptive nature of the latter's claims—its coercive, parochial, and chauvinistic view of education—we believe nonetheless that it appropriately argues for a moral/cultural vision of the purpose of education. The Right's prescription places education on what is for us the correct and most desirable discursive terrain: Education must primarily be defined in terms of its relation to the community's moral vision. Education must be seen in the context of the crucial social and human condition of our time, and it must be rooted not only in a prophetic commitment to raising social awareness about the dangers and suffering of our world but also in the praxis of deep personal and social change. More specifically, it is our belief that the struggle for a genuinely new public discourse of education depends on our capacity to offer a cognitively convincing and, more especially, a morally compelling vision of our possibilities as a culture and a society. The struggle for transformative social change—whether about education or anything else—depends now on a politics that is ready and able to articulate the future in the framework of a compelling moral vision rooted in the material, emotional, and spiritual needs of our lives.

This is one of the lessons of the political success of the Right in the 1980s and 1990s. This argument has been eloquently and forcefully made by *Tikkun* editor Michael Lerner, who notes that the thirst for moral meaning is one of the deepest in American life. Moral vision, he says, far from being a "soft issue" is potentially the guts of American politics.[10] It powerfully fuels the "traditional values" crusade of the Right that continues to haunt and obstruct attempts at a more progressive politics. Failing to grasp this fact (by staying away from the moral needs of the people), the Left in America has been unable to mobilize a strong sense of commitment.

The power of the Right's discourse has been that its moral language addresses the psychological deprivation that has grown out of the failure of communal life in the United States. While liberals and the Left have championed the poor and those who face overt racial and sexual oppression, they have ignored the pain that many others, especially middle-class people, have experienced in the not strictly legal or economic arenas—in their families, in the absence of community and an ethical frame to life.

Implicit in conservatives' "profamily" and "traditional values" politics, argues Lerner, is a compassion that counteracts the self-blaming that dominates personal life today. Whether it be personal happiness, economic well-being, or social success and recognition, everything is supposedly in the hands of the individual. The pop-psychology formulation of "Take responsibility for your own life" and "You can make it if you really try," he says, reinforces in new ways the cornerstone of American ideology, namely, the belief in meritocracy. If you want happiness, you will get it; if you don't have it, you have only yourself to blame.

Lerner argues that conservative politics depends not on the specifics of its program but on the way in which it acknowledges the crisis in personal lives while pointing the finger at a set of social causes (feminism, gays, "liberal permissiveness") that are not the fault of individual Americans. Lerner continues:

While strongly rejecting the conservatives scape-goating, we can also see that by encouraging people to find a social cause for family crisis they decrease self-blame and increase self-compassion.

This analysis helps us to understand the popularity of Reagan in the first six years of his presidency. Reagan's picture of an America in which people could find true community and pride in their lives offered a seductive alternative to self-blaming. We need not adopt or accept a similar patriotic chauvinism, but we do need to be able to understand the seductiveness of such an appeal.[11]

It is easy to see similar factors at work in the Right's educational agenda—the homogeneity and uniformity of a core curriculum and a common standard of cultural literacy, the question of prayer in school or the demand for an end to busing, a return to neighborhood schools and the explicit inculcation of "traditional" moral values in schools. The conservatives' moral language is a call for a communal life that would buffer the insecurities and uncertainties of daily life.

Paradoxically, of course, this desire for security is undermined by the very economic system that the Right trumpets unquestioningly. While, as Lerner notes, decent human relationships depend on trust, caring, and the ability to give to others, today the "successful" American spends much of his or her day manipulating and controlling others. The kind of people who will be rewarded with promotions, clients, and customers must learn to continually manipulate and sell themselves. They must develop personalities in which their own feelings and emotions become distant and alienated, which precludes authentic and deep relationships with other human beings, whether in families or in friendships. The conservative philosophy of selfishness and individualism expressed in a worship of the capitalist marketplace and its disdain for the poor contradicts relationships that are open, loving, and caring—the cement of a compassionate and supportive communal life.[12]

Notwithstanding the distortions of conservative discourse and the phony remedies, there are important lessons here for those of us committed to the possibilities of a more just and equitable society. Not the least of these lessons is the power and importance of rooting our concerns in a vision that speaks to our moral and spiritual needs as a community. Without this vision, progressive politics becomes what it so often is, namely, a laundry list of worthy but disparate issues (health care, equal pay, day care, environmental protection, tax reform, etc.)—a set of unquestionably important concerns but without the moral and spiritual vision that moves people and in which people find themselves affirmed.

The Left's current preoccupation with "difference" reduces politics to the clamor of a warring tribalism. Instead of a communal moral and spiritual vision, the Left offers an image of a world balkanized into an endless proliferation of those who can claim some history of oppression and exclusion. Such oppression becomes a jealously guarded experience about which no one outside of it dare speak (without the accusation of acting imperiously and arrogantly).

Again, our goal here is not to disregard difference or to deny the experience, language, and distinctiveness, of people's lives. The world, as we know too well, has been hideously deformed by the way in which whole groups of human beings have been silenced and made invisible through the power of other people's discourse. While the validation of these disregarded voices is necessary, it is not a sufficient condition for radical social change. It too easily becomes a politics that divides people, excludes, and emphasizes our separation. It becomes a holier-than-thou sectarianism, very far from the image of a world in which we can all see ourselves valued and loved.

While we emphasize irreducible differences and distinctiveness, the Right and the religious fundamentalist will bludgeon us into a "recognition" of our common heritage, tradition, and values. Perhaps the image of the "quilt" with its validation of the distinct patches whose singularity is enhanced by their contiguity with others and the richness of the whole is the metaphor for a liberating communal life that we like the best and think appropriate for our time. Despite the multiplicity of identities in modern society and the complexity of demand, claims, needs, and wants, we should not imagine that this lessens the power or significance of a morally and spiritually rooted communal vision as the leitmotif for a renewal of a politics of progressive social change.

THE POLITICS OF EDUCATIONAL TRANSFORMATION

Of course, the struggle for a different definition of the purpose and goals of education in many ways turns on the matter of social agency: Who will support and respond to an alternative language or vision of educational concerns?[13] Yet the world we have entered—the postmodern world as it is sometimes called—makes it harder than before to identify some kind of "natural" progressive constituency.[14] For example, who is to identify with the victims of oppression and who with the perpetrators? Who will respond with enthusiasm for an alternative educational discourse agenda that concerns itself, say, with issues of social justice, social responsibility, and democratic empowerment? The shifting, more fluid nature of identity in today's culture and the multiple forms of suffering, indignity, and deprivation felt by human beings in the world makes the ground on which we struggle to banish or at least mitigate oppression and pain a slippery one, without a secure or stable point in which we may situate ourselves and understand who we are in relation to those around us.

The human catastrophes of drug addiction or emotional illness, for example, create new forms of solidarity among people separated in other ways by social class, race, or other forms of identification. Within this context in which human beings find themselves united in shared desperation and need, different kinds of politics can emerge that pose questions about society, its compassion, and its supportiveness. Addiction and emotional illness reflect deep veins of suffering and need that run through the society; these forms of indignity and exclusion criss-cross the culture. Like the crisis of the environment, this represents a context of human experience that lends itself to new forms of shared concerns and expectations and, thus, to new languages and images that may reorient the larger vision for our society and our expectations and hopes for education.

While we wish to emphasize the fluid and relatively open way in which political struggles—including those around education—might be constituted, it would be foolish to suggest (as some have) that the lines that distinguish oppressor and oppressed have lost all meaning or relevance and that we are all, for example, equally culpable for the ills and injustices in the world. The exploitation of labor by capital continues to be readily discernible. Corporate greed and disregard for the needs of the working and middle class is all too visible. Military and political elites in this country support and supply material to Third World authoritarian governments that continue to suppress those who call for more equitable and democratic social and economic systems. At home, women suffer the structural violence of poverty and economic injustice, as well as personal violence at the hands of men, for whom there are real social, cultural, and economic advantages in the existing gender arrangements. While in some ways we may all be responsible for the current degradation of nature, this must not be confused with the guilt of those powerful political and economic interests who plunder the earth's limited resources.

Yet know that none of us operate in sealed and unidimensional social spaces. We slide quickly from roles in which we exploit and dehumanize others to those in which we ourselves are the object of others' instrumental attitudes and exploitative treatment. In the complexity of the contemporary world, we occupy, at once, positions where others are targets of our prejudice, venality or manipulation, and places where we are objects of manipulation by others. In the loose and shifting sands of our world, few of us are unscarred by the indifference, callousness, and indignity endemic to our private and public worlds. For some, this psychic and spiritual wounding is more visible, more unrelenting, and sometimes more total. For people of color, women, gays and lesbians, the handicapped, the aged, the mentally ill, the poor, and all of those who come to be, in our society, designated as "other," the pain of exclusion and abuse is obviously palpable. Even domination, however, exacts its price in suffering. Robert Bly and others have, for example, begun to make the case for a male liberation from the drivenness and emotional stuntedness of masculine middle-class life, the consequences of which is male rage that more and more seems to explode on our streets and in our homes.[15]

Again, we do not wish to suggest that all of the suffering is on a par. The deprivation of homelessness, poverty, racism, or sexual abuse is certainly more brutal and more terrible than other forms of human suffering. The issue here is not whether we may find equivalence in the forms of pain and oppression. For some, oppression and victimization are unrelenting, wherein survival itself is a matter of unrelieved struggle. Rather, we wish to recognize that there is no "privileged" bearer of oppression or suffering in our society. There is not a simple duality that distinguishes people as *either* those who dominate, exploit, or inflict pain on others *or* those who are the recipients of the same. Political topographies that categorize the world in this way end up with rigid, predetermined images of "us" and "them" or "us" versus "them." They lead us to the reassuring simplicities of "enemy thinking." Demographically these maps have carved up the population so that it is clear from the outset who is politically "progressive" and who is not. The political images and understandings that people adopt are, from this point of view, merely waiting in the wings for the curtain to rise before making their appearance according to an already rehearsed dramatization.

Yet such interpretations, in their rigidity and dogmatism, start by ignoring the complexity of human experience and identity and the increasingly problematic nature of our political affiliations and the preferences that confront us. As Sharon Welch courageously acknowledges, we may assume concurrently the roles of both oppressor and oppressed. She writes as both a woman in a patriarchal culture and as a professor at an elite university that is a cornerstone of the system of class privilege in the United States. Such contradictions are not uncommon. We may move routinely between positions that seem privileged and offer us authority and status to situations in which we are degraded, disempowered, and victimized. Such is the routine character, for example, of many women's lives.[16]

To understand all this is to appreciate the importance of Michel Foucault's critique of the Marxian concept of power and categorization.[17] There is no *single* axis around which all relations of power and domination, struggle and resistance are plotted. There are, instead, a multiplicity of fields in which human beings struggle for freedom, justice, dignity, and a fuller realization of their lives. These fields overlap and cut across one another, thus producing a complex social map of human aspirations and struggles. Such struggles have their own dynamic, character, and set of possibilities. Families, schools, religious communities, neighborhoods, workplaces, cultural institutions, state institutions, and so forth, sustain and focus deep, even explosive, tensions. While such tensions are fueled by the unrealized aspirations and disappointed hopes generated from within the culture, these tensions cannot easily be assimilated within one another, reduced to one overarching problem that, if resolved, would herald a utopian transformation of the world—solving at one stroke all our problems and concerns.

Relinquishing such an apocalyptic tale of revolutionary change may be disappointing to those who hunger for the simple, the universal, and the either/or explanation of events. However, it does not diminish our sense of radical possibility and the hope of human transformation and social change. Quite the opposite! Released as we are from the old Left fixation on finding the historically "privileged" agent of social change or revolution, or the one real focus for radical struggle, we can now open our eyes and see a world replete with human aspirations for fulfillment, plenitude, dignity, justice, compassion, love, and spiritual significance and replete with the struggles to realize such possibilities in modern society.

Of course, our different situations inflect our hopes and struggles in different ways. The possibilities for change are shaped and delimited by their multiple discourses. Even within the life of one person, relative satisfaction at work, might give way to fury and agitation at the inability to be safe from harassment on the streets; economic well-being might be accompanied by the fear of family disintegration or the despair of a spiritual emptiness, and patriotic sentiments might coexist with a religious faith that impels one to work for the sanctuary of those who are the victims of U.S. collusion with fascist governments in Central or South America.

The politics that emerge from the fluidity and complexities of identity in contemporary America do not, it must be emphasized, negate those historically important social struggles. We, in no sense, wish to underestimate, for example, the long and difficult struggles by labor in this country to ameliorate exploitative economic relations or to advance the welfare and occupational conditions of working people. Nor do we wish to detract from the crucial value of movements like those for racial justice, for peace, or for sexual equality. Our goal is, however, to offer an educational language—and later, an agenda—that can be as inclusive in its appearance as possible, able to recognize the fullest possible range of human struggles and concerns at this juncture in time.

EDUCATIONAL DISCOURSE AND THE CRISIS OF MEANING

We believe that life in the United States at this time has become so painful, alienating, ethically compromised, and spiritually impoverished, that education must speak first and foremost to this human and social crisis. The crisis is pervasive and multidimensional in its effects: sometimes material, sometimes psychological and emotional, and sometimes spiritual (and often all of the above). The crisis reaches into the very corners and crevices of our society, producing the pauperization of some and the miseration of many.[18] Its consequences are in the form of shame, deprivation, indignity, and psychic distress.

The desperate need for a transformative politics and an educational vision and language commensurate with this leads us to attempt to construct a discourse and an agenda that can speak to the widest range of people who might be responsive to the need for deep social change and who might recognize that our present cultural, moral and economic path as a nation (and as a planet) is destructive and dehumanizing. This is not a time to speak to the converted (as, sadly, so much of critical educational scholarship tends to do) or to stay within predictable and expected social constituencies, or to seek what is ideologically "correct" but politically ineffective.[19] Our struggles here are not ours alone. They belong to all those who are sincerely attempting to renew a socially transformative vision and language.

Such a renewal requires questioning seriously the tried and traditional language of Left and liberal politics and the subjects of such politics.[20] We are convinced, for example, that an "economic" discourse alone—that is, the question of how wealth is to be divided between classes—is necessary but insufficient to mobilize the kind of support that is needed. Nor is it enough to attach the politics of transformation solely to the language of political, civil, or social rights or to the expansion of a democratic culture.

As important as this is, such an emphasis does not speak clearly enough to the emotional distress and spiritual despair of a world that does not offer the support, solidarity, and compassion of a loving community.[21] As important as is the language of economic justice, it implies, in and of itself, little about how we should break out of the ecodestructive conditions of industrial societies that currently bind both working class and the captains of industry to a global path that is suicidal.[22]

Nor can we find convincing anymore the equation of a radical vision of a world that is thoroughly rational and, therefore, fully engineered. For many of us, especially the young, what seems especially attractive is rather a world in which the spontaneous, the unpredictable, and the ecstatic flourish and in which individualism and freedom find deep and vibrant expression. What has been called the post-Fordist phase of capitalism, with its computerized capacity for unprecedented novelty, diversity, and creative fluidity, has made the old heroic production-oriented images of socialism seem repressive and archaic. In such conditions, the demand for diversity and pleasure in everyday life cannot be derided as purely romantic escape or capitalist excess.[23] Nor is there much attraction to the Marxian promise of a society wherein everything is fully transparent and accessible to reasoned intellect. Such a vision seems positively perverse in its denial of the mysterious, the unfathomable, and the wondrous. While, for example, we might insist on women's reproductive rights, we need also to acknowledge the difficulties and dilemmas that do indeed surround the question of how and when the precious phenomenon of human life comes into being. As our life-world is corroded and subjugated by the technocratic order, with its depersonalization and abstract rationalities, men and women understandingly turn to the religious, the spiritual, and the mystical as means of asserting the ineffable qualities of human life and experience.[24]

The Left's long marriage to modernism, with its narratives that are so determinedly secular, rationalistic, and instrumental, has wrought a vision at odds with many of the most powerful and moving discourses of human freedom and resistance in the world today.[25] But to accept and include such discourses in a language of transformation means to shed any remaining illusions about our capacity to describe the world as it really is, rather than in metaphors that offer resonant and evocative images concerning human existence and possibilities. Perhaps the difficulty of doing this is reflected in the reluctance of critical intellectuals in the United States to fully embrace the languages that have emerged from Liberation, Feminist, and Creation theologies—surely some of the most moving and powerful revolutionary discourses in existence today.[26] To include the spiritual and the religious in our language of social or educational change is to acknowledge that political struggle is not so much about "truth" but about how we and others can image or re-image the world. It is about the way we can envision human possibility, identity, and a meaningful existence.

Just at the moment when the Left has come to recognize so clearly the mass psychic impoverishment that both capitalism and bureaucratic socialism have wrought, it has been captured by a sensibility that makes it both increasingly cynical and increasingly reluctant to articulate the value of universal human rights, liberation, community, and social justice.[27] Such notions are dismissed by critics as but part of the metaphysics of modernity and so-called enlightenment. What is offered instead is nothing but the endless transgression of cultural limits and the proliferation of differences among people. Yet, for many people, this "postmodern bazaar" is repulsive and terrifying. It is part of the problem, not the solution. It offers little that validates tradition, it provides little that connects us across time and space, and it says little about what might transcend the particular, the local, and the contingent and about what might speak to the whole human condition.[28]

EDUCATIONAL DISCOURSE AND
THE POLITICS OF INCLUSIVENESS

Therefore, we want to offer the elements of a public discourse for education that privileges no one group of people and that tries to speak to and include the experiences, needs, and hopes of a broad spectrum of individuals. Together, these constitute what Stuart Hall referred to as a "popular bloc," a political movement composed of a diverse set of social groups who might favor deep social and educational change.[29] The language that we offer here is broad, inclusive, and rooted in aspects of our national culture. It seems to make possible the articulation of the multiple concerns of human beings who in obviously different ways might be moved by a vision of education whose overriding task is what has been called "tikkun olam"—the healing and repair of our society and world. In this sense, we seek here to offer a discourse for education centered in a moral language that can embrace and express the variety and complexity of wounds, indignities, and exclusions that are the experiences of our fellow citizens.

To construct this bloc means finding ways in which dissimilar people with distinct, sometimes divergent, interests can come together and find common ground. It means to seek a language—and an agenda—for education that reflects the particular struggles and aspirations of social groups and that can reconcile their differences without denying or subordinating any of them. A transformative educational discourse requires a language and an agenda for educational reform that insists on educating the young for a socially just, socially responsible, democratic, and compassionate community. Proposing that the work of education be conceived of in these terms means, on the one hand, to envisage an education that works for the transformation of our culture in ways that emphasize the overarching moral imperative of a compassionate, solidaristic, and participatory society. Yet, at the same time, this vision must not turn into some monolithic moral straitjacket that dictates educational concerns in narrowly defined ways.

The struggle for a fuller, deeper, and more humane community may, in some set of circumstances, mean that education be about ensuring literacy; elsewhere, the possibility of jobs; and in some other places, political participation and empowerment. Given the complex nature of identity and the diversity of ways in which people may conceive of a humane transformation of our world, our educational language and agenda must not be confused with the dead hand of some programmatically "correct" instructional curriculum or form of pedagogy. Our overriding concern is quite distinct from questions of exactly what and how we teach in the classroom (even when this is conceived in the radical forms of critical or feminist pedagogy). Although this is not irrelevant to reshaping education, it should not be confused with our present task, which is to formulate and offer a broad and inclusive discursive framework through which a diversity of people can see the concerns and hopes that they have for themselves and for their children given expression and related to the purposes of education in this country.

The struggle here is not about pedagogy as much as it is about education's place in what we earlier referred to as the political imaginary. It is about how to reconceive the purpose and goals of education so that it is explicitly linked to the transformation of the social and cultural realities that we live. Notwithstanding the obvious importance of classroom methodologies, modes of teaching, and so forth, we do not want to be caught in the trap of technique, of an obsessive focus on matters of practice, or of questions about how to do things in the classrooms. To avoid this, it is worth running the risk of urging a different kind of conversation—one that might be dismissed as removed from real school concerns—but that insists on referencing the larger human, cultural, moral, and spiritual vision within which we wish to educate our children. It does not aim to displace matters or questions of practice, but only to act as the reference point (or points) for how we are to conceive of the value and purpose of what education ought to be in this society at this time.

Educational work is made more meaningful and vital by its situatedness in this vision. The political effectiveness of this vision (i.e., the extent of its appeal and support) depends on how well it is capable of drawing in and articulating the diverse and divergent needs and concerns of ordinary people. It depends on how well an education oriented to this vision can be seen as speaking to people's lives and, more important, to the lives of their children. The danger of ignoring this is apparent in the emphasis today in radical educational circles on critical or feminist pedagogies, or on defining educational change as a revitalization of what it means to be a citizen and pursuing what has been called a critical democracy. The issue is not that these are not valuable and valid aspects of what we on the Left have to offer education in the present situation. It is that they are too limited in emphasis, too circumscribed in whom they address, too one-sided in their definition of what constitutes educational renewal.

The result is—as is quite clear from the limited enthusiasm or acceptance of the whole critical pedagogy project—an agenda for education that is simply not sufficiently resonant with the concerns of many people.[30] That is glaring in its disregard for a whole range of human concerns, like the role of the traditional, the spiritual, community and obligation, responsibility and discipline. Making the expansion of democratic life the leitmotif of radical change in contemporary society[31] strikes us as a necessary but insufficient way to image our future social reality. Radically extended popular empowerment in economic, cultural, and political life is certainly a crucially important goal of a society more and more subject to a quality of existence emptied of any meaningful democratic experiences. Reform or changes in education directed toward a deepening of the meaning of democratic rights and responsibilities in the public sphere is certainly a crucial concern for progressives.

However, the discourse of an education that can speak to a healing and a repair of our world must say more than this if it is to be heeded. It must touch people's spiritual and emotional lives through what have been called the feminine moral images—of wholeness, compassion, care, and responsibility. This the discourse of social rights and democratic empowerment cannot do: These concerns are necessary but insufficiently evocative for a transformational politics in the closing decade of this century. The politics of radical change in these years will belong to those who can successfully articulate the postmodern—or antimodern—impulses that are increasingly being unleashed in the world.[32] In the case of education, the Right and the religious fundamentalist have, for the most part, been more adept at this task. They have been (for obvious reasons) both more successful and the more ready to use this kind of language. They have been able to step into what we know from our work with teachers and community groups as the discursive emptiness of the present moment— where educational talk is conducted without reference to some prophetic vision of society or human life, a discourse bereft of the mobilizing power of a moral focus that links the work of education to the needs, hopes, and possibilities of the larger culture. Such a focus would link our educational concerns, policies, practices, and goals to the question of the quality and character of our personal and communal lives. It would insist that educational questions are always, at the same time, questions about what it means to be human and about how we as humans ought to live together.

EDUCATION AND THE HUMAN STRUGGLE: A VISION QUEST

In the following pages, we respond to the necessity as educators to affirm the basic beliefs and commitments that ground our work as professionals and citizens. We do so in the recognition that such a process is a necessity that also yields limitations, possibilities, and problematics. We have endeavored to provide a framework that attempts to be in-clusive; and though knowing that it cannot possibly accommodate all positions and orientations, we will offer a discourse that endeavors to be rational and rigorous but that nonetheless includes a language of a more elusive and evocative nature. Our orientation is rooted in both history and myth, in both the nightmare of contemporary realities and the dreams of the ages, and in both the promise and violation of our social and cultural covenants. We offer these views in the light of our preceding analysis, which proposed an educational vision in the postmodern world that recognizes the perils and problematics of both righteousness and moral evasion, of both dogmatism and inanity, and of both certainty and relativism. We are quite clear that educational discourse *must* reflect significant moral and political concerns, although we welcome further debate and dialogue on the particulars of our moral and political orien-tation. It is imperative that educators strive to engage in a continuous process of reflection and practice that helps to illumine our historical aspirations and our continuing response to them.

In this spirit, we associate ourselves with some of our culture's most treasured traditions. We affirm and celebrate with others the recognition of the mystery and the belief in the sanctity of life and its corollary, the significance of all life and the worth of all individuals. We celebrate the incredible energy and imagination that humans have across time and space devoted to developing processes and institutions that impel us to make these beliefs palpable and vital. Over the centuries, human genius has provided us with extraordinary ideas, including the very basic notions that life is to have meaning and that we as a people have the capacity to conceive and create a better life. We are heir to a wealth of ideas on what constitutes a better life, on how we can better understand the complexities involved in creating a better world, and on how we can attain these goals. These processes have produced brilliant and dazzling ideas and have led to extraordinarily ambitious human endeavors. We have available to us powerful religious texts (the Bible, the Koran, numerous liturgies and theologies) and enormously influential political documents (the Rights of Man, the Declaration of Independence, the Bill of Rights). We also have been enriched by magnificent philosophers, theologians, and teachers like Moses, Jesus, and Socrates, who have provided us with the intellectual and spiritual energy to conceptualize and actualize these visions.

We also sadly must confront the failures of such efforts in the face of other, darker human impulses—those forces that impel oppression, greed, cruelty, hatred, and callousness. These failures have produced incredible suffering, pain, anguish, and misery over the centuries in the form of any number of human inventions—war, poverty, racism, sexism, hierarchy, classism, privilege, and slavery.

We also acknowledge the powerful contribution that great minds have made in providing us with ways of understanding, conceptualizing, and responding to the immense chasm between our vision and our realities. Thinkers like Freud, Marx, Dewey, Locke, and Rousseau have provided us with modes of recognizing and naming that which divides us within and among ourselves.

We are witness, therefore, to amazing stories of our existence as a people. These stories of conflict and struggle, in which great nations and notions have risen, reveal an incredible range of human responses— sacrifice as well as greed; pacifism *and* violence; cynicism *and* transcendence; vulgarity, crudeness, and primitiveness, along with beauty, grace, and sophistication. Our history is about the Sermon on the Mount and Auschwitz, is rife with slavery and liberation, is about war and peace, and is witness to penicillin and the hydrogen bomb. We have put people on the moon and made hell on earth, and our heritage includes both the Golden Rule and the principle of the survival of the fittest.

As educators, we locate ourselves, therefore, as both heirs to and participants in this continually disheartening, turbulent, and exhilarating struggle to create a world of peace, justice, love, and joy. We recognize that as participants what we and our colleagues do will, for better or worse, have an effect not only on our lives, but on those that come after us. We also reaffirm our faith in the belief that careful, thoughtful, and reasonable reflection and inquiry can significantly help to clarify the struggle, as well as help provide direction for the amelioration of, if not the solution to, our problems.

As educators, we must stand fast in our faith that understanding and insight are vital to the struggle for liberation and that the development of intellectual capacities for this purpose remains a central concern. However, our view of education is that its processes must extend beyond the intellectual realm since it is clear that humans do not learn to live and love by intellect alone. We as a people respond also to the rhythms of the body, the light of the soul, and the voices of the spirit. We are also mindful of human psychology and, hence, of the tyranny and distortion that can emerge from our propensity to evade, deny, and rationalize in the service of self or group. Therefore, our commitment to education for social justice and personal fulfillment must at all times be informed by the imperative of remaining critical, skeptical, and humble.

EDUCATION AND THE HISTORICAL MOMENT

We have in other places sketched out a broad framework for an educational orientation specific to the particular struggles of our time.[33] It is a framework that posits our historical moment as incredibly perilous, dangerous, and unconscionable. Our view is that educational planning and theorizing must have, as its most crucial point of departure, the harsh realities and extraordinary possibilities of our present existence. The dominant text for educators must clearly and explicitly reflect recognition of the enormous dangers and opportunities that define our historical moment. The planet is at risk because the environment has been plundered. The world is at risk because intense national rivalries have produced weapons with immensely destructive capacities. Our civilization is at risk because we have produced and tolerated untold human misery, poverty, and degradation. We, as a people, are at risk as a consequence of a consciousness of alienation and meaninglessness that seeks solace in drugs, hedonism, violence, and materialism.

We recognize, with others, the volatility, ambiguity, and danger of addressing such questions. What is less recognized and affirmed is the enormous risk involved in not addressing them. Fundamentally, human history is about trying to define and act on what is good and, simultaneously, trying to examine and overcome the resistance to that impulse.

At this moment in time, we note with pain and bewilderment that we live in a world of unnecessary human suffering that can only be described as barbaric, if not demonic. So much so, that all people—including, of course, educators—must ground their work in the responsibility to participate in healing the pain of this suffering by joining in the effort to liberate us from oppression and the impulse to oppress, thereby engaging in the tasks of creating a more just and peaceful world.

Our educational and social orientation is broadly based on powerful themes of Western culture, with particular reference to the tradition of Socratic critical reflection; prophetic moral outrage and poetic inspiration; and the religious, moral, and political traditions that speak to the centrality of justice, love, community, peace, and joy. Those traditions recognize that humans are flawed and fully capable of inflicting pain and misery but also have the capacity to transcend a consciousness of savagery. There is also a recognition that this transcendence is not a matter of choice or destiny but of will, requiring the concerted efforts of human agency.

Vital to this orientation is the recognition that democratic processes represent the most resonant political model of working toward these goals. We, therefore, join with others in demanding that educators work diligently with others to renew and revitalize our democratic traditions and sensibilities. Ironically and tragically, our present educational system, for the most part, erodes democratic traditions in ways that are both highly visible and marked. Clearly, concerns for the development of democratic processes is no longer central in even the rhetoric of dominant educational ideology.

Competition (masked as excellence) and authoritarianism (masked as effective schools) have replaced democracy as the chief rallying calls of educational practice. At a deeper level, the corrosive force of grades, tests, and tracking act even more fiendishly to weaken the basic moral commitment to human dignity. We find ourselves anguished and captured by a consciousness in which our worth and dignity are not inherent and self-evident, but instead are to be "earned." Schools are part of an institutional arrangement in which dignity is awarded, parceled out, and distributed. Our moral traditions urge us to exercise the Golden Rule and to love our neighbor, but the Iron Rule of schools is to love, if not envy, only those neighbors who achieve.

The harshness and severity of social competition that is so vividly acted out in educational institutions is root and symptom of the increasingly dangerous tendency to promote what Dorothee Soelle calls "hyper-individuality." Robert Bellah and his colleagues have poignantly and eloquently documented how community is perhaps our most significant "endangered species." However, ironically enough, community is threatened not only by concern for self but also by the polarization engendered by the proliferation of narrowly focused communities.

The poison that has produced the epidemic of distrust and division is the competition that is embedded in our structural inequality. Our system of social justice continues to produce a harsh economic class system in which the benefits of life are immorally distributed. This system demands intense competition for the available rewards under the guise of a free system open to anyone willing to work hard. Schools add fuel to class division as well as to the internecine warfare within classes by legitimizing this gross and debasing warfare as meritocracy, presumably an equitable way to achieve the American Dream.

What our society and schools irresponsibly and unconscionably fail to make clear is that the American Dream involves success at the expense of others. In this sense, the American Dream becomes the moral nightmare of those forced to pursue individual rather than communal fulfillment by rejecting the vision of an America with liberty and justice for all. Competition American style, provides a winner-loser consciousness in which individuals and groups are pitted against each other in a game of very high stakes.

We have also come to see that a major element of oppression is one in which certain people are seen as objects to be manipulated and directed in the interest of those who are subjects. This same subject-object relationship, in which people are seen as resources to be utilized, has also had disastrous effects upon our environment, resulting in the very real possibility of global extinction. Moreover, this consciousness reflects not only greed, rapaciousness, and stupidity, but also poignantly demonstrates the tragedy and horror of a people unable to develop a sense of their connection to each other, to the planet, or to the universe. The pollution and plunder of the planet indicates little or no sense of how we are connected to the awesomeness and mystery of our origins and destiny. To educate must involve consideration of who we are in relation, not only to each other, but to the environment, the globe, and the universe.

The history of human existence reveals a persistence, therefore, of paradox and dialectic—of progress and retrogression, of hope and despair, of a series of "the best of times and the worst of times." This is not to be taken as a reason for complacency and serenity, but rather as a reminder of our responsibilities as citizens and educators to be alert to the continuous possibilities of danger and liberation. Our history is, as we have said, replete not only with horror and misery but also with the consciousness that such experiences are not inevitable: Indeed, human genius has enabled us to resist and overcome such experiences. The American experience includes slavery and emancipation, the Ku Klux Klan and the civil rights movement. Its history encompasses women's exclusion and the women's movement, robber barons and muckrakers, jingoism and pacifism, labor bashing and the labor movement. Our icons include Simon Legree and Sojournor Truth, Lincoln and Booth, Ivan Boesky and Ralph Nader, David Duke and Martin Luther King, Jr., the Grand Inquisitor and Dorothy Day.

We see the task of educators as that of nourishing a consciousness that would facilitate a significantly more just, peaceful, and harmonious world. Basic to such a consciousness would be an awareness of both our individuality and our dependence on each other, our culture, society, planet, and universe. As people who grapple with the clear and present demands of life (work, family, relationships, shelter, food, health), such dependence is required, necessary, sensible, and pragmatic. As people who wrestle with meaning and fulfillment, interdependence is integral and inevitable. It is, however, not enough to recognize our oneness with nature and the reality of our human solidarity. We also must affirm a moral commitment to that connection. It is one thing to say that we are in fact connected to each other and quite another to figure out how to respond to that reality.

Surprisingly enough, there is a very high degree of agreement on what should ground this response. Our traditions and instincts urge us to seek harmony, peace, and justice and to conduct this task with a sense of care, love, and compassion. Language and images surely differ, as do interpretations and understandings of these notions, but we cannot but be sustained by the persistence of these commitments. Even if we suspect that this rhetoric can and has been used cynically and manipulatively, we can take solace from the fact that it is relied on so heavily, for as La Rochfoucault put it, "Hypocrisy is the tribute that vice pays to virtue."

A consciousness of caring, compassion, and justice is related to notions of the beauty and sacredness of life itself—and with that comes the centrality of the idea of dignity for all. The mystery, awareness, and drama of life are acted out in and within all life-forms. Every life becomes precious and invites us to become ever more aware of that which endows us with the energy to seek meaning. Within such a view, humans have pursued the possibilities of fulfilling the promises of human destiny by creating institutions designed to support the struggle for human dignity and meaning. Fundamental to such institutions is the principle of democracy, the spirit of faith in the human capacity to be free. Democratic procedures are more than benign techniques for facilitating decision making. They are also concrete manifestations of the affirmation that life is sacred, and therefore our greatest responsibility is to pursue liberty and justice for all.

AN EDUCATIONAL CREDO FOR A TIME OF CRISIS AND URGENCY

Educators are primarily moral, political, and cultural agents charged with the responsibility of grounding their specialized insights in a cultural political, and moral vision. An educator without some kind of moral and cultural grounding is either tragically alienated, cynically deceptive, or naively shallow. John Dewey reminds us that education is about learning to create a world and that our most vital and demanding task as educators is to be mindful of the kind of world that we want to create. Absolutely essential, therefore, in the ethics of education are the twin pillars of freedom, namely, responsibility and choice. As educators, we are required to respond to the challenges of life and to choose among the many moral, political, and cultural possibilities open to us.

We Choose, Celebrate, and Affirm These Propositions:

1. *We recognize the wonder, mystery, and awe that surrounds our life and that beckons us to contemplate, examine, and make meaning of it and of our part in it.* As educators, we must encourage and help students to separate mystery and awe from ignorance and superstition, but we must be careful to witness and be informed by what is beyond our present human capacity to comprehend. As educators, our responsibility is to present with respect varying interpretations of life's meaning. But our most compelling responsibility is to renew and reenergize the commitment to pursue lives of individual and communal meaning.

2. *We renew our faith in the capacity to celebrate diversity and difference while working to create a world of harmony, peace, and justice.* As educators, we must avoid the perils of pride and arrogance that emerge from a posture of cultural superiority. We recognize that meaning and fulfillment derive, in part, from cultural identity, and we must therefore strive to revere and respect, not patronize and romanticize, the ethos of particular cultural, racial, and ethnic groups. This consciousness requires basic trust in the recognition that harmony is not synonymous with homogeneity, that peace is not to be equated with control, and that justice is not to be blurred with freedom.

   As educators, we must move from a consciousness of mastery, domination, submission, and docility in which some persons are subjects and others are objects. As educators, we must strive to see our students not as black boxes, not as clay to be molded or minds to be trained, but as sentient beings deserving of dignity, love, and fulfillment. As educators, we must not require people to earn their dignity, but we must strive to celebrate the sanctity, miracle, and preciousness of life. This consciousness does not bring us to punishment, tracking, grading, and honors programs, but to an education that reveres life as sacred and inviolate. Such a consciousness does not urge us to get ahead, but to stand with; does not idealize competition, but venerates dignity; does not legitimate privilege and advantage, but rather seeks to heal the deadly quarrels that divide the human family.

3. *We renew our faith in the human impulse to seek to create a world of justice, compassion, love, and joy, and in the human capacity to create such a world.* As educators, our responsibility is to nurture these impulses that have permeated human history not only by increasing awareness and understanding of them but by confronting the equally human impulses to oppress, dominate, and objectify. As educators, we can be guided and comforted by the immensity of human intellectual, creative, and intuitive potential to re-create our world; and at the same time, we should be sobered by the human capacity to be destructive, cruel, and callous. We speak to an education that is grounded in our strongest and deepest moral traditions, which urge us to love our neighbor, to seek justice, and to pledge ourselves to a nation committed to liberty and justice for all and a government of the people, by the people, and for the people. We speak to an education based on traditions that urge us to beat swords into ploughshares, not to develop more deadly swords; a vision in which lions lie down with lambs, not one in which we train lambs to be lions; and a universal dream of milk and honey for all, not the American Dream of champagne and caviar for a few.

4. *We reaffirm our commitment to the joys of community, the profundity of compassion, and to the power of interdependence.* As educators, we must become aware of the spiritual disease of alienation, loneliness, fragmentation, and isolation and must act to reduce the perilous effects of an education directed toward success, achievement, and personalism. As educators, we have the responsibility of nurturing the impulse for meaningful and cooperative relationships and for exposing the myths and dangers of individual achievement. Education must not act to convert the uncivilized, but neither should it serve to create a myriad of individual universes. Compassion serves neither to distance nor to blur or annihilate differences, but rather seeks to share the struggles, pain, and joys that are common to us all. If we are to compete, we as educators need to confront the significance of the race not only for the winners but also for the losers. If we are to be committed to individual excellence, then we must know if it is achieved at the expense of others. More important, we as educators must participate in the process of creating a society in which people are more united than divided, where differences are not translated into hierarchy, and where pain and anguish are occasions for neither pity nor exploitation but for compassion and solidarity.

5. *We affirm the central importance of nourishing a consciousness of moral outrage and social responsibility.* As educators, we must go far beyond informing, describing, and analyzing and must free ourselves from the destructive force of moral numbness. We must help our students to become aware of our failures to meet our moral and cultural imperatives and to help them inform their intellectual understanding with moral judgments. An education that engenders a posture of promiscuous tolerance, scholarly detachment, or cynical weariness toward unnecessary human suffering is an abomination! We must avoid the temptation to teach only what makes one feel good or to teach that social problems are only "interesting." Education is not about finding out things, but about finding ourselves. It is not enough to say further research is needed when what is needed is not more information but more justice. To know without a sense of outrage, compassion, or concern deadens our souls and significantly eases the struggle of demonic forces to capture our consciousness. We need an education that produces moral indignation and energy rather than one that excuses, mitigates, and temporizes human misery. Heschel reminds us that although only a few are guilty, all are responsible. Our task as educators is therefore to teach students to identify the guilty, to have compassion for the victims, and to exercise their responsibility to reduce, if not eliminate, injustices.

POSSIBILITIES AND PROBLEMATICS OF THE DISCOURSE: FROM EDUCATIONAL RHETORIC TO POLITICAL DIALOGUE

We therefore offer a discourse that is unapologetically moral, spiritual, and political and that is rooted in imagery of justice, freedom, joy, and peace. Although our commitment is deep, we are not unmindful of at least some of the problematics of such a discourse. We are aware of the dangers of self-righteousness and of moral zealotry, and we recognize that tyranny and oppression often are associated with political movements grounded in such visions. Our discourse has its share of inner tensions and paradoxes—affirmation of both criticality and commitment, of firmness and flexibility, community and individuality, freedom and equality, harmony and diversity. As intellectuals, we cannot but be wary, skeptical, and critical of any creed, formulation, or manifesto; but as moral agents, we cannot be paralyzed by complexity and tolerance. Our discourse, therefore, needs to be enriched by considerations of promoting serious dialogue on how to sophisticate and enlarge our vision. We must also take seriously the existence of other vital discourses, orientations, and visions, and we must be mindful of the necessity of developing sufficient consensus among these groups in order to constitute a coherent and significant political movement.

It is important to reiterate that we are speaking to public as well as professional discourse on education. A sophisticated and informed public dialogue on education is absolutely required for both ideological and strategic reasons. Because our nation was founded on the moral and political traditions of democracy, it is essential that our educational policies emerge from a well-informed and energized public will. Moreover, it is clear that significant educational changes can happen only when there is strong social and cultural demand, understanding, and support for them. Professionals have a special responsibility in this process. So also do those who do not consider themselves to be professional educators but who seek to participate actively in educational debate.

This responsibility (in addition to others, such as research, teaching, and consulting) involves the profession in helping to frame the public dialogue in a more sophisticated and textured manner. While it is the public who has the responsibility and the power to determine cultural, social, and political matters—and, hence, educational policies—the public looks to the professional for guidance in determining the nature and scope of the issues. In a word, professionals have particular and special responsibilities in the critical task of problem posing. By this, we do not mean that the public should be totally dependent on just another kind of expertise—"We'll tell you the problems, and you solve them." What we do mean is that our leadership responsibilities involve seriously engaging the public in the process of framing and posing important questions and issues. Such responsibility is merited to the extent that the profession exercises its critical capacities and its understanding of the social, cultural, political, moral, economic, and religious context and the significance of more technical matters. This is to move away from a notion of a professional rooted in narrowly conceived pedagogical and technical matters to one inevitably and intimately involved in major political and social concerns.

Those of us interested in significant educational change must be committed to significant cultural and social change. If educators are concerned with not only understanding but also changing the world, then they must integrate their work with political and social movements. This requires, among other things, overcoming the insularity of educational theorists as well as the divisions within their ranks. Thankfully, there has been a considerable discussion of this process as expressed in the exposition and analysis of the concept of *inclusiveness*, meaning a movement that seeks to include and involve rather than to exclude and alienate.

Enemies: A Love Story

Inclusiveness is meant not simply to convert more people but rather, or in addition, to validate and incorporate beliefs from the previously excluded or ignored. It is not a marketing or promotional endeavor, but the exemplification of the intellectual and democratic processes of free, open, and good-faith exchange. Chief among the challenges involved in attempts at inclusiveness are, on the one hand, clarifying the difference between deepening commitments and distorting them, and on the other, developing the ability to distinguish potential colleagues from closet adversaries.

Indeed, a major dimension of radical discourse of both Right and Left has been the use of the metaphor of "enemy," which emerges as oppositional language rich with references to "class warfare," "social conflict," and "the battle between the Right and the Left." There are at least two major issues here. The first has to do with how we should regard those who seem to support ideas that we feel are clearly inimical to a just and peaceful world; and the second, with how we can maintain our principles and commitments in the face of plausible, if not persuasive, resistance.

The first question involves the matter of how to name those who seem bent on reactionary policies and practices. Are such people wicked and evil? Perhaps they are not evil, but sick or neurotic, or emotionally unbalanced. In any event, as we have already discussed, we would be naive to believe that critical analysis and rational persuasion can, by themselves, significantly alter neuroses or conquer evil. Perhaps then it would be better to consider them misinformed, if not ignorant. In this case, we can have more confidence that traditional educative processes can be enlightening and efficacious. There are, of course, many other explanations for destructive behavior and attitudes, including sociological (upbringing, subculture, class origins, etc.) and biological ones (genetic disorders, brain abnormalities, etc.). In any case, shall we name those who are misinformed, deformed, and/or possessed as "enemies"? What are we to do with enemies? Normally, enemies are to be battled and vanquished and perhaps, if we are gracious, eventually rehabilitated.

Others, of course, have suggested another response to enemies—to turn the other cheek and even to love them. Despite the heroics of martyrs and the efforts of the churches, this formulation, although extraordinarily attractive and popular, has not exactly caught on. For one thing, it seems well nigh impossible to juxtapose the concepts of love and enemy as anything but a psychological oxymoron. In addition, to love thy neighbor is to invite the possibility of weakness, wishy-washiness, and appeasement. Can we passionately observe and adequately protect our covenants and still stoutly defend the faithful through such passivity, weakness, and naivete? Should we love a neighbor who does not do these things? How are we to regard neighbors who dishonor our parents or covet our spouses; who lie, steal, ravage, despoil, and violate? Are there no principles that we will not passionately oppose? No outrage that we will not tolerate? No ideas that we reject? Are there not monsters out there who are beyond the confines of sanity and safety?

The paradox of being wholeheartedly committed to principled decision and just as firmly committed to tolerance, diversity, and openness is as knotty as it is crucial. Our intellectual and moral energies direct us to confront the enormity of human malice, arrogance, and stupidity and to feel a sense of moral outrage. The evidence of unnecessary human suffering brought on by unnecessary human stupidity or intolerable evil is overwhelming. However, what is not so clear is its etiology and treatment. Who, if anyone, is to blame? Who and where are the culprits and what should we do to them? The paradox is intensified by our own consciousness of fairness, rationality, careful analysis, and skepticism—we become hoist by the petard of our commitment to reasonableness. We have come to see the horrors that emerge from ideological, philosophical, and theological certainty and dogma. We have learned about the contingencies of knowledge, how our beliefs are shaped by history, interests, circumstance, culture, family, and so forth. We are very much aware of the power of rhetoric, of how language can frame the debate, and of the endless narrative possibilities open to us.

Yet, as moral uncertainty and intellectual ambiguity grow, so does our fear about them. We note that the forces of oppression, greed, and privilege seem not to be deterred by theoretical misgivings or professional concerns for fairness. We are very much aware of how uncertainty feeds into existing and rampant apathy, indifference, alienation, and powerlessness. We are increasingly frustrated by the failure of progressives to ground their movement in a discourse of passion and faith.

Converting the Enemy

In this time of peril, we must risk not only a strong affirmation of a vision of justice, peace, and freedom but also a full-hearted commitment to the struggle to make this vision real. We urge, however, that we inform and infuse this struggle with a deep sense of humility and compassion. When we speak of humility, we do not speak of abasement or false modesty since we have ample reason to celebrate what we as a people already have learned and accomplished. Rather, we need to accept that whatever talents we as people might possess have come to us undeserved and unearned. In addition, we speak to the humility that comes from the recognition of the awesomeness of the mystery of life, the extraordinary complexity of human beings, the incredible diversity of human expression, the yet-to-be determined nature of human possibilities, and the unbelievable richness of human experience.

When we speak of compassion, we do not speak of pity, sympathy, or even empathy alone, but rather to a sharing of the burden involved in the struggle for meaning and dignity. To suffer with others is not only to empathize with the difficulties, paradoxes, and conflicts involved with the struggle, but also to participate in it in solidarity. We are both united and divided by our differences, with good reason to believe that differences within people mirror those between them. To act in good faith is to assume that we all seek improvement, amelioration, progress, even as we disagree on what this means and indicates. Acting in good faith means that we allow for the possibility of error, distortion, and misinformation in all of us and that failures to agree are matters of regret and sadness rather than rage and dismay.

By definition it would seem that it would be extremely difficult to act in good faith with "enemies." Perhaps it is time to deconstruct the concept, or at least to examine the value of the term. Does it really help to maintain the dualism of enemy/ally or friend/foe? What is the source of this distinction that is so prevalent, so deep, and so destructive? Indeed, it runs so deep in our consciousness that even Jesus seems to affirm it by contributing to its reification, since he does not urge us to reconceptualize the concept of "enemy," but only to change our attitude toward the enemy.[34] It has been suggested that the concept of enemy is an atavistic one, rooted in a primordial but now anachronistic consciousness in which the species had literally to fight for survival. Perhaps our most compelling educational responsibility is to move our consciousness away from one in which people must be in conflict because of scarcity to one in which a consciousness of sufficiency obviates the need for deadly conflicts. We must learn not to fight fire with fire but with warmth; to cool passion, not with ice but with compassion; and to seek to understand, rather than vanquish, those who differ with us. Such a task is obviously not easy, and it has within it the danger of sentimentality and the denial of real differences of enormous consequences. However, it seems a manageable enough task to reduce rather than increase our "enemies," or at least to diminish our contempt for them.

At the risk of oversimplification, it is clear that educators lack the particular conceptual tools that can help us understand the psychological mechanisms involved in the impulses to oppress and to liberate. Notwithstanding our faith in critical rationality, we must admit that a pedagogy that relies primarily on rational analysis and critical reflection for transformation of consciousness is bound, at best, to have limited effect. As educators, we must have the courage to look unblinkingly at what seems to be as real an educational fact as there is, namely, that even very bright, intellectually able people are significantly involved in developing and administering policies directed at preserving inequality, hierarchy, and oppression. We must examine ways in which we can add to the texture of a pedagogy of critical rationality rooted in the commitment to social justice and personal liberation. It surely is clear by now, and perhaps gratuitous to mention again, that humans are extraordinarily complex, contradictory, and paradoxical beings, capable of acting divinely and/or demoniacally.

Confessions of a True Professional

Education theorists also must do again what would seem obvious—that is to see ourselves and our colleagues as human, finite, and fallible people subject to conflicting and questionable impulses. In so doing, we act not only in an intellectually and morally honest way but also in a way appropriate to our responsibilities to provide leadership to the public. This responsibility includes being much more open and candid with the public about our strengths and limitations, which can help us to avoid the dangers of professional hegemony and can also help liberate all of us from the fantasies of certainty, perfection, and objectivity. We must seek for similar reasons to escape the prison of narrow professionalism and the chains of the academic ethos. This ought to be relatively painless for those who, on intellectual grounds, reject the posture of detachment and objectivity as misinformed or pompous or both. It would seem that the writings and talks of at least these people ought to reflect more subjectivity and personal reflection. The risk in such an endeavor, of course, is increased personal vulnerability and the possibility of being intellectually discounted.

This risk is heightened and made real by virtue of the intensely competitive nature of professional and academic life. Ironically enough, cultural criticism is a kind of growth industry in academia, and we are witness to the absurdity of people gaining power, privilege, and status as a consequence of pointing out the evils of power, privilege, and status. We must find ways to resist the forces that impel us to attack others in the guise of critique and the temptation to establish our professional identities at the expense of our colleagues. We must recognize in our own dialectical wisdom that this professional ethos of competition, hierarchy, and self-servingness emerges from the intersection of institutional demands and personal intentions.

We must therefore be prepared to be more understanding, honest, forgiving, empathic, and compassionate not only about others but also about ourselves. There certainly are powerful intellectual reasons for significant self-examinations—never mind the moral and psychological requirements for honesty, openness, and candor. Within a context of the blend of affirmation and humility that we have been discussing, we suggest that the concept of confession might help. By confession, we mean simply the process of continuous, candid self-reflection, self-criticism, self-affirmation, and self-renewal. It is a process that is grounded neither in our sinfulness nor in our purity, but rather in an understanding that we are sentient beings constantly engaged in a struggle within and among ourselves. Such a process would enable us to affirm and reaffirm; to remind us of our strengths, weaknesses, predilections; and to go on with our individual praxis as we acknowledge and forgive our weaknesses and affirm and celebrate our strengths. Confession to us is not about guilt but about responsibility, that is, about becoming more aware of our ability to respond to our commitments. It is a process that must happen within and among us, for we need the support and insights of each other to strengthen both our individual selves and our sense of solidarity. Professional community cannot help but be divisive, if it continues to be firmly rooted in individual achievement, discipleship, and ideological loyalty. Collegiality, if we are to be intellectually honest and morally responsible, must extend to concerns for the problematics of being human. Since our work is to heal and liberate, our task can only be made easier when we learn to heal and liberate ourselves from the doubt, envy, scorn, fear, and hostility that haunts and has the capacity ultimately to destroy us.

To affirm our commitments with humility, we must consider the possibility of letting go of some basic elements of our consciousness—for example, enemies, competition, hierarchy. We believe that it is very difficult and problematic simply to will greater openness, but that a consciousness of affirmation, humility, and confession will lead us to a much greater degree of openness. If we are to engage the public in a dialogue on the moral and political dimensions of education and in a discourse that involves the problematics of human agency, then we ourselves must engage in this very praxis. In this way, we celebrate both the particularities of our work and our solidarity with the public.

We see, for example, very real possibilities for developing significant openings to groups and orientation now marginal to radical educational theorists. These groups and individuals include, among others, those who believe that rationality does not exhaust the possibilities of knowing and that intuitive and esthetic experiences also can provide insight and understanding. Moreover, there is powerful evidence that the human experience has always involved and continues to involve religious and spiritual aspirations and sensibilities. We must, at the very least, learn not to deny and discount such widespread and deeply felt convictions since it would be infinitely more constructive and healthy to be responsive and open toward them. Do we seriously believe that those who value intuition, the body, and self-reflection are entirely primitive, naïve, and narcissistic? If so, then do we really believe anything is gained by urging these people to consider that their lives are shallow and meaningless? Do we really believe that the millions of people who are grounded in religious faith are ignorant and superstitious and that we should ask and expect them to deny that which has given them meaning, fulfillment, and solace? Is it not also possible that important insight and wisdom is contained within the consciousness informed by esthetic, subjective, and spiritual sensibilities?

In a parallel way, we also must learn to affirm those colleagues who have taken on diverse and varied roles, functions, situations, and projects. We indicated before that the highly competitive ethos of academic and professional life tends to encourage a great deal of dismissiveness and discounting of the work of others. Radical theorists, in particular, tend to be very suspicious of so-called moderates or liberals who work on making relatively modest changes within the existing school system—because they do not see the big picture or, worse, will become dupes of the power structure. We confess to sharing the fear that such so-called realistic efforts can, at best, distract us from more basic considerations and, at worst, deceive us into blurring change with transformation.

We are more persuaded, however, that while it is probably desirable to maintain this skepticism it is also important to affirm and celebrate efforts that are simultaneously modest and significant. For example, tutoring children in a working-class neighborhood on the SATs may be modest, in that only relatively few children are involved, and also may tend to perpetuate hierarchy and monitoring. However, in the short-run and in the context of other more fundamental projects and given the particular circumstances of the particular children, it would seem that such a project has important redemptive dimensions, that is, doing well on the SAT probably and very likely will help to empower these children by giving them the intellectual skills and cultural capital necessary to participate in cultural politics.

We must demonstrate our awareness of and learn to respond to the reality of a culture that operates on several levels. There is the continuum of time (e.g., immediate, short range, middle range, longer range, ultimate, etc.) and there are the varieties of important contexts (e.g., changes within individuals or within culture/society/institutions; change of consciousness, outlook, paradigms; transformation of institutions, etc.). As individuals, we constantly move between, within, and among these levels, usually at a very rapid and dizzying rate. Shall we change our cereal, our diet, or our total outlook on food? Do we see family traditions as generally satisfying, as bourgeois artifacts, or as vital and enduring elements of tradition? Responses to such questions inevitably involve our own individual existential circumstances. How do we respond to questions about education for liberation when our teenage children want to drop out of school and get married? How do we handle our disgust and outrage at grades when our students write poor term papers? What do we do when our colleagues with heavy financial obligations are too terrified to protest?

Again, within the context of a consciousness of confession, we must show compassion for others and for ourselves when we find ourselves in contradictory and paradoxical situations. Although it is surely possible to significantly reduce the degree of contradiction through reflection and analysis, it is also likely that many contradictions emerge from the necessity to operate simultaneously in several of these levels—to have to deal with both short- and long-range issues—to deal with the preservation of institutions simultaneously with the necessity of totally transforming them. There is, indeed, extremely important work to be done in the name of justice, peace, and freedom in all of these levels and contexts.

There are risks and problematics involved, but here again we can have confidence in our capacity to be critical and compassionate within a context of good faith. We need to learn that there are always possibilities and limitations involved in the particular work that we do. This requires both intellectual and moral considerations. Intellectually, it is clear the boundary sites and areas of cultural politics are fuzzy, unclear, overlapping, discontinuous yet interconnected. From a moral perspective, we surely can have compassion for those who struggle earnestly in their particular ways and varied situations and, at the same time, insist that these struggles be grounded in a quest for peace, justice, and freedom.

Within a consciousness of confession and humility, we must come to accept the limitations under which we all work. Healing and transforming the world will not be the result of the work of one or a few giants. Nor will it emerge from one or a small number of strategies. It will emerge from the cumulative and continuous efforts of a great many people working in a great many arenas, albeit generated by a few basic moral and political principles and commitments. We need the courage and confidence to continue our work while realizing its insufficiency and incompleteness, and we need the humility to celebrate the contributions that our colleagues working very differently from us can make to our common quest. However, we must avoid the sentimentality of nostrums that ease the pain and anguish of our insufficiency, such as the piety of "Everything works out for the best," the narcissism of "Aren't we all wonderful," and the preciousness of "the solidarity of the marginal and oppressed."

Within a consciousness of critical and skeptical rationality, therefore, we must be wary, if not suspicious, of glibness, wishy-washiness, and evasion. We need to be particularly wary of being captured by the tyranny of trying to be politically correct and of being held hostage by doctrinaire ideology. Along with the struggle to rid ourselves of the consciousness of "enemy" should come the capacity to be more discerning about the meaning and significance of our highly diverse social movements and ideas. Our society grows increasingly diverse, but our dominant culture is reluctant to cede its canons of judgment. We must persist in our determination to be affirmative and flexible in the realization that there are psychological, intellectual, and moral barriers to being nonjudgmental. Furthermore, we must recognize the depth and significance of the impulse to affiliate with particular groups, cultures, and movements.

A compassionate, humble, yet penetrating criticality can help us see more deeply into the paradoxical and complex consciousness of both "good" and "bad guys." For example, people who resist affirmative action may be misguided and misinformed, but they also are likely to be responding, however inappropriately, to genuine and legitimate fears. People who demand, on the other hand, such commendable and legitimate aspirations as community participation in the schools may very well have extremely limited and conventional ideas on curriculum and instruction. Teachers are surely oppressed, underpaid, and overworked, but some are also capable of cruelty, inconsiderateness, and stupidity. Radicals who provide moral energy and conceptual breakthroughs can also have quite conventional and narrow notions of scholarship.

Oppressed and marginal groups and individuals have a right to demand to be heard, and those in power have a responsibility to at least ease, if not remove, mechanisms of silencing. We need at the same time to learn not to patronize such groups and individuals by endowing them with special powers or sensitivities or to exclude them from the responsibility to pursue the reduction, rather than the exploitation, of divisiveness. Camus has said that we are all murderers, Welch confesses that she is both oppressor and oppressed, and Freud can help us understand why this would be so. This understanding is surely vital, but it is an understanding that should inform and not paralyze judgment and will. Our critical consciousness can help us become more aware of the ramifications and implications of what we are doing and why, but it is our moral consciousness that helps us determine what we should be doing.

We therefore return to our concern about how we are to participate in the great continuous human drama that shapes and directs our lives. As educators, we have special responsibilities to engage in the human enterprise of creating a life of dignity, justice, peace, joy, and meaning for all. We must ground our expertise in this endeavor and put our special knowledge in the service of this project. We are not merely experts, but first of all human beings who respond to the call for cultural, moral, and political leadership from the perspective of those who work in educational institutions. We have faith in the human capacity to create a just world and confidence that this capacity can be further enriched by deepening awareness and possibility through the nourishment of our intellectual, critical, esthetic, and moral sensibilities. We are intolerant of and outraged at unnecessary human suffering and the oppression of the human spirit. We are dedicated to using our energies to transform that which enables oppression and inhibits transformation. We do so humbly but with determination and in the faith that our work is neither sufficient nor unnecessary. We must avoid the triviality and banality of professionalism, the smugness and arrogance of scholarship, and the suffocation of self-righteousness. We also, however, must celebrate the energy of a professional ethic that is grounded in democracy and justice, the liberation that comes from critical rationality, and the meaning that emerges from a moral vision.

In the next and final chapter of this book, we have attempted to lay out the dimensions of an agenda for educational reform. We found it difficult, however, to separate in any neat way the concern with, and the pursuit of, an alternative discourse for education from the issue of an agenda. Perhaps in our fixation on language, we are victims of the current preoccupation with the text in academic life. Yet, what is clear to us is that there really is no way in which the struggle for a deep change in our educational concerns can be separated from a focus on the terms, meanings, and definitions of educational work. Not to do this consigns us quickly to the limited—and, for us, ultimately unacceptable—parameters of prevailing educational policies and practices.

In making this point, we do not wish to ignore or denigrate important ongoing struggles that are part of a progressive reform agenda in education. These include attempting to win equitable funding for schools and school systems; giving more managerial power to teachers and improving the status and conditions of their work; ensuring wide access to early childhood programs of high quality; fighting class, race and gender bias in the evaluation and assessment of students; reducing or eliminating tracking or other forms of separation in schools and school systems that stigmatize or exclude students; providing broad opportunities for meaningful sex education; resisting censorship of books in classrooms and school libraries; and supporting efforts to make curricula fully embody multicultural and multiethnic and nonsexist approaches to teaching, and so forth. Yet, if we are to go beyond this and "unpack" educational goals and concerns in some more fundamental way, we will need an agenda that stays in touch with—indeed, continually refocuses—our energies on the underlying motives and impulses of the educational enterprise itself.

While chapter 6 might disappoint some by not offering a sufficiently systematic, point by point, series of proposals for reform, we believe we have stayed true to our project of trying to shift the ground on which educational work and effects are ultimately predicated. Clearly for us, too, there is no easy separation between words and deeds. The struggle to redirect how we analyze the nature and purpose of education is as real and as practical a task, we believe, as any true policy objective might be.

NOTES

1. The assertion of "totalizing" political thinking and its inherent dangers has been central to the critique of Marxism by both postmodern and feminist writers. See, for example, David Kolb, *The Critique of Pure Modernity* (Chicago: University of Chicago Press, 1987); Jean-Francois Lyotard, *The Postmodern Condition* (Minneapolis: University of Minnesota Press, 1984); Michel Foucault, *Power/Knowledge* (New York: Random House, 1981); Linda Nicholson, ed., *Feminism/Postmodernism* (New York: Routledge, 1990).

2. Alvin W. Gouldner, *The Two Marxisms* (New York: Seabury Press, 1990); Martin Jay, *Marxism and Totality* (Berkeley: University of California Press, 1984); Russell Jacoby, *Dialectic of Defeat* (Cambridge, England: Cambridge University Press, 1981).

3. A growing concern with the emphasis on "difference" in left political thinking at the expense of a notion of community is found in a number of writers. See, for example, Marshall Berman, "Why Modernism Still Matters," *Tikkun* 4, no. 1 (January/February 1989), pp. 11–14, 81–86; Barry Kanpol, *Towards a Postmodern Theory of Teacher Cultural Politics* (forthcoming); Wendy Kohli, "Postmodernism, Critical Theory and the 'New' Pedagogies: What's at Stake in the Discourse?" *Education and Society* 9, no. 1 (1991), pp. 39–46; Suzanne Moore, "Gender, Post-Modern Style," *Marxism Today* (May

1990), p. 91; Henry Giroux, *Border Crossings: Cultural Workers and the Politics of Education* (London: Routledge, 1992).

4. See, for example, Steven Connor, *Postmodern Culture* (New York: Basil Blackwell, 1989); David Kolb, *Postmodernism Publication* (Chicago: University of Chicago Press, 1990); Douglas Kellner, *Jean Baudrillard, From Marxism to Post-Modernism and Beyond* (Oxford: Polity Press, 1988).

5. Fritjof Capra and Charlene Spretnak, *Green Politics* (New York: Dutton, 1984); Carl Boggs, *Social Movements and Political Power* (Philadelphia: Temple University Press, 1986).

6. Rudolf Bahro, T*he Alternatives in Eastern Europe* (London: NLB, 1978).

7. See, for example, Richard A. Cloward and Francis F. Piven, *The New Class War* (New York: Pantheon, 1982); Boggs, *Social Movements and Political Power* (Philadelphia: Temple University Press, 1986); Jurgen Habermas, *Legitimation Crisis* (Boston: Beacon, 1975); Richard Flacks, *Making History: The Radical Tradition in American Life* (New York: Columbia University Press, 1988).

8. Douglas Kellner, *Critical Theory, Marxism and Modernity* (Baltimore: Johns Hopkins University Press, 1989).

9. See, for example, H. Svi Shapiro, *Between Capitalism and Democracy: Education Policy and the Crisis of the Welfare State* (Westport, Conn.: Bergin & Garvey, 1990); also, Stanely Aronowitz and Henry Giroux, *Education under Siege* (South Hadley, Mass.: Bergin & Garvey, 1985); Ira Shor, *Culture Wars: Schools and Society in the Conservative Restoration* (Boston: Routledge, 1986).

10. Michael Lerner, "A New Paradigm for Liberals: The Primacy of Ethics and Emotions," *Tikkun* 2, no. 1 (1987), pp. 22–28, 132–38.

11. Ibid., pp. 24–25.

12. Ibid. See also Christopher Lasch, "What's Wrong with the Right," *Tikkun* 1, no. 1 (1986), pp. 23–29; and Robert Bellah et al., *Habits of the Heart* (Berkeley: University of California Press, 1985).

13. For an analysis of the question of social agency in the quest for radical school reform, see H. Svi Shapiro, "Beyond the Sociology of Education: Culture, Politics, and the Promise of Educational Change," *Educational Theory* 38, no. 4 (Fall 1988), pp. 415–30; see also Geoff Whitty, *Sociology and School Knowledge* (London: Methuen, 1985).

14. There is now a large literature that attempts to address this issue. See, for example, Stanley Aronowitz, *The Crisis in Historical Materialism* (Minneapolis: University of Minnesota Press, 1990); Stuart Hall, *The Hard Road to Renewal* (London: Vergo, 1988); Raymond Williams, *The Year 2000* (New York: Pantheon Books, 1983).

15. R. Todd Erkel, "The Birth of a Movement," *Networker* (May/June 1990), pp. 26–35.

16. Sharon Welch, *Communities of Resistance and Solidarity* (New York: Orbis, 1985).

17. Foucault, *Power/Knowledge*; see also, Nancy Hartsock, "Foucault on Power: A Theory for Women," in *Feminism/Postmodernism*, ed. Linda J. Nicholson (New York: Routledge, 1990), pp. 157–75.

18. The list of authors who have contributed to our view of the ethical and spiritual crisis of the nation is a long one. It includes Cornel West, Michael Harrington, Robert Bellah, Barbara Ehrenreich, Theodore Roszack, Matthew Fox, Beverly Harrison, Maya

Angelou, Michael Lerner, Philip Slater, Richard Sennett, Sharon Welch, Dorothee Soelle, Harvey Cox, Peter Clecak, and Sallie McPhague, among others.

19. This criticism must not be interpreted in a personalized manner. In no sense is this statement meant to invalidate the overall powerful and important work of critical educational theorists that has been, and continues to be, done. It concerns accessibility of what has been written and the need for a discourse about schools that can go beyond the limited constituencies that are now its primary audience.

20. Among these are Michael Lerner, Cornel West, Dorothee Soelle, Isaac Balbus, Stuart Hall, Douglas Kellner, Stanley Aronowitz, Sheila Rowbottom, Andre Gorz, Murray Bookchin, Jean Cohen, Terry Eagleton, bell hooks, and others.

21. See, for example, Sharon Welch, *A Feminist Ethic of Risk* (Minneapolis: Fortress Press, 1990); Beverly Harrison, *Making the Connections* (Boston: Beacon, 1985); Matthew Fox, *A Spirituality Named Compassion* (Minneapolis: Winston Press, 1979).

22. See, for example, Andre Gorz, *Ecology as Politics* (Boston: South End Press, 1980); Murray Bookchin, *The Modern Crisis* (Philadelphia: New Society Publishers, 1986); Petra Kelly, *Fighting for Hope* (Boston: South End Press, 1984).

23. See, for example, *Marxism Today* (October 1988), special edition on "New Times"; see also Alvin Toffler, *Powershift* (New York: Bantam Books, 1990).

24. See, for example, Peter Gabel, "Creationism and the Spirit of Nature," *Tikkun* 2, no. 5 (1987), pp. 55–63; Michael Harrington, *The Politics at God's Funeral* (New York: Holt, Rinehart, 1983); Harvey Cox, *Religion in the Secular City* (New York: Simon & Schuster, 1984); see also the work of Marion Woodman, Dianne Stein, Theodore Roszak, or Fritjof Capra.

25. See, for example, Isaac D. Balbus, *Marxism and Domination* (Princeton, N.J.: Princeton University Press, 1982). See also, Terry Eagleton, *The Ideology of the Aesthetic* (Oxford: Basil Blackwell, 1990).

26. See, for example, the work in this country of Sharon Welch, Beverly Harrison, Dorothee Soelle, Matthew Fox, Walter Breuggemen, Starhawk, and Judity Plaskow.

27. This is perhaps best reflected in the wave of admiration for the work of the French guru of postmodern social theory Jean Baudrillard, with its cynical, self-indulgent assertion of the meaninglessness of social and political struggle. For an excellent discussion of the phenomenon, see Douglas Kellner, *Jean Baudrillard: From Marxism to Postmodernism and Beyond* (Oxford: Polity Press, 1988).

28. Of course, it is this which is embodied in the fearful conservatism of intellectuals like Allan Bloom, Daniel Bell, E. D. Hirsch, William J. Bennett, and others.

29. See, for example, Stuart Hall, "Blue Election, Election Blues," *Marxism Today* (July 1987), pp. 30–35.

30. See, for example, H. Svi Shapiro, "Educational Theory and Recent Political Discourse: A New Agenda for the Left?" *Teachers College Record* 89, no. 2 (Winter 1987), pp. 171–200.

31. Chantal Mouffe and Ernest Laclau, *Hegemony and Socialist Strategy* (London: Vergo, 1985); see also, Samuel Bowles and Herbert Gintis, *Democracy and Capitalism* (New York: Basic Books, 1986).

32. See, for example, Cox, *Religion in the Secular City.*

33. David Purpel, *The Moral and Spiritual Crisis in Education: A Curriculum for Social Justice* (Granby, Mass.: Bergin & Garvey, 1988).

34. We are indebted to Dr. Marshall Gordon for this insight.

An Agenda for Educational Reform and Cultural Transformation

There is a tension at the heart of our wish to propose an agenda for educational change or reform. Such reform must, on the one hand, be sufficiently concrete and practical to constitute a realistic set of proposals. Yet, on the other hand, there is a danger that in the effort to be practical, we will lose the connection to a vision truly transformative of education and society. We insist that nothing less than a fundamental change in how we view human life and social purpose would be sufficient to address the calamities that now beset humanity. While agendas that seek to offer immediate remedies to our ills are seductive (for both their authors and their audiences), they provide only an illusory comfort. We wish to avoid this trap—the bane of even the best educational reform efforts. Yet there is a great danger in addressing problems at only the level of a moral vision of social potentialities. Such a vision seems inspiring but futile, necessary in the long-run, but perhaps quite remote from short-term concerns and needs.

Our struggle here has been to hold "both ends of the chain"; to attempt to elucidate purposes, strategies, and approaches grounded in the everyday world of educational concerns while trying to ensure that these are not severed from the long-range need for a fundamental shift in our human and social priorities, in our basic worldview. We wish to be practical or realistic without slipping into a frame of mind in which techniques, programs, or tactics become our dominant focus. We know how easy it is for an agenda to become reified—to become separated from the moral/political vision that originally gave it life and become simply an end in itself. We want to avoid a form of educational policy making that appeals to program administrators and specific interest lobbies but has lost any real connection to other people or to some more embracing human and social vision. Our fight is with the impulse toward fragmentation and technicalization in the educational world that rapidly disconnects whatever marvelous proposals are put forward from the human struggle for a more just, compassionate, and democratic community. Reform objectives should open up spaces in society where radically different, sometimes unsuspected, possibilities can become the subject of human aspirations and struggle. We have seen this time and again in the course of history.

We know, too, how the complex interplay between long-range vision and short-run proposals affects the question of hope. An overemphasis on the former, however right and necessary it may appear, leaves us nothing to do but wait. All our immediate preoccupation and efforts seem timid, puny, or irrelevant to the larger issues. Yet, to emphasize only our immediate efforts is to fall prey to a reassuring irresponsibility or sentimentality about the human or social crisis. There is here a false incrementalism that suggests that every little bit that we do leads us to some promised land of equality and opportunity. From our own work with both educators and the lay public, we know the importance of language that stresses that our individual or institutional efforts are inadequate to the larger crisis *and* that these efforts are necessary and valuable. We are compelled to offer a version of Antonio Gramsci's famous, if paradoxical, epigrammatic expression on hope and possibility, "pessimism of the intellect but optimism of the will." We must work as if our efforts will be fruitful even as we understand the enormity of our tasks.

With this in mind, we make no claim to offer a definitive agenda for educational reform. What we offer is, we hope, illustrative of the kind of direction that reform strategies and change approaches might take. At times, our language is broad and schematic; at other times, it is quite prescriptive. We sometimes address educational concerns within the larger matrix of human development; at other times, these concerns are framed in the institution of school. We are not interested in elaborating a blueprint for educational reform so much as issuing an invitation to educators and interested citizens to begin to remap our educational tasks, concerns, priorities, and possibilities, in the light of the difficulties and pain of the contemporary world. Consequently, our efforts are to be seen as a limited contribution to a process of educational change that must finally be debated and enacted within the spheres of public life and communication (however eroded or corrupted these are in so-called democratic societies).

Consonant with what we have argued throughout this book, we do not wish to cajole people into an agenda in the spirit of forcing spinach on resistant children who have been told that it is good for them whether or not they like it. Nor do we wish to present our agenda as the moralistic preaching of those who know what is best for others. We are quite sure that a democratic polity means that people must see why specific policies or proposals make sense in the context of their lives, hopes, and needs, and in the way people can support such ideas because they represent rational options and choices. "Persuasion" through guilt inducement, deceptive argument, or coercion is not what we have in mind when we speak of an agenda resonant with people's lives. We have sought to compile our agenda on what can reasonably be argued are the real needs and concerns of people's lives.

We have, of course, argued that these needs and concerns must be understood more broadly than progressive politics often has conceptualized them. They include not only the quest for economic security and opportunity but also the emotional demand for self-esteem and dignity, the sense of community life bound by moral commitment, and the spiritual need for personal meaning and purpose. An agenda for educational reform must speak to these powerful and compelling dimensions of our lives. We hope that by the book's end we will have accomplished this.

We are also, of course, cognizant that, as with all choices, there are risks. To adopt a new set of priorities may mean to put oneself—and even more frighteningly, one's children—in danger of losing certain advantages and inducements. At the same time, our agenda remains within the broad sphere of our national, cultural, and historical life—its promises, hopes, dreams, and images. We remain convinced of the proposition made recently by Michael Walzer that a prophetic or critical social language, if it is to succeed in its appeal, must take society to task in terms of its failure to make good on its own best promises and commitments. The radical impulse flows from the desire to eliminate or make good on the degraded images that have become unbearable in our public life.

The question of who is most likely to receive and embrace the kind of agenda that we offer is a difficult and troubling one. It is a complex question of which individuals or groups in our society (if any) would be most receptive and supportive of radical change. Quite clearly, we must speak to more than the most discriminated against or marginalized groups in the population—though these must certainly be a part of any constituency for change. Yet, that strategy is destined to fail that cannot articulate the concerns and needs of a wide variety of people in the country especially those in the middle class.

We have made the argument in the previous chapter that we must be open to understanding the multifaceted nature of pain, indignity, injustice, and suffering in the culture; that we must break out of stereotypical categories of those who constitute progressive *or* reactionary forces in the society. We wish to reject the easy view of political identities as if, for example, some people are congenitally right-wing. We wish to avoid such a reified view of identity and affiliation, preferring instead the view that people's allegiances are more fluid and mutable and that needs, concerns, anxieties, and so forth, can be articulated through a variety of agendas for change, some more positive and some more negative. Whatever else might exist, there is always, we believe, a demonstrable interest in more freedom, democracy, and justice among many different people in the United States. This "good sense" must be set beside the "bad sense" of racism, misogyny, chauvinism, authoritarianism, and intolerance.

The width of the spectrum of those who might be open to this kind of agenda is unclear. Yet, there are certainly boundaries. Our agenda is deeply antithetical to those whose clear allegiance is to the national security state and its obsession with military might and domination. What we offer is incompatible with the ideology of capitalism, whose motive forces are monetary profit, the exploitation of human labor, and the destruction of nature. And we question deeply all hierarchic arrangements of power and human value that so deeply scar the landscape of our global culture. We seek no facile resolutions of such commitments since these diverge from the social norm. While we seek an agenda whose foci are broad, flexible, and encompassing, we, too, have our bottom line. Our agenda is predicated on validating people's experience, respecting their concerns, taking seriously our national culture's own historical commitments, reaffirming our moral responsibilities, and giving credence to the multiple forms of human oppression and injury.

Such breadth and flexibility does not, however, signal an interest in acceptance of what we offer on any terms; we do not wish to put our agenda on the auction block to be sold at any price. In this time when public life here and around the world is so marked by cynicism and betrayal, we know the importance of meeting people where their lives and needs are. Yet, we insist, this meeting ground should not provide the place for some tawdry escape into victory parades, nor can it be a place where the simple remedies of first-aid will suffice to heal our wounds. The world and our times demand more than circuses and Band-Aids.

PRESENT CLAIMS, TRANSFORMATIVE POSSIBILITIES: TOWARD A "MIDDLE-RANGE" AGENDA

Whatever else may be said about present educational problems, it must be acknowledged that they are very real in the sense that they generate energy, concern, and resources within the public and professional realms. Consequently, we accept the responsibility to respond to this de facto agenda in a way that accepts it as a legitimate expression of public concern while also contesting the way in which issues are construed and problems defined. Our starting point consists of those issues, problems, and concerns that shape the educational agenda in this country at this time. We seek, of course, to inflect this agenda in new ways. Starting from the familiar signposts of education and social issues, the roads we follow take us in policy directions radically different from the usual prescriptions and pronouncements, although this effort is still framed, more or less, by the problematics of the dominant educational discourse: basic education, schooling and jobs, social responsibility, and disciplined behavior among the young. Later in this chapter, we will point toward an agenda that situates itself in discursive territory well beyond the issues, problems, and concerns that typically focus educational discussions. In this sense, the chapter moves from an agenda forged out of the immediate claims and demands of the present to one that depends on the forging of new claims and imperatives out of the perhaps less tangible, but certainly no less urgent, press of modern life.

Basic Skills: Toward a Curriculum for Survival

One of the central rallying cries of those who have seen the schools as cheating youngsters out of their educational "rights" has been the need to emphasize—or reemphasize—the basics. On the surface, at least, what the basics are seems straightforward: the need for a curriculum that ensures that kids learn to be both literate and numerate—how to read, write, and do arithmetic. At one level, there is an unassailable sensibleness to this demand. It is, of course, entirely debilitating, disempowering, and deeply injurious for any citizen or worker, consumer, parent, or community member to find themselves without these skills. There is in the expectation that schools will instruct children so that they are functionally literate and numerate an obvious logic that is daily reinforced by the experiences of working-class and middle-class parents. To the extent that radical or progressive educators have appeared to take issue with the priority of basics in the schools, these educators have seemed out of touch with the everyday concerns, needs, and demands of people's life-worlds. Their ideas appear naive or irrelevant to what working people know are the facts of life in an industrial (or postindustrial) society—one needs to know how to write or read if one is to have any chance of economic survival. No agenda for education can possibly succeed if it seems not to take seriously the question of reading, writing, and numeracy.

One of the still not clearly understood political phenomena of recent years is the identification of the Right with the public discourse about the basics. Those who championed the demand that public education be responsible for the acquisition of the skills of literacy among children were conservatives. The Left, on the other hand, was held responsible for the decline in the ability to read or write. Even worse, the Left's educational practitioners were seen as hostile to the salience of the basics in the curriculum of schools. There is good reason to argue that this was a misrepresentation or obfuscation of reality. Nevertheless, framing the educational debate in these terms has been disastrous. The long-run struggle for social justice in America has appeared to be in opposition to the more immediate concerns of parents. Literacy as the concern of schooling has been counterposed to the goals of an education that might help bring about a more equitable social order.

Of course, in this alignment of political forces and educational discourses, there was a good deal of clever manipulation and deception. There was, for example, the claim that liberals' influence over public education in the 1960s and 1970s was responsible for a decline in reading skills. In fact, careful analysis of the documented data shows that such a claim is not easily supportable.[1] The growth of a far more diverse and socially heterogeneous population of students whose performance was included in the overall assessment of basic skills in the nation was not usually made clear in the assertions about educational decline. Instead, the teachers and educational reformers who tried to combat the disempowering and dispiriting effects of basal readers and texts and that of pedagogues who denied the lives, languages, and cultures of so many students in the public schools were portrayed by conservatives as the villains who had undermined school standards. Amidst the concerns of economic stagnation in the 1970s and the cultural and moral disarray supposedly unleashed in the preceding decade, the Right harnessed the collective anxieties and organized them into a crusade against the apparent erosion of instruction in the basics. Here, it was proclaimed, was one of the culprits in the declining economic opportunity for the younger generation *and* the disintegration of the moral order.

In this, of course, the discourse concerning basics evoked images and concerns much wider than reading, writing, and arithmetic. Those observers who have described a reactionary aspect to the "basics" mentality are surely correct. There is a wish among some social groups for schools to prepare youngsters for jobs and roles like the ones they grew up among, thus perpetuating a world these groups understand.

There is, too, in the notion of the basics (as well as in the related concepts of "minimal competencies," "performance standards," and so forth) the implicit expectation of self-sufficiency and self-reliance— compelling ideas in a time of economic and social insecurity. Curriculum experiences that promise the fundamental knowledge or skills to make possible one's survival—and ensure a minimum degree of agency in the pursuit of one's livelihood form a powerful focus for the mobilization of educational opinion. The power of the basic skills phenomenon is associated with the way in which schooling is directly connected to ensuring that one has the basic ability to negotiate one's way in the world. This discourse connects schooling with the acquisition of those skills or knowledge that might, in some way, protect individuals from the insecurity and predatory nature of our social and economic environment. Of course, defined in this way, education becomes an expression of the concern for survival in a hazardous, fragile, and precarious world. Looked at from this point of view, the basic skills phenomenon can be understood, at least in part, as rooted in what Christopher Lasch has called the "Survival Mentality." Such a mentality, he argues, is the product of "people who have lost confidence in the future. Faced with . . . rising crime and terrorism, environmental deterioration, and long-term economic decline . . . the problem of survival overshadows loftier concerns. It has entered so deeply into popular culture and political debate that every issue, however fleeting or unimportant, presents itself as a matter of survival."[2]

The concern with survival, notes Lasch, is connected with the widely shared perception that all of us are victims or potential victims. Today almost everyone is vulnerable to disaster—to the collapse of the family and marriage, to catastrophic illness, to the deliberate manipulation of inflation and unemployment, to grossly unfair taxes, to pollution, to unsafe working conditions, and to the greed of the oil companies. This mentality is reflected in the outpouring of popular books on survival and survivors and the huge psychiatric literature on "coping," as well as in the grim rhetoric of everyday life. Even competition as a central value of our culture now centers not so much on the desire to excel as on the struggle to avoid a crushing defeat. The purpose of success has been reconceived as a daily struggle for survival.

We understand and affirm parents' desire for their children to master the basic skills of reading, writing, and expression. We are sympathetic to their desire for their children to possess the skills and knowledge that they need to survive in the world. We do not dismiss this desire as a reactionary response of know-nothings wishing merely to repeat their own poor school experiences and stubbornly refusing to try anything new. Yet, if alarm over survival, for ourselves and our children, drives the wish that kids master the basics and become minimally competent, it is a sadly restricted and unimaginative notion of what it might take to survive.

While the emotion-laden discourse of basics is deeply rooted in the experience of individuals daily struggling with the crisis of survival—material, moral, spiritual, and psychological—in its present limited form it offers very little to help us cope with existing realities. As with other aspects of survivalist discourse (which stress the importance of narrow, clearly defined objectives), basic skills–oriented schooling offers a curriculum with little or no attention to questions of personal meaning. There is little concern with the transmission of a cultural literacy that might provide the kind of narrative threads that allow one to grasp one's place in the totality of our social life. To the contrary, this curriculum is a discontinuous and unconnected inventory of skills, information, and behaviors remote from an education that could foster the intellectual capacity to connect history with the present or to link individual experience with that of the collectivity. In this sense, it is profoundly individualistic—an approach in which our joint problems and difficulties must be faced by the solitary individual who, with the help of schooling, has learned to "cope" with the world alone.

The basic skills perspective, in this sense, mirrors an orientation to the world in which life consists of isolated acts and events without pattern, structure, or unfolding narrative. Time and space have shrunk to the immediate present and the immediate environment. The basics approach to curriculum has little interest in making sense of the world, in connecting experience with meaning or meaning in one part of our world with that in another. The knowledge conveyed through such schooling is fragmented and experienced as isolated bits of information.

Unconcerned with matters of awareness, insight, or imagination, it supplies, instead, a set of skills and the knowledge needed to simply (if not easily) get by in the world. Curricular concerns are, at best, predicated on the need to cope with or adapt to the existing reality and to avoid any significant intellectual or moral engagement with the dangerous and catastrophic problems that confront humanity. In this sense, the usual basic skills approach represents a version of self-sufficient individualism.

Avoiding any real attempt to critically confront our shared human predicament and needs, it attempts only to facilitate an individual's adaptation to the shoals and currents of our turbulent and threatening reality.

While we affirm that education today must be about surviving and survival, that schools must deliver on those basic competencies that will help with this, and that reading, writing, and arithmetic are necessary components of a curriculum concerned with surviving, we also want to expand this discourse and attach its concerns, to broader, more transformative goals. Schools should indeed instruct students in those skills, knowledge, and abilities that will empower them to deal with, cope, and address the demands of the everyday world. This means that schools must help students learn to decode words and sentences. It also means that students are capable of dealing with the obviously distorted and manipulative messages that young people are inundated with through the news media.

Literacy is a necessary but insufficient expectation of schools; there must be a critical literacy wherein young people attain the capacity to penetrate the surface descriptions that commonly represent (or misrepresent) our world. Reading (as it has been said) must enable kids not only to read the word, but to "read the world." There is certainly great interest and support for helping youngsters learn to decipher and discriminate the complex, often confusing or deceptive messages of television, advertising, and other mass-mediated images. We have here popular sympathy for a radical expansion of what it means to be literate in America.

Widespread apprehension of corporate and governmental abuses of the process of public communication has deepened the awareness of what it means to be *communicatively competent.* Survival and the capacity to deal with one's environment clearly now requires an ability to "read" the distorted, often exploitative messages that saturate print and broadcast media. Indeed, there is a widespread sense that our young people are endangered by the abuses of public communications and that children and adolescents are enormously vulnerable to powerful interests and the images they generate. In this sense, notions of "decoding" television, movies, and advertising have increasing resonance among parents and community members. Such "basic skills" become a front-line for protecting children from the relentless influence and seductions of corporate capitalism.

To insist that basic skills today means communicative competence is to give a transformative twist to the existing public discourse of education. It is to root the basic instructional work of schools in the work of empowering young people to cope with the complexity and confusions of the contemporary social world. Such a discourse places us fully on the side of the need for achieving literacy, but this time a more comprehensive and relevant version of it. There is reason to believe that expanding the discourse of basics in this way will meet with real communal support and will become a salient item in an alternative agenda for educational reform. Such expansion takes nothing away from the clearly resonant language of basics while more clearly rooting it in the confusion and vulnerability of everyday life.

This language can be expanded to include a range of "social competencies" that enable young people to survive in the world. We might remember here Jesse Jackson's evocative assertion that graduates of our high schools should come across the stage grasping their high school diplomas in one hand and their voter registration cards in the other. In this sense, the preparation for active citizenship in our society may be seen as indispensable to matters of survival. It means possessing the capability of responsibly confronting and dealing with the often hazardous or disordered circumstances of our lives—what for many (especially the young) feel so often like a world out of control. Of course, survival here means something quite distinct. Instead of adapting to or coping with the difficult and threatening circumstances of social reality, this approach emphasizes the possibility of intervening in what exists and changing that reality—or at least challenging the "facts" of our social world.

In emphasizing the need to make society adaptive to human concerns and needs (rather than vice versa), the curriculum must stress the knowledge and skills that might ensure a more responsive culture. This is an education for the purpose of active citizenship and participation in civic and communal life. Citizenship here embraces a concern for those spheres of human activity that impinge on our lives as individuals and as members of a collectivity—as students, as workers, as consumers, as neighborhood residents, as voters, as women or members of minorities, or in other ways. Citizenship education is rooted in the issues, concerns, and struggles of the everyday world, not in the rarified abstractions typically found in school book discussions of democracy. A civic education also stresses how we can affect the conditions of our everyday lives, which requires a social rather than simply a personal form of empowerment. Instead of emphasizing only individual self-reliance and self-sufficiency, there is the notion of an interdependent community in which individual capabilities and skills are pooled in order to exert a shared control of our social world.

Of course, dealing with issues of survival in this way means that education must point to the way in which distress, alienation, disrespect, and exploitation limit the broader shared experiences in our institutional world. The basic skills of survival are ones that provide a means through which the anxiety, confusion, disintegration, degradation, and suffering of everyday life can be seen as rooted in the common circumstances of our lives and can be responded to in this way. If education in our world must enable our young to live and survive in this world, the basics must include, but also go beyond, their limited and traditional definitions. A new agenda for education must encompass this quest for the survival of our children.

Work: Powershift and Educational Reform

A resonant progressive agenda for education must deal with the connection between jobs and schooling. Whatever disdain radical and progressive critics may have for the increasing vocationalization of schooling—the reduction of broad educational goals to specialized or technical skills—its importance to people cannot be denied. Decent employment stands at the center of most of our attempts to establish the conditions for family security and material well-being. And school is the means by which most people hope to attain these goals. A vocational dimension is vital to any effective radical agenda on education. Without it, such an agenda is bound to be perceived as irrelevant to the lives of most people. Of course, such a strategy cannot represent an endorsement of the usual, narrowly conceived, specialized forms of vocational or technical training.

Fortunately, support for a broader conception of education for work has begun to grow among a number of influential constituencies. Concern over low or declining productivity has directed attention recently to the problems of human capital formation—the need for an educated, trained, and skilled work force capable of adequately meeting the demands of an advanced industrial infrastructure and defending itself against the effects of low-wage competition from developing countries.[3] In facing the human problems of low productivity, a number of commentators have emphasized strategies aimed at wider participation in economic affairs. Such participation would center around measures to ensure broader control of investment decisions, a democratization of the structure of the workplace, support for the introduction of "democratic technology," and the need for a more responsive and accountable corporate sector.

Commentators have argued that only through such changes will it be possible to address the economic (as well as the social and human) needs of the United States in the coming years. The influential work of William G. Ouchi, Thomas J. Peters,[4] and many other similar studies have loudly touted the human and productive advantages of greater democratic participation in the workplace. The popularly noted, if limited, experiments in decentralized management, quality circles, job rotation, and cooperative decision making, as well as the widespread interest in Japanese forms of corporate management, have opened up unprecedented possibilities for an expansion of the responsibilities of and control by workers and middle-level employees.[5]

In considering what forms of education might be apposite to the nature of a more flexible, democratically structured workplace, it is clear that a greater integration of human tasks necessitates something broader than specialized technical training. While specialized training will certainly have its place, attention might be given to "training" in democratic processes, the capacity to critically evaluate social needs, and the human and environmental consequences of economic decisions. Such an education would have to be oriented toward concerns wider than simply training students to operate as instruments of production. It would have to take seriously the functioning of institutional democracy, the politics of control, the assumption of collective responsibility, the negotiation of priorities, the elaboration of procedures, and the resolution of conflicts—all of which can be learned only through opportunities for genuine democratic participation and governance in our educational institutions. It goes without saying that given the hierarchial authoritarian character of most schools in America such change would be every bit as radical as the changes proposed for the control of industry itself.

In addition to this democratic restructuring of educational institutions, education would have to renew its commitment to the notion of a broader "cultural" education. While a human capital focus implies only the need for an appropriate specialized education, the social restructuring of industry to unite the concern for both the execution and conception of tasks requires an education that allows individuals an understanding of the broader purposes and ends of production and other activities in their society—an understanding that includes a critical examination of existing purposes as well as possible alternatives. Popular participation in the fundamental industrial planning and investment decisions implies awareness of and insight into the interrelatedness of such decisions with matters of social, human, and cultural significance; the effects of the allocation of human and material resources; the consequences of industrial development on the environment; the issue of human needs and appropriate or necessary levels of consumption; productivity and the relation between work and leisure time; the relationship between forms of technology and human experience; and the interconnections of the world economy.

A more democratic approach to the management of economic institutions requires moving from an education in which a highly circumscribed knowledge is emphasized to one embracing the totality of social concerns and relationships. Specialized training gives way to an education concerned with broad human understanding of the meaning and purpose of productive life. In an important sense, education for economic democracy implies a renewed commitment to cultural education—one in which central concerns are human life, its meaning and significance, and the social order in which these are constituted. The questions that are integral to an education for economic democracy transcend answers derived from the simple utilization of technical criteria. Issues of allocating resources, environmental effects, technology and worker experience, work and leisure, and so forth, cannot be dealt with through an instrumental rationality in which ends are presumed. Such issues are indissolubly connected to wider considerations—aesthetic, ethical, and existential. These can only be decided through an examination of the purposes of production in our society and culture.

While the technical education of human capital embodies a rationality in which ends, purposes, and effects of economic activity are, to a large extent, presupposed (the "bottom line" is always efficiency, the minimization of costs, and the maximization of profits), the notion of meaningful economic democracy implies choice regarding the possible goals of our productive energies. The education that follows from this would likely question the wisdom or necessity of centralization and concentration of industrial development, the possibility of forms of technology that enhance rather than reduce craftsmanship and worker creativity, the development of labor-saving technologies versus full employment, and the social need or usefulness of current industrial priorities (e.g., the emphasis on private modes of transportation). Such questions are inextricably linked to issues of human values, social priorities, and ideological commitments.

It must be noted that the new robotic and cybernetic technologies have frequently produced effects quite opposite to those that we have described. The use of these technologies has intensified the pace with which jobs have become fragmented, controlled, and alienating. Testifying before a committee of the House of Representatives, William W. Winpisinger, the then-president of the International Association of Machinists, pointed to the effects of the new technology on skilled labor.[6] He argued that the search for short-term profits has dove-tailed with labor-saving technology to encourage job-fragmentation. Machinists, he said, have been replaced by low-skilled machine operators backed up by a relatively small number of specialized service people. While unemployment has been one result of the new technology another result has been the lowering of the skill level of the average worker.

Nonetheless, despite these trends, a wide variety of voices recently have argued for the necessity of a different strategy to solve our crisis of production and industrial competitiveness. The report by the National Commission on the Skills of the American Work Force, argued in 1990 that the country is "headed toward an economic cliff." Unless the nation redesigns its businesses to become more productive—by putting more authority in the hands of workers—"we may all slide into relative poverty together."[7] There must be, the report insists, more responsibility and authority at the work site.

In a similar vein, the report by the Office of Technology Assessment, a nonpartisan government agency, insists that economic development in the United States in the coming decades will depend heavily on how much trust U.S. businesses put in the capabilities of the workforce.[8] The development and utilization of new technology will demand, the report says, the availability of broadly educated workers who have been encouraged to develop creative approaches to their work, to be intellectually flexible and critically minded, and to have the capacity to assimilate unfamiliar, complex, and often inconsistent knowledge. The futurologist Alvin Toffler, in his 1990 book, *Powershift*, puts the issue quite clearly:

The inner life of the corporation must change. The old smokestack division of a firm into " heads" and "hands" no longer works. Just as owners once became dependent on managers for knowledge, today's managers are becoming dependent on their employees for knowledge. The knowledge load and more important, the decisions load are being redistributed. In a continual cycle of learning, unlearning and relearning, workers need to master new technologies, adopt to new organizational forms and generate new ideas.

As a result "submissive rule observers, who merely follow instructions to the letter, are not good workers" says a study of employee relations and productivity in the giant Sony Corp. in Japan. . . . Only regulations which are endorsed by the majority of the work force have a chance of being abided by. But to invite workers into the rule-making process is to share power once held exclusively by their bosses—a power shift not all managers find easy to accept.[9]

Social Responsibility: Schooling for an Ethic of Communal Care

Across a wide and divergent set of social constituencies too, there is a sense that American society has become an irresponsible one. From Left to Right it is argued that there is a deep moral crisis that centers on selfish, narcissistic, and careless attitudes and on a lack of mutuality and obligation to others. Of course, what is emphasized or seen as most symptomatic of this crisis varies significantly. For some (more often conservatives), it is the dependency of those on welfare, the spread of an ethos of entitlements without any concomitant sense of obligation, and the desire for immediate gratification and pleasure. Such opinion focuses on the "epidemic" of pregnancies among young unmarried women and the lack of paternal responsibility, the "culture of dependency" among the poor, the wide-spread pursuit of unrestrained indulgence, the decline of patriotic duty, and so forth.

An overriding concern is that a reckless, amoral, hedonistic selfish-ness has led to a disintegration of the communal fabric of American society. The explosion of drug dependency throughout the society with all of its antisocial consequences is perhaps the most visible face of the "moral panic" associated with the development of this irresponsibility. For others, irresponsibility toward the society is manifested most sharply in the get-rich-quick philosophy of the 1980s that seems to have so shaped the industrial and economic decline of the United States in the 1980s and 1990s. Its face is the savings-and-loan scandal, the merger mania and financial double dealings on Wall Street, and the flight of capital and industrial plants from the United States to cheaper labor markets in the developing world. It includes, too, the misuse and abuse of natural resources and indifference to the dangerous, hazardous, and wasteful environmental consequences of corporate behavior. The focus is also on the development of a society that seems to treat with in-difference or callous disregard the growth of widespread homelessness, poverty among children, and degradation of public utilities and amenities (such as public transportation, health care, roads, and rail systems).

Of course from Left and Right explanations of the crisis of social responsibility differ. The Right blames the permissive moral climate that emerged in American society in the 1960s: Rock music, lackadaisical parenting, the breakdown of the family, the women's movement, and the welfare state have undercut the traditional demands of communal life—duty, obligation, accountability, and restraint. On the Left the Reagan and Bush years are seen as having produced an ethos in which greed, human indifference, and lack of compassion flourished.

An emphasis on individualism, private enterprise, and governmental deregulation resulted in the nightmare of a society in which freedom became the license to act without regard for anything but one's own narrowly defined interests. Paradoxically, while Reaganism promised to put an end to a society that spent without earning and sapped the self-responsibility of people and communities, it produced a society with unprecedented personal, corporate, and government debt and unparalleled indifference to those least well-off (obliquely acknowledged in presidential candidate Bush's assertion of the need for a "kinder, gentler nation").

Strangely, and despite its poor record, the Right has continued to be the tribune of moral responsibility in America. Interestingly, as Geoff Mulgan has suggested, the Left still shies away from the implications of a strong ethos of individual responsibility.[10] It still feels more comfortable concentrating responsibility in the hands of the state and remote collective institutions. These problems, he suggests, are not solved by simply emphasizing the need to devolve power. Words like *empowerment* and *citizenship* can easily be seen as the dispersal of power, rights, and entitlements without any emphasis on an ethos that makes moral demands on those receiving them.

Of course, the Right's prescription for greater individual responsibility has been thoroughly inadequate. The notion that private property and private interests lead to a more responsible society has produced increasingly disastrous results. Property rights produce care within narrow limits and at the price of carelessness in relation to the rest of society. As the overall metaphor for our moral conduct and human relationships, the marketplace encourages a focus on private interest and produces an evasion of concern for the wider community, dishonesty and deception in our public dealings, amoral attitudes toward the products of one's work, and a disinterest in the effects of our actions on later generations.

Mulgan has suggested that an attitude of responsibility toward others in society should be encouraged for a number of reasons. People are social as well as individual creatures. They develop a sense of themselves through their group and collective identities and through the obligations that these entail. Responsibility to others brings out the best in human nature. Without a sense of responsibility for both individuals and institutions, the world becomes a place of alibis and evasions. Without a strong sense of natural obligation, society runs the risk of sliding into mutual indifference and growing injustice. Without ensuring collective provisions, society becomes a jungle where the weak are left to their own suffering and inadequacies. And finally, there needs to be a moral balance between power and responsibility. Power needs to carry accountability. Those who exercise power must also become responsible for how it is used. Wherever possible, political systems should seek to establish a congruence between power and responsibility.

The language of individual responsibility toward society finds resonance within diverse elements of the national culture. This diverse appeal, of course, is the strength of such a language. There is, too, the danger that it can become all things to all people. "Ask not what your country can do for you but what you can do for your country" lends itself as easily to militaristic patriotism as it does to concern for the social ills of our nation. Yet, we think the risk is worth taking. While most of us might agree that there is a greater need for social responsibility, it will take a discursive battle to ensure that this means not mindless flag waving but compassionate concern for those in our community who are poor, excluded, and victimized. Indeed, we need to be mindful that the intensity of emotion that surrounds the question of the flag and patriotism expresses the desperate desire for a strong sense of community in a highly fragmented, atomized, and egotistical culture.

There is, we feel sure, potentially great support for a dimension of schooling that seeks to inculcate in youngsters a sense of the importance of service to the community; the development of an attitude of caring for and stewardship of our natural environment; the value of aiding the sick, the elderly, and those who are alone; the importance of doing for others, not simply taking for oneself; and the value of addressing the consequences of social injustice, whether among the poor, immigrants, the homeless, the handicapped, or those subject to discrimination and racism. How these impulses might be addressed, developed, and nourished in schools is best left to teachers and schools. Within the broad concern of the individual's responsibility for society, what particular inflection or emphasis might be given by educators will depend on the place and character of their school and on the community that it is a part of. Whether the modality of concern is through forms of community service, specific kinds of curricula, or a more general infusion of a "social responsibility" ethic in the classroom or school will depend on the particularities of the school and community and must be the result of the initiative, creativity, and the interests of students, teachers, and administrators. Here we wish to limit ourselves to the specific recommendation that the agenda for schools include as a central component the moral imperative of cultivation of a concern among the young for the welfare of the larger community.

Linking education to the individual's responsibility to society requires addressing a widely perceived crisis in citizenship. The degeneration of active, meaningful, and involved citizenship is most readily discernible in voting behavior, though it is also apparent in the now well-documented apathy and disinterest among young people toward national and international events and affairs. In the elections of the 1980s, voter turnout fell to historically low levels. In the 1984 and 1988 general elections, less than half the eligible electorate voted. Even in the record turnout of 1992, only 55 percent of the eligible electorate voted. American voting turnout is the lowest, by far, among industrialized democracies. Certainly, this is an embarrassment for a country that claims leadership of the "democratic world."

It would be naïve to believe that this situation of voter apathy is not welcomed by many of those special interests who benefit from widespread citizen apathy and the effective depoliticization of public life, especially since nonparticipation is highest among the poorest, most dispowered group—those who would have the most to gain from a real shift in social and economic policies. At the same time, a variety of concerns (ranging from future social stability to renewed local political initiatives) have prompted calls for a more active electorate. In emphasizing the need to take citizenship education out of the textbooks and into the community, a progressive educational agenda might find allies among those who have been advocating community service as part of normal academic requirements (in both high schools and colleges). Such community service would expand democratic participation and deepen civic awareness and understanding as well as enhance the concern for social justice. The crisis of electoral apathy and civic disaffiliation might provide an important opening to an education for greater political empowerment.

Outside of school, concern about the influence on children of mass-mediated culture has often blurred the lines between Left and Right. There are a growing number of shared concerns: sexual exploitation, unrelenting violence, the promotion of alcohol and tobacco, pornography, the flaunting of wealth, and other issues. These frequently create common grounds for concern among feminists, consumer protection activists, professional educators, as well as religious and other morally oriented groups.

The corrosive moral effects of mass-mediated images of success, power, achievement, and ambition have produced what the conservative commentator Kevin Phillips has called the "politics of cultural despair."[11] This feeling of despair connects widely divergent groups in the society, from parents in the black community sickened by the exploitation of their children by fashion merchants and cigarette promoters to white middle-class parents angered by the shoddy, exploitative programming for children on commercial television (which is viewed as often little more than a very crude vehicle for advertising without any artistic or educational merit).

Some of the campaigns for greater responsibility in these broader media arenas of socialization contain a rampant authoritarianism that certainly endangers freedom of expression. At the same time, however, these campaigns reflect the growing unwillingness to leave cultural resources that have enormous educational effects on the young to the invisible hands of advertising executives or the fashion and popular culture moguls. The conflict between private interest and public influence over the moral and intellectual development of the young has increasingly called into question the self-serving autonomy of the "culture industry" in America.

A progressive agenda for education must surely support this attempt to subject to some kind of popular accountability the cultural powers of largely unregulated corporate interests. It must insist that the goal of such attention is not censorship but the need for socially responsible attitudes among those who wield enormous influence over the young—attitudes that, it is widely perceived, are absent today, at enormous human and societal cost. A progressive educational agenda must forcefully support the proposals that have been developed by groups like Action for Children's Television who demand careful regulation of the commercial media to ensure that manipulation and exploitation of the young is minimized and to make possible much greater resources for producers of cultural work that might cultivate a humane and critically aware citizenry.

Of course advocating that the production and dissemination of culture be subject to greater popular consideration and control carries with it real dangers of parochialism and intolerance. Yet to continue to leave the domain of popular culture and the production of social values and meanings to the shallow criteria of the marketplace is to be complicit in the continuing and visible irresponsibility of the most powerful educational forces in our society. Such a decision would be morally dangerous and politically shortsighted. It is now possible, we believe, to constitute a "popular bloc" that might effectively focus attention on the wider powers of education in American society and call for a public media that might more legitimately reflect the educational needs of a democratic, caring, and environmentally sensitive society.

Discipline: Unlearning the Culture of Narcissism

The question of discipline in schools ranks very high among the concerns of parents and other members of the public and cuts across races and classes. Survey after survey demonstrates that schools are expected to teach disciplined behavior to the young. Consistently parents and other citizens have voiced alarm about the failure of schools to ensure that young people develop sufficient respect for authority and appropriate attitudes and behavior. Not surprisingly, this concern has been, throughout the 1980s and 1990s a central element of conservative discourse about schools and a focal point of its educational agenda. And for a number of powerful reasons, the Left has found itself hostile to the widely supported public demands given expression in this agenda. Yet, as we have tried to argue throughout this book, such demands need to be looked at more carefully and sympathetically. They need to be seen as expressing something more than an irrational authoritarianism among those determined to inflict order and control on the young.

The call for order and discipline surely has elements of a deeply rooted psychological interest in squelching all those playful, erotic, and anti-authority characteristics found in the young. After the work of Wilhelm Reich, Erich Fromm, Theodore Adorno, Jules Henry, and, more recently, Alice Miller, there can be little doubt about the power of this protofascist drive toward producing a world that is intensely regulated, highly predictable, and deadeningly unchanging. The spirit-destroying, anti-democratic impulses of the authoritarian personality have been well described by many observers of the schools in the 1950s, 1960s, 1970s, and 1980s.

The order-and-discipline educational legitimacy derives from an anti-social view of what is thought to constitute human nature. Untamed or uncontrolled, this nature threatens to overwhelm civilization through its youthful destructive and sexual urges. Such a view is certainly still an important component of what has been described as the "small-town" traditionalism of American culture. For those who espouse this view, only strong discipline and compliance with the authority of teachers, parents, and other significant adults can ensure the survival of the community.

Of course, we know, too, that for many parents—especially working-class ones—their lived experiences teach them the importance of learning to deal in an accommodating way with authority and authority structures. Without the right demeanor or attitudes their children will, in all likelihood, have a much harder time holding down a job and ensuring some degree of security for themselves and their families. For these parents, being "good" means learning to conform (or appear to conform) to the rules and regulations that structure institutional life—whether in school or at work. Being "bad"—flouting rules, subverting authority, playing instead of working—is the road to punishment, insecurity, and indignity.

The widespread concern, even panic, about the lack of discipline among the young, may speak also to other aspects of our society and culture. We cannot deny that the 1960s and 1970s saw an unprecedented upheaval in the social and cultural fabric of the nation. Few elements of our moral and normative world were not seriously questioned and, in some cases, upended. The "Great Refusal," as it has been termed, referred to a widespread critical negation of habits, identities, values, practices, and beliefs that formed the dominant ideology in the United States. Everything from military values and patriotism to sexual attitudes and the value of a career and family life were, at some time, brought into question and frequently derided.

While some commentators have seen the ascendance of conservative politics in the succeeding period as a "return" to a pre-1960s sensibility, morality, and outlook, this oversimplifies and misrepresents the enduring nature of the changes that have occurred. Feminism, the antiwar movement, cultural and artistic dissent (especially rock music), the consumer and environmental movements, the diversification of fashion and style, struggles against racism, continued corruption in government and big business, and so forth, have permanently undermined the pre-1960s consensus about identity, morality, and legitimate authority. The mere fact that two weeks after the United States launched its war against Iraq more than a quarter of a million, largely young people participated in nationwide antiwar protests (something that did not happen until into the fifth year of the war in Vietnam!) is testament to this change.

Movies for the teenage market typically provide cynical commentary on the meaningless nature of schooling and ridicule, in particular, the authority of teachers and principals. Sexual activity continued throughout the 1980s and 1990s to occur at an earlier and earlier age despite calls for restraint, the AIDS crisis, and the high levels of teenage pregnancies. Whether under the banner of feminism or not, women of all ages and walks of life have continued to resist and question masculine prerogatives, advantages, attitudes, and values. Corporate, political, and religious scandals have continued to erode the legitimacy of those with power or influence. Rock music and the postmodern music bazaar have continued to scorn and ridicule established norms of appearance, sexual preference or behavior, or, indeed, any fixed identity. Notwithstanding the, at times, flourish of "traditional" values of patriotic, family-centered, career-minded values, there has been, simultaneously, the enduring legacy of disbelief and cultural/moral flux that has made cynicism, as Peter Sloterdijk noted, the characteristic attitude of our time.[12]

The rampant escapism of drugs, alcohol, even ear-blasting sound systems, reflected a crisis of identity-forming structures (especially the family) and dissolution of a stable, securely grounded ego—a self that could be situated in an enduring, coherent, and meaningful social world. In this context, concern for more discipline, order, and structure in schools (and in families—note the growing popularity of so-called tough love) is more than the expression of irrational, authoritarian tendencies among educators and parents. It is an eminently understandable response to a world in which both self and community have lost the dependability and security of social boundaries and communal limits, in which structures that demarcate our autonomy as well as our connections have dissolved into a disorganized anarchic condition.

This is a crisis of both the internal self and of our social relations, though, in conservative discourse, it is "repair" to the former which is given most serious attention. In "tough love," authority figures try to hammer the young ego into an obedient, rule-abiding mode of behavior. In the "traditional" school, discipline, subservience to authority and conformity to rules are emphasized. The goals of each are to restrain and retrain the erotic, resistant, and transgressive drives unleashed by cultural changes and the delegitimation of social authority, so that individuals become less willful and more submissive to authority.

Whatever its reasonableness in present conditions, the usual expression of this concern for discipline and restraint fails to extend beyond an emphasis on coerciveness, conformity, and a blind submission to power. That is to say, the usual inflection of the public discourse on discipline remains narrowly focused on behavior. In this sense, discipline in schools becomes understood as keeping kids under control, managing their behavior, getting them to act in compliance with the rules of the institution— whether or not there is any real comprehension of why they exist or whom they are intended to benefit. As a response to the need to promote thoughtful self-regulation among the young regarding the effects of their actions on others, such an approach to discipline is self-defeating and futile. Its demand for mindless restraint and conformity brings into further disrepute and contempt among the young the real value of discipline as a dimension of human conduct.

Our agenda for education must affirm the validity—and, indeed, the dire necessity—of discipline as a way of being human in the world. The Left's inability to incorporate the importance of human discipline into their educational project has allowed the Right to monopolize an issue of enormous public concern.[13] Yet, our condition as a national and international community cries out for an alternative, socially sensitive, humanly transformative notion of discipline—not the rejection of discipline among the young as an educational goal, but its redefinition. We should reject discipline as a practice concerned with an unreflective and unthinking obedience toward authority or as a mindless conformity to institutional rules. To insist on such behavior among the young is, for obvious reasons, antithetical to the education of citizens for a thoughtful, questioning, democratic culture in which individuality and dissent are valued and prized.

Yet, in a society rife with unbridled egoism, greed, excessive consumption, the misuse of limited resources, and indifference to the effect of how we live on the lives of others, there is an urgent need for a discipline that might instruct the young about the need to moderate one's demands and to act with restraint and care. We wish to nurture in our young a discipline that makes clear its connection to the care and respect for others and the earth. It stands in opposition to a culture that encourages the profligate, selfish, and unrestrained gorging of our resources, the irresponsible destruction of our air and water, and unbounded consumerism. Conservation, sensitive treatment of our natural environment, and self-control over what and how we consume are all aspects of a meaningful notion of discipline. Discipline in this context means learning what it means to limit one's own demands and impulses because of their detrimental effects on the lives of others. It is an essential component of a more socially responsible and socially just world.

To act without such discipline is to recklessly put one's own needs, concerns, or inclinations ahead of all others. To act without discipline means to push ahead of someone else, to act without respect or concern for someone who is elderly or handicapped, to smoke without regard for its effects on others, to blast out music without concern for its invasiveness, to heedlessly waste resources and materials, to drink alcohol and drive, to engage in sexual relations without a concern for their possible consequences. It is also, collectively, to condone the use by 5 percent of the earth's population (our society) of 30 percent of its nonrenewable energy, to seek to amass money or profit without apparent limit and without concern for how this affects the lives of working people, to pursue a way of life based on "more is better," and to pursue a course of international behavior in which military might and not the rule of law determines our actions as a country.

For us, then, to act with discipline is to act with regard to limits: to curtail what one wishes to say, do, or have because of its potentially deleterious consequences on others. Discipline, in this sense, is a key element in acting with responsibility to and for others. To transform the meaning of discipline into this sense of self- and collective restraint is to become cognizant of the dangers of behavior whenever our expectations, desires, or assumptions go unchecked or whenever there is no critical moral reflection. It is to become aware of the hurt we inflict on others when we waste or destroy precious resources; when we squander time, energy, or money; when we imperiously assume that everyone around us shares our religious faith, language, history, or culture. Whenever we act without learning to limit our needs thoughtfully, without curtailing our power and prerogatives, or without checking our assumptions that everyone is just like us, then we have acted recklessly and without discipline. So it is that we wish to affirm the public's alarm about the lack of discipline among the young—and the importance of schools in changing this—while insisting that this not be a mindless, unthinking knuckling under to institutional rules, but rather a relational, morally sensitive, and reflective process of learning to live with others in community.

FUTURE CLAIMS, DREAMS, AND POSSIBILITIES: TOWARD A "LONGER-RANGE" AGENDA

Beyond the discussion and resolution of intermediate issues of policy making and practice, there remains the continuing responsibility for reframing these problems into more meaningful patterns that involve changing our consciousness, transforming our culture, and restructuring our society. In this section, we suggest a few ways in which such a process might take place, recognizing here that the danger lies in the ephemeral and utopian qualities of such an endeavor. In addition, the agenda issue that we will now discuss requires even greater risk and courage than those described in the previous section. It surely is important to take seriously the articulated and overt concerns of the public, but it is also vital that we seek to go beyond our short-term fears and distrusts. We must also develop an agenda that engages us in the struggle to create a more trusting, generous, open, and aspiring community. We recognize however, that responding to concerns like those discussed in the preceding section is very likely a necessary precondition for engaging in an enterprise concerned with fundamental transformation.

However, this process can be facilitated by recognizing that we as a people have shown the capacity to frame our concerns beyond "the bottom line." Indeed our interests need not be defined by a concern only for our immediate needs and pressing demands. The human community repeatedly manifests its readiness to sacrifice in the name of deep commitments and profound aspirations. The struggle for civil rights, planetary survival, and political liberation provide powerful testimony to the human impulse to work diligently and to take serious risks not for the short run, not for personal gains, not for partisan advantage, but for the welfare of those in faraway places and times. Surely, there are leaders and educators who fail to nourish these impulses and who instead exploit our immediate and pressing fears, but such people fail in their higher responsibility to fully grasp the depth of the human covenant to strive for a better world.

The separation of short run from long run and the division between self-interest and communal interest are false and misleading in human terms. People have a spectrum of concerns, but it is to their own interest to live under conditions in which they can respond to *all* their impulses—to survive *and* to grow; to be fed and to nourish others; to be empowered and to empower others; to succeed, but not at the expense of others; and to extend the warmth, caring, and tenderness of family beyond the hearth. Our faith is that people are not fulfilled unless and until they can contribute to a "greater good," and indeed we believe that educators must respond to this human need as much as to the human demand for survival skills. This, of course, will require a very different educational discourse than one of competition, personal achievement, and materialism.

A discourse of cultural transformation should provide us with a language with which to redirect our theoretical and applied energies from an education of privilege, advantage, and individual success to an education for compassion, cooperation, and harmony. Such a language will necessarily require a discourse that not only has roots in empirical analysis but also utilizes our images and metaphors of a language of acceptance and integration. Central to such a discourse is a vision in which wealth and power are not goals in and of themselves but are modes of creating a world of justice, love, and joy. Such a vision, deeply and profoundly grounded in our traditions, can be made possible through the creativity of contemporary genius, as energized by the future hopes of millions of people around the world.

We reject the proposition that our educational system should contribute to America's efforts to maintain worldwide military, political, and economic superiority. We therefore not only reject the notion that what is required is keener competition, but maintain that such competition will not only not solve but will actually exacerbate our crisis. We strongly believe that our crisis is not about foreign competition but about human suffering. It is not about the drive for individual success but about the pain of personal alienation, and it will not be eased by promoting power but by searching for meaning. Our nation—indeed, our planet—is surely at risk, not because our students do not know enough about computers or because they are lazy, but because we are severely lacking in a consciousness of community and meaning.

Our culture's obsession with privatism, individual success, competition, and achievement surely has promoted an astonishing amount of goods, services, and wealth. It also has facilitated greed, narcissism, cynicism, instrumentalism, and callousness. The price is well known and staggering—social inequality, injustice, and polarization; individual alienation, anomie, and despair. What we require in response to this crisis is surely not an education designed to intensify the very competition, alienation, instrumentalism, and mindlessness that is both essence and symptomatic of the crises. We require, instead, an education directed at renewing and regenerating our undernourished impulses to search for community, justice, compassion, and meaning.

Rather than panic over our dependence on other countries for cheap raw materials while desperately and futilely searching for the magic of independence, we would be better served by at least accepting the reality of our interdependence. Interdependence need not be seen as a harsh reality to be swallowed but rather as an opportunity to exercise our responsibilities to create a world of connection, sharing, and nurturing. Interdependence in our present consciousness of individualism and competition tends to be seen as an obstacle and a hindrance to personal fulfillment and, therefore, as a condition to overcome. In a consciousness of community and harmony, however, interdependence can be experienced as the human connection that enables us to celebrate both our diversity and our common destiny. Having said this, we must also be wary of the problematics of any particular orientation, for interdependence and community come not only with the promise of shared redemption but also with the danger of social division and oppressiveness. Our history and our heritage tell us of the desire to seek justice and community but also of the human proclivity to sabotage and subvert the process.

However, at this particular moment in history, we are in the midst of a crisis that reflects more of the excesses of individualism and competition than the dangers of community and sharing. Unfortunately, the present social discourse does not emphasize solidarity and community but reflects more of a commitment to nationalism and patriotism. We have drifted increasingly into a situation in which public education is seen as an ancillary and support of state policies—that is, driven by consideration of official governmental policies. As we have already indicated, the most prominent of the recent reports on public education is not entitled a *culture*, a *people*, or a *planet* at risk but a *nation* at risk. The agenda for educational policies is being increasingly shaped by politicians—the president, governors, legislators—who see educators as handmaidens of their economic and political plans.

Educational policies are seen as politically instrumental and in the service of such concerns as foreign policy, economic development, and manpower training. Educational institutions are clearly becoming less autonomous, critical, and independent and, instead, are functioning much more as bureaucratic appendages to state agencies and initiatives. We are urged, for example, to offer more work in science, mathematics, and computers, not primarily because they may be intellectually rewarding or liberating, but because they are needed to support the particular economic and political policies of the nation and the states.

There is, of course, a great deal of irony and contradiction within this discourse of nationalism, competition, success, and achievement. For example, although this educational discourse is directed toward national salvation, it is infused, not with the obligation of personal sacrifice, but with promises of significant individual benefits. It is a discourse that promises that the national policies of military and economic domination are (1) good, (2) good for the world, (3) especially good for the United States, and (4) very, very good for those individuals who make valuable contributions to these policies. In a word, there is an opportunity for some individuals to profit from national superiority. Everyone is to work very hard, compete seriously, and be well disciplined so that America will be great. Some will make a great deal of money, and everyone has a chance to avoid poverty. The particular kind of individuality being promoted is that which contributes to this competition and which resonates with particular national policies. Such a consciousness facilitates the worst dimensions of individualism, egocentrism, self-servingness, and self-protectionism. It is a consciousness concerned, not with promoting authenticity and diversity, but with self-obsessiveness and social divisiveness.

There is the further irony that the very rewards offered to those willing to commit themselves to these instrumental tasks are themselves problematic even within the dominant cultural ethic. What presumably lures people to work industriously at meaningless tasks is the attraction of discretionary money to buy pleasure—for example, through expensive vacations, travel, or material possessions. In other words, we are to work hard almost all of the time in order not to work hard some of the time. The work ethic has been replaced by the pleasure principle, and with it has come an extraordinary amount of alienation in the workplace. The bottom-line mentality involves narrowness not only of what constitutes gain but of what constitutes patience—that is, we want a lot of money and we want it now so that we can have fun now. We believe workers want and need decent salaries, but they also want and deserve meaningful work and a world where escaping is not a necessity.

What then is the vision of the dominant culture? We are asked to commit ourselves to a vision in which the United States will always be the richest and most powerful country in the world. To ensure this, we are to study a lot of science and mathematics, develop computer skills, and compete with each other in order to train an elite cadre as well as a compliant work force. As a consequence of this, we also will have a great deal of pride in our country and in ourselves, and a large number of us will be very, very rich. The very, very rich will have the opportunity to purchase and enjoy magnificent services and products, thus providing steady employment for American workers.

Educators are asked to facilitate this vision by upgrading the quality of teachers and materials, by developing more sensitive measurements of achievement and by creating powerful mechanisms of quality control. Key to this social and educational vision are discipline, hard work, high standards, and an ethic of fair competition. Educators are to level the playing field in order to be fair and also, not incidentally, to increase the pool of talent. The winners will win a great deal and the losers will presumably gain pride from participating in fair competition and learning to lose in a sportsmanlike way.

What we must confront, however, is the disturbing reality that the current vision that we have so harshly criticized as dominant is a vision that is broadly and deeply accepted by a great number of people across race, class, and gender. Even many of us who are genuinely committed to transformation find ourselves caught up in the attractions, with all their contradictions, of a cultural and educational orientation that is steeped in competition, success, and achievement. It is easy enough for any of us to rationalize and/or be distracted by the attractions and benefits of the dominant discourse.

It will also take a great deal of discipline to let go of some of the hallowed traditions of radical discourse. For what is required for a true discourse of transformation to emerge is a creative and bold criticism not only of our basic problems but also of our traditional solutions to these problems. For example, virtually all educational reformers, whether Left or Right, almost always speak to the necessity of supporting the public schools, albeit for differing reasons. Yet, it would seem to be a contradiction for those of us interested in a significantly more just society to support an institution that is as captured by policies grounded in structural inequality, division, and hierarchy as are the public schools.

We must immediately acknowledge the paradoxical and complex nature of the struggles involved in transformational movements and must reiterate our position that the struggle needs to be carried on in any number of settings. Having said this, it then becomes necessary to speak to a discourse of an agenda for educational transformation that seeks to both supplement and extend the suggestions that are in the first part of this chapter. The task of creating and supporting ways of promoting progressive and liberating classrooms and schools is certainly necessary and surely not sufficient.

While the first section of this chapter speaks more to the application of our vision to an agenda of more or less professional concerns, the second section of the chapter moves the focus of the discourse slightly by addressing ways in which professional reforms can be applied to a discourse of social and cultural transformation. While we do not accept the romantic notion that the schools can be a major agent of cultural and social transformation, neither do we accept the overdetermined notion that educators are a passive and impotent lot who merely pass on a prepackaged consciousness. Indeed, educators are well situated to observe and note how school policies come to change in relation to changing social currents. Moreover, educators, as human beings, surely have a right to engage in their profession within a context of meaning and purpose. Most important, we strongly affirm the responsibility of educators, as cultural and social leaders, to ground their expertise in a vision that represents our noblest commitments.

We say this in the knowledge, of course, that the dominant culture itself derives much of its legitimation and energies from very powerful and deeply revered traditions and images. Our task need not be daunted by this reality, for as educators we can be mindful that we too have the imagination to tap into the power of these traditions and images—not to bolster greed and domination but to enrich, inspire, and energize efforts to transcend the stagnation, vulgarity, and emptiness of the dominant culture. We believe that it is vital to reclaim those images and ideals that were once created to move us to pursue equality, freedom, community, justice, but instead have been co-opted to legitimate a culture obsessed with achievement, success, and materialism.

We add our voices to those who reject this vision and cry out in pain and outrage that what this vision has helped to do is to produce great wealth and great inequality, provide enormous privileges for some, afford considerable freedom for many, and cause immense suffering for a great many others. There are other strong and vibrant alternative traditions in the American experience that aspire to freedom, equality, and justice for all, not just for the competitive, talented, fortunate, and aggressive. We are not at all limited in our quest for meaning by images of rat races and striving to be Number One. Although much of our lore and mythology is steeped in the language of rugged individualism (e.g., the cowboy hero at home on the range), there are other powerful images of community, solidarity, and sharing (e.g., the communal Thanksgiving).

Even the maverick cowboy is a hero by virtue not only of his solitary being but of his unblinking dedication to justice, decency, and peace. The mythic figure of Abraham Lincoln also represents this struggle and quest as shown in his ability to prosecute vigorously a bloody civil war and yet at the same time to press for healing and forgiveness, providing powerful testimony to the nation's yearning for an end to its traditions of violence, conflict, and terror. The coda of Lincoln's Second Inaugural Address, although delivered over a century ago, speaks not only to our times but more importantly to our dreams, hopes, and aspirations: "With malice towards none; with charity for all; with firmness in the right, as God gives us to see the right, let us strive to finish the work we are in; to bind up the nation's wounds; to care for him who shall have borne the battle, and for his widow and his orphan—to do all which may achieve and cherish a just and lasting peace among ourselves, and with all nations."

This is a vision, not of competition, achievement, and domination, but of compassion, caring, and community. The fact that it is spoken at a time of bitter division and bloody war is not a matter of hypocrisy but a reflection of our paradoxical capacities to harbor both hatred and compassion. Indeed, it was the unanticipated pain and agony of the prolonged war that moved Lincoln in his Second Inaugural Address to go beyond a consciousness of conquest and punishment. "Neither party expected for the war the magnitude or the duration which it already attained. . . . Each looked for an earlier triumph and a result less fundamental and astounding. Both read the same Bible, and prayed to the same God; and each invoked his aid against the other. . . . The prayers of both could not be answered— that of neither has been answered fully."

Lincoln's Gettysburg Address is an eloquent restatement of our basic purpose as a nation and as a people: "It is rather for us to be here dedicated to the great tasks remaining before—that from these honored dead we take increased devotion to that cause for which they gave the last full measure of devotion: that we here highly resolve that these dead shall not have died in vain; that this nation, under God, shall have a new birth of freedom; and that government of the people, by the people, and for the people, shall not perish from the earth."

Lincoln here invokes a profoundly serious national purpose and implores us to find redemption in a horrible war that goes beyond mere victory and political gain. He reminds us that our struggle is to create a democratic structure truly responsive to the people and to freedom and that this struggle is embedded in a spiritual and moral vision. We are reminded that we are the first modern nation to establish itself within a principled framework: "a new nation conceived in liberty and dedicated to the proposition that all men are created equal." The essential themes here are of liberty, equality, and democracy within a framework of moral and spiritual impulses—themes that contrast sharply with the vulgarity of the notion that our destiny is about economic and military hegemony.

Almost four-score years after the Gettysburg Address, President Franklin Roosevelt, immersed in a global conflict and depression, provided us with further insight into the dimensions of the struggle for freedom. He proclaimed the Four Freedoms—Freedom of Speech, Freedom of Worship, Freedom from Want, and Freedom from Fear. This formulation gives us a still clearer sense of what freedom involves and, more important, gives us more understanding of the significance of the question, Under what conditions can people be free? It is surely a hollow mockery to be able to vote but not have enough food to eat, and a perversion of liberty to be able to speak our minds but not be able to stay healthy.

Freedom and equality lose their antipathy for each other when we come to accept the basic principle that we must not gain advantage at the expense of another person. We should be committed not so much to individual freedom as to the freedom of each individual. Since we are a social species, we inevitably and significantly interact with each other. In a word, we are deeply involved with each other's lives. We are profoundly interdependent, and we need to accept this not only as inevitable but as something to be cherished. We have the extraordinary opportunity to create a culture in which *all* people can be free—one in which we gladly accept the responsibility that comes with the realization that freedom is indivisible, that there is a great deal of unnecessary human suffering, and that we have the capacity to eliminate that suffering. At the very least, we must abhor and abominate gains that emerge from unnecessary human suffering rather than rationalize or deny the depth of human pain.

We can only sketch a few contexts and areas in which this dialogue might take place, as well as suggest some starting points for other action. Again, what we are putting forth here is not a program but an agenda, a framework, and a discourse. Indeed, our agenda, framework, and discourse are such that they preclude us from offering blueprints and instead impel us to create a common ground in order to work cooperatively and synergistically to develop particular policies and programs. We accept our responsibility to make affirmations and to be committed to them, and in our case we are committed to the collaborative struggle to create a compassionate, just, and peaceful world. It is this struggle that gives humanity its dignity and meaning, and it is imperative that we in no way impair anyone's opportunity or responsibility to be engaged in that struggle. This struggle goes on in a variety of settings, such as family, workplace, and schools—each important and all interrelated. Rather than engage in the simplistic notion that one or a very few of these settings are central, it is vital to reflect on the possibilities that all of them offer.

Family Values

For example, much has been said of the so-called erosion of "family values" and the breakdown of the nuclear family and how this has contributed to our social and cultural woes. Sometimes this criticism seems like another example of the "blaming the victim" syndrome, so that we must be very careful not to oversimplify the problem or to single out particular groups for blame. We must ask ourselves not only to reconsider the validity of conventional family models but more importantly to reflect on the forces that contribute to and promote family instability and deterioration. Perhaps most important, we need to remember those dimensions of family that are most conducive to stability, meaning, and coherence.

Families often are accused of not providing sufficient order, discipline, or structure, and, in the case of children in schools, of not providing an appropriate learning environment. At a deeper level, however, what the family ideally offers is unconditional love, total caring, and protective sanctuary. This is surely not to say that families do, in fact, always or even usually provide this, but only to say that this is the family ethic—this is what we demand and expect of families.

Indeed, we are very critical of families—our own and others—when they fail to nurture, support, and care. Heartless and cold parents are, rightfully, scorned and rebuffed, since parents are expected, perhaps unrealistically, to be all loving, all caring, all supportive. There are surely disagreements on what it is that constitutes loving—some say, for example, that strict discipline should be enforced as an act of love—but there is consensus at least on the basic criteria, that is, whatever we do in the family should be done in the name of love, safety, and caring. Why these efforts so often fail is obviously highly complex and extremely difficult to discern, but clearly it involves dialectical relationships among family members and the culture.

Since our culture makes such a strong connection between achievement and worth and since self-esteem and dignity are in our culture contingent on performance, families, like schools and other institutions, become sites for the struggle for dignity and worth. Parents find themselves pointing with pride (or disappointment) to their children's (even infant's) achievements, siblings develop intense rivalries for attention and affection, and intergenerational warfare erupts over the validity of the current youth culture. What is required is for families to disavow the forms of achievement, competition, and performance that produce hierarchy and conditional love and to affirm the basic, but often undernourished, human impulse to provide total support, love, and care.

Organizations often pride themselves on "being family," presumably meaning that members feel so close to each other that they are able to value caring and concern over production. The irony, of course, is that many families are less "family" in that they have taken on the consciousness of organizations emphasizing production and achievement. The poignance and tragedy of this situation emerges from the growing realization that most of us seek the comfort, support, and acceptance of the family ethic both in families *and* in the workplace. Families need to be liberated from the demands of achievement, control, and competition; and, indeed, it is the traditional family values of loving, caring, and security that can liberate the society from its impulses to be insensitive and cruel in its obsession with production, achievement, and advantage.

Let us as a society work to renew both traditional family values—compassion, nurture, unconditional love—and the tradition of our American democratic values. Democracy in America extends the family ethic of inherent dignity for each person to the political and social realms and involves consent of an informed electorate, grass-roots participation, social responsibility, and commitment to liberty and justice for all. All citizens have an opportunity to participate in this glorious and grand American experiment to infuse these spiritual and moral beliefs into our daily lives.

As was discussed in the preceding sections, business and industries can strive to involve workers in decision making, to provide work environments that are esthetically pleasing, and to offer wages and benefits that liberate employees from the fear of want. They can use their immense intellectual, creative, and material resources to maximize the quality of their goods and services, being guided less by short-term profits and more by the opportunity to contribute to a better life for all. Let us develop yardsticks that help us measure the appropriate ratio of personal profit to public benefit, for capitalism clearly has generated immense wealth and an astonishing diversity of goods and services. What is needed is the imagination and the will to channel that creativity and energy into processes that at minimum can produce this wealth without creating inequality, injustice, and unnecessary human suffering.

The Development of Community: Implications for Curriculum and Instruction

Engaging in the struggle for a more just and equitable society surely involves educational processes, both formal and informal. Schools and universities are obviously important sites for developing not only skills but also modes of relationships. They clearly are places where people, rather than angle for advantage, could study intensively and reflect upon the meaning, significance, and implication of these various modes of relationships, by examining the moral, political, and historical dimensions of social and cultural organizations. Formal educational settings provide the opportunity to reflect on these matters in the light of prior, ongoing, and collective experiences in an organized setting that itself is based on assumptions about human nature and that has its own social and political ethic. Members of our educational communities have an opportunity not only to study other communities but also to reflect on their mode of participation in their own community. Students and staff, therefore, have the opportunity to vicariously study and existentially act on their struggle to affirm their own dignity and the dignity of others and to search for ways to work as individuals in community and diversity.

This is not indoctrination but an honest effort to struggle and come to grips with the challenges required by a commitment to creating a world of love, justice, dignity, and freedom for all. This struggle clearly involves disagreement, debate, doubt, confusion, and uncertainty, but it is a struggle in which many activists, theorists, and educators have long been engaged. Human history is replete with ingenious and imaginative efforts to create caring and productive communities with liberty and justice for all. There are also existing traditions of cooperative efforts in the classroom and a significant lore of practice rooted in a pedagogy of respect, care, and affirmation of all students. Teachers know a great deal about creating a context of trust, caring, and respect in the classroom in more appropriate ways than simply imposing and requiring them.

Obviously such an educational orientation would require considerable shifts in many conventional practices and policies. It would mean, for example, seriously reexamining tracking and grading policies with a concern that these practices not be used to legitimate hierarchy and to offer affirmation for some students at the expense of others. Testing for purposes of diagnosis and feedback are vital to the educative process, but procedures can and have been devised that do not serve as masks for perpetuating privilege. We surely can agree that some students learn faster than others and that there is a continuum of talent distributed across the population, but we need to struggle with how to respond to varying educational needs without punishing people for being in particular places on these continua.

Part of our human struggle is to find ways to acknowledge differences and to celebrate talent without loss of human dignity. Moreover, when such differences are experienced as deficiencies and handicaps, they provide opportunities for others to express their compassion, interdependence, and responsibility rather than their pity. Another major challenge of human destiny is to find ways to be empathic without being distant, compassionate without being sentimental, and helpful without being patronizing. True charity does not consist of donations by the powerful to the weak but is the affirmation of interdependence and the celebration of life-affirming moments. Schools provide countless opportunities to study, experience, and experiment with these challenges, not as work or assignments, but as the opportunity to "play at life," to imagine and create better lives. Confronting the phenomenon of "handicapped" must provide an opportunity to go beyond easing the pain and distress of the victimized. We must also reflect on the cultural roots of "handicapped" and continue to struggle to create a society in which differences do not constitute deficiencies.

We surely need to learn more about the conflicts, controversies, and divisions that contribute to unnecessary human pain. We need to be informed not only by their taxonomic descriptions but by their historical, cultural, and psychological sources. Why do poverty and war exist? What explains the distribution of wealth within our community, state, and nation? How do we explain the wide variation in wealth within and among nations? Why are there such amazing and unacceptable gaps in life expectancy, medical care, educational opportunities, and political freedom? These questions by themselves constitute an entire curriculum for all of us.

Such studies will no doubt create frustration, perhaps even a sense of despair and futility. We must be careful, therefore, not to stop at analyses and descriptions of catastrophes and atrocities, but to study and reflect on our traditions of struggling to heal historic wounds and to create a consciousness of peace, dignity, and community. There is available to us a great deal of research and experience on efforts to resolve conflicts peacefully and nonviolently. Such research and experiments need to be intensified not only by academics but through the praxis of students and staff. Obviously, schools and universities are complex organizations that require an orderly process for decision making and conflict resolution. However, educational institutions have a special responsibility to model a compassionate and humane approach to these organizational require- ments. Schools and universities, staff and students, have the opportunity to study and act on their respective rights and responsibilities and to struggle to resolve their differences, not with coercion, cleverness, or bureaucratic finesse, but in ways in which dignity for all is affirmed.

Learning to live peacefully and harmoniously in community is extraor- dinarily difficult and risky. Learning requires order, civility, and respect; the pursuit of wisdom cannot thrive in an environment of fear, coercion, and violence. We are mindful that students are fully capable of being cruel and violent to each other as well as to teachers, and we must not and cannot tolerate such behavior. Students share with teachers the impulse to lash out and to hurt; yet we believe that all also share a yearning for peace and harmony. Firm as we are in the commitment to creating an environment of caring and harmony, we are under no delusions that this can be created by proclamation. The distrust, disharmony, and rage in the classrooms reflect parallel feelings in families, communities, neighborhoods, and society. Schools provide opportunities for the study of their sources and for experimentation with more appropriate ways of living together.

An education grounded in an effort to emphasize cooperation rather than competition, justice rather than privilege, and peace rather than violence perforce will be highly rigorous and creative. Creating a world of caring and compassion requires serious and deep reflection on our history, our traditions, our ideas, and our possibilities. It requires careful study of language and major modes of inquiry, as well as deep insight into social, political, and economic theories and institutions. It surely requires the cultivation of the human spirit, the nourishment of imagination, and the impulse for self-expression. A culture of freedom for all would include an opportunity for study and research for the sheer joy of it for all who share this interest.

The development of an appropriate pedagogy certainly will require further research and experimentation, but such efforts can proceed from existing knowledge. We are not at all talking about "innovations" in the sense of variations within the existing system, since we are convinced that a fundamental restructuring and transformation of mainstream edu- cational practices is required. However, the direction of the transforma- tion that we are suggesting, although radical, is not new since it is rooted in our oldest, most revered traditions and our most cherished aspirations.

We need renewed thinking, ideas, images, metaphors, and practices, and we are blessed with enormous resources for this task. We have not only rich traditions and energizing images, but extraordinary talent, untapped creativity, and a restless, unfulfilled energy to create a world of compassion, justice, and joy. This task is indeed daunting, but the failure to engage in it is even more terrifying.

A DISCOURSE OF TRANSFORMATION: GENERATING A "SUBLIME MADNESS"

Listing problems is easy and suggesting satisfying solutions is exhilarating, but contemplating the reality of these obstacles and resistances is sobering. Although we live in the hope that our lives must and can be improved and in the faith that the educative process is central to that possibility, the horrors and catastrophes of the twentieth century have turned optimism, hope, and possibility into endangered concepts. Perhaps the most severe casualty for progressive educators has been the collapse of the promise represented in the broad vision of Deweyan education, grounded in the energy and optimism of traditional American revolutionary consciousness as informed by its robust and no-nonsense pragmatism. The so-called modern project of creating a more just and peaceful world through rational and scientific discourse not only has badly foundered but, even more devastatingly, has seriously eroded confidence and trust as we increasingly fester in frustration, distrust, pessimism, anger, and powerlessness, if not cynicism and hostility. The proposition that poetry, hope, and reason died at Auschwitz and Hiroshima remains persuasive and pervasive.

In fact, it is much easier to make a rational case for not pursuing such elusive and utopian goals. The culture is not clear on its goals. We are disillusioned by failures of various gods, visions, and programs. We have witnessed and experienced limitless cruelty, injustice, pain, terror, and destruction—and almost all of it in the name of some lofty and noble ideal. Our existence is fragile, and we often feel, in John Donne's phrase, "alone and afraid in a world I never made." When we contemplate change, we face enormous resistance, apathy, or divisiveness in some combination. When we work for change, we face the risk of losing not only what we seek but what we already have, since there is very good reason indeed to despair, ample evidence of futility, and an abundance of ammunition for cynicism.

The tragic impotence of American educators in responding to these crises resides partly, we believe, in two denials. The first is a denial of reality on the part of mainstream educators who refuse to recognize the severity of our cultural and social crisis and its relation to education. This blindness, however unintended, has the effect of sustaining the crisis and draining energy away from the struggle for cultural transformation. The agenda for reform developed by mainstream educators certainly involves some attainable and attractive projects, but their very modesty represents a denial of the profundity of the issues.

There is, however, another denial that contributes both to the timidity of the reformers and the despair of the transformers. This denial concerns the inability of many educational critics to relent on their faith in the very processes (rationality, technology, dialogues, objectivity, etc.) that went up in the flames, smoke, and ashes of Auschwitz and Hiroshima. This stubborn reliance on analysis, reflection, and critique is not only anachronistic but increasingly ironic since this same academic tradition has helped make rationality, objectivity, and certainty highly problematic. We are encouraged however by the increasing recognition among such critics of the need to probe deeper than the intellect to find that which impels us to engage in the struggle for a better world.

As educators we find ourselves, therefore, in the paradoxical situation of urging ourselves to be rational and to have hope when there is little reason to have hope, and to believe sanity will prevail when there is little reason to believe it will. Indeed, we acknowledge, even as we present an agenda for educational change, that this or any agenda will be meaningless and sterile unless it is enveloped in a spirit that energizes us to engage in such risky, if not dubious and fool-hardy, activities. Perhaps the most important part of this agenda, then, is to participate in efforts to facilitate the process by which we can be open to creating and receiving such energy.

As we have indicated, the theme that runs through our vision is a commitment to creating a world of caring and compassion. We believe that humans have a deep capacity and impulse for caring but that such energies are not being nourished and instead are being diverted into self-serving and individualistic channels. Although the current psychological discourse tends to posit a model of human nature that stresses selfishness or self-serving altruism, we must struggle against this as we would against any hegemonic structure. Indeed, some psychologists are involved in challenging the conventional professional wisdom about the human capacity for caring and empathy. For example, C. Daniel Batson, in reviewing the pertinent literature, concludes:

I believe the evidence is very strong indeed that the ultimate goals of empathetically aroused helpers is to increase the welfare of the person for whom they feel empathy, as the empathy-altruism hypothesis claims. If the empathy-altruism hypothesis is true, then I think we must radically revise our views of the human capacity for caring. For to say that we are capable of being altruistically motivated is to say that we can care about others' welfare as a terminal not just an instrumental value. We can seek their welfare for their sakes, and not simply for our own. If this is true, then we are far more social animals than our psychological theories, including our most social-psychological theories, would leave us to believe.[14]

Such probing, significant as it is, does not fully satisfy since it persists in seeing humans as "animals" and, hence, begs the far more vital question of the mystery of human existence. Why do humans care for others? Why do they risk their lives, and why do they ask such questions? How is it that we venture to challenge and deny our apparent limitations, and what impels us to go beyond them, that is, to seek transcendence? Educators concerned with changing consciousness cannot avoid such questions, nor can they afford not to engage in such discourse. The awe-inspiring mystery of the universe—and, with it, the mystery of human existence—are eternally present, and our capacity and propensity to ignore them are as perilous as they are astonishing. Dorothee Soelle, in her efforts to forge a theology that enhances Marxist and feminist principles, chides those who participate in such avoidances:

Only nonorganic intellectuals or theoreticians feel themselves superior to religion; only these white, male, city-bred, culturally bourgeois, educated, abstract beings regard religion as something inferior and connect it with the sex and color of the powerless, or generally with unenlightened phases of human history. Any self-critical understanding of Marxism, on the contrary, must today admit that atheism has affinities to a certain class that overvalues reason, achievement, productivity, and progress.[15]

She goes on to challenge the conventional wisdom of the Left that meaning is humanly constructed or, as she puts it, "The experience of God as present in this life is a way that is opposed to the modern, rationalistic way of thinking whereby it is we who create life's meaning."[16] Her thinking not only reopens the questions but helps us to see the problematics of a struggle framed primarily in political terms. In a passage on the Marxist philosopher Milan Machovec, she characterizes him as one who "witnesses to a knowledge that life is not made, but given to us. . . . The fundamental experience is that it is not I who create my life, and therefore I cannot take yours away from you either. . . . There is a kind of reverence that preserves this point: that human dignity is not created by us, but exists before us. It is not derivable from anything else and does not depend on someone else's agreement—the state's, let us say."[17]

We need language and images that can put us in touch with that force that "exists before us" and that engenders human dignity. That force or spirit is that which explains courage, endurance, and hope, and it is to that spirit that we look to energize and sustain our continuing efforts in this time of crisis. We need an energy that allows us to work for transformation in the face of a strong unlikelihood of success. We also need a spirit that can connect the concrete and specific things we do with the larger and broader principles and goals that inform them. We require the courage to act when we are fearful, when we are not sure what to do, and when we fail. We need the strength to continue the struggle when we are outnumbered, outmaneuvered, and written off. We need a spirit to create a deep bond with our colleagues and companions who have struggled before us and who will continue after we are gone. In the words of Reinhold Niebuhr, we need the faith that "sees good in spite of evil and evil in spite of good and in this way we can avoid both sentimentality and despair." It is a spirit that can connect the mysterious with the real, the whole with the particular, the sacred with the secular, and the eternal with the present.

We see perhaps the best possibilities for such a discourse in the work of a number of modern theologians who strive to renew and reinvigorate the messages of the biblical prophets. Such work can be seen in Liberation Theology and in such theorists as Matthew Fox, Dorothee Soelle, Cornel West, and Sharon Welch. These writers, in particular, have done a great deal of work in addressing our political and social crisis in the wake of the devastating effects of moral relativism, intellectual uncertainty, and cultural fragmentation. Although fully acknowledging the depth of these problems, these writers continue to find hope and energy in their connection to a deeper faith.

Cornel West has been especially helpful in developing a discourse of hope and commitment in a time of despair and uncertainty. West is quite clear that his own orientation, what he calls prophetic pragmatism, is rooted in his experience as an African-American reared in the traditions of Christianity as informed by Marxist analysis and American pragmatism. In his embrace of these traditions, he is careful to note which dimensions he accepts and which he rejects and is able to craft an orientation that has particular meaning to him but is also provocative and evocative enough to be helpful to others with varying and different experiences. This is to say that although West's orientation may not be appropriate to all, neither is it so particularistic that it can be seen as merely "interesting" and idiosyncratic. We believe that West's efforts provide a very helpful model for those who seek to ground a political and moral orientation in a larger, more cosmic framework.

West sees the world as a paradoxical one where our treasured traditions can liberate as well as oppress, where utopian dreams are necessary but ultimately futile; and where people have both romantic and tragic perceptions. He rejects both the grand theories of idealism and the modest agendas of liberalism. West confronts the contradictions of human consciousness, believing that cruelty, cowardice, and moral courage coexist in all of us. Although he does not flinch from his tragic view of human history, neither does he allow himself and others the luxury of despair: "The brutalities and atrocities in human history, the genocidal attempts in this century, and the present-day barbarities require that those who accept the progressive and prophetic designations put forth some conceptions of the tragic."[18]

West believes that his Christian faith empowers him (and others) to respond to the tragedy of this-worldly life by providing solace and meaning to the existential fear and dread of death, loss, and meaninglessness. It is, according to West, the promise of "ultimate salvation" (eternal redemption) that can free humanity to engage in the well-nigh hopeless and interminable struggle against the forces of evil, a struggle that affords the possibility for "penultimate salvation" (political and social liberation). This blend of ultimate hope and intermediate possibility provides a framework that embraces the nitty-gritty of current struggle with the profundity of ultimate meaning. It is a framework that combines irrational hope with a shrewd sense of human limitations, that allows for the coexistence of energy and doubts, and that "denies Sisyphean pessimism and utopian perfectionism." To West, prophetic pragmatism is

the possibility of human progress and the human possibility of paradise. [At its center is a] struggle guided by a democratic and liberation vision, sustained by moral courage, and existential integrity, and tempered by the recognition of human finitude and frailty. It calls for utopian energies and tragic actions, energies and actions that yield permanent and perennial revolutionary, rebellious, and reformist strategies that oppose the status quos of our day. . . . Prophetic pragmatism attempts to keep alive the sense of alternative ways of life and of struggle based on the best of the past. In this sense, the praxis of prophetic pragmatism is *tragic action with revolutionary interest, usually reformist consequences, and always visionary outlook.*[19] (Emphasis added)

Again, West emphasizes how his own religious convictions influence his views on prophetic pragmatism but does not see religious orientation as a barrier to affirming such a consciousness: "The mark of the prophet is to speak the truth in love with courage—come what may. Prophetic pragmatism . . . neither requires a religious foundation nor entails a religious perspective, yet [it] . . . is compatible with certain religious outlooks."[20]

Clearly, not everyone can be comfortable with the images of Christianity or, for that matter, of any organized religion. However, the reality remains that as a people we hunger for meaning and strive to connect the particulars of our daily lives with timeless images. We urge educators committed to a life of peace, love, and justice to respond to this human necessity by engaging in the most basic of all discourses, that is, that which addresses the mystery of our origin, purpose, and destiny. Our views on these questions will clearly shape our responses to the demands, challenges, and opportunities that face us as educators and citizens in this moment of intense danger.

It, therefore, becomes possible rationally to engage in an agenda of education and social transformation only when we can be inspired to do so, that is, only when we can be captured by a spirit that turns such a dubious and risky engagement into a deeply and profoundly moving imperative. That this is basically an irrational act was recognized by Reinhold Niebuhr, who, writing on the eve of World War II about those who would be involved in such a project, said that "justice cannot be approximated if the hope of its perfect realization does not generate a sublime madness in the soul. Nothing but such madness will do battle with malignant power and 'spiritual wickedness in high places.' [Such an] illusion is dangerous because it encourages terrible fanaticism. It must therefore be brought under the control of reason. One can only hope that reason will not destroy it before its work is done."[21]

NOTES

1. See, for example, the excellent analysis of reading test scores in Ira Shor, *Culture Wars: Schools and Society in the Conservative Restoration* (Boston: Routledge, 1986).

2. Christopher Lasch, *The Minimal Self* (New York: Norton, 1984), pp. 95–96.

3. Robert B. Reich the secretary of labor in the Clinton administration, is one of the best known of those advocating such a strategy. See, for example, Robert B. Reich, *The Work of Nations* (New York: Knopf, 1991).

4. See, for example, Thomas J. Peters, *In Search of Excellence: Lessons from America's Best-Run Companies* (New York: Warner Books, 1986). See also, Martin Carnoy and Derek Shearer, *Economic Democracy* (New York: Sharpe, 1980).

5. "Workers' Technology Bill of Rights," *Democracy* (Spring 1983). We are disregarding the more obviously manipulative and cooptive aspects of these job reforms.

6. "Report of the National Commission on the Skills of the American Work Force," *Education Week* 9, no. 39 (June 1990), pp. 41–43.

7. Alvin Toffler, *Powershift* (excerpted in *Newsweek*, October 15, 1990, pp. 86–92).

8. "Technology and the American Transition" (Report by the Office to Technology Assessment), *Education Week* 7, no. 34 (May 1988), p. 1.

9. Toffler, *Powershift*.

10. Geoff Mulgan, "The Buck Stops Here," *Marxism Today* (September 1990), pp. 22–27.

11. Kevin Phillips, *Post-Conservative America* (New York: Random House, 1982).

12. Peter Sloterdijk, *Critique of Cynical Reason* (Minneapolis: University of Minnesota Press, 1987).

13. In developing this view, the authors have been influenced by the critique of the Left and the discussions of the lower-middle-class culture found in Christopher Lasch, *The True and Only Heaven: Progress and Its Critics* (New York: Norton, 1991).

14. C. Daniel Batson, "How Social an Animal: The Human Capacity for Caring," *American Psychologist* 45, no. 3 (1990), pp. 336–46.

15. Dorothee Soelle, *The Window of Vulnerability* (Minneapolis: Fortress Press, 1990), p. 33.

16. Ibid., p. 37.

17. Ibid., pp. 37–38.

18. Cornel West, *The American Evasion of Philosophy* (Madison: University of Wisconsin Press, 1989), p. 228.

19. Ibid., p. 229.

20. Ibid.

21. Reinhold Niebuhr, *Moral Man, Immoral Society* (New York: Scribners 1960), p. 277.

Selected Bibliography

Apple, Michael W. "Systems Management and the Ideology of Control." In *Ideology and Curriculum*, pp. 105–22. London: Routledge & Kegan Paul, 1979.

Apple, Michael W. *Education and Power*. Boston: Routledge, 1982.

Apple, Michael W. "The Politics of Common Sense: Schooling, Populism and the New Right." *Strategies* 2 (1989), pp. 24–44.

Apple, Michael W. *Teachers and Texts*. New York: Routledge, 1988.

Aronowitz, Stanley. "The New Conservative Discourse." In *Education and the American Dream*, ed. Harvey Holtz, Irwin Marcus, Jim Dougherty, Judy Michaels, and Rick Peduzzi. Granby, Mass.: Bergin & Garvey, 1989.

Aronowitz, Stanley, and Henry Giroux. *Education under Siege*. South Hadley, Mass.: Bergin & Garvey, 1985.

Bahro, Rudolf. *The Alternatives in Eastern Europe*. London: NLB, 1978.

Barber, Benjamin. "The Philosopher Despot." In *Criticism* (Fall 1988), pp. 61–65.

Bastian, Ann, Norman Fruchter, Marilyn Gittell, Colin Greer, and Kenneth Haskins. *Choosing Equality: The Case for Democratic Schools*. Philadelphia: Temple University Press, 1986.

Batson, C. Daniel. "How Social an Animal: The Human Capacity for Caring." *American Psychologist* 45, no. 3 (1990), pp. 336–46.

Belenky, Mary Field, Blythe McVicker Clinchy, Nancy Rule Goldberger, and Jill Mattuck Tarule. *Women's Ways of Knowing*. New York: Basic Books, 1986.

Bell, Daniel. *The Cultural Contradictions of Capitalism*. New York: Basic Books, 1976.

Bellah, Robert, et al. *Habits of the Heart*. Berkeley: University of California Press, 1985.

Bennett, William J. Quoted in *Education Week* 7 (January 1988), p. 27.

Bennett, William J. *James Madison High School: A Curriculum for American Students*. Washington, D.C.: U.S. Department of Education, 1989.

Berger, John. *And Our Faces, My Heart, Brief as Photos*. New York: Pantheon, 1984.

Berman, Marshall. *All That Is Solid Melts into Air: The Experience of Modernity*. New York: Simon & Schuster, 1982.

Berman, Marshall. "Why Modernism Still Matters." *Tikkun* 4, no. 1 (January/February 1989), pp. 11–14, 81–86.

Bloom, Allan. *The Closing of the American Mind*. New York: Simon & Schuster, 1987.

Boggs, Carl. *Social Movements and Political Power*. Philadelphia: Temple University Press, 1986.

Bowles, Samuel, and Herbert Gintis. *Democracy and Capitalism*. New York: Basic Books, 1986.

Bowers, C. A. "The Reproduction of Technological Consciousness." *Teachers College Record* 83 (Summer 1982), pp. 529–57.

Bowers, C. A. *Elements of a Post-Liberal Theory of Education*. New York: Teachers College Press, 1987.

Capra, Fritjof, and Charlene Spretnak. *Green Politics*. New York: Dutton, 1984.

Carnoy, Martin, and Henry Levin. *Schooling and Work in the Democratic State*. Stanford, Calif.: Stanford University Press, 1985.

Castells, Manuel. *The Economic Crisis of American Society*. Princeton, N.J.: Princeton University Press, 1989.

Cloward, Richard A., and Francis F. Piven. *The New Class War*. New York: Pantheon, 1982.

Coleman, James, Thomas Hoffer, and Sally Kilgore. *Public and Private Schools*. Washington, D.C.: National Center for Education Statistics, 1981.

Coons, John E., and Stephen D. Sugarman. *Education by Choice*. Berkeley: University of California Press, 1978.

Cox, Harvey. *Religion in the Secular City*. New York: Simon & Schuster, 1984.

Davis, Mike. *Prisoners of the American Dream*. London: Vergo, 1986.

Erkel, R. Todd. "The Birth of a Movement." *Networker* (May/June 1990), pp. 26–35.

Everhart, Robert. *Reading, Writing, and Resistance*. Boston: Routledge, 1983.

Fine, Michelle. *Framing Dropouts*. Albany: State University of New York, 1991.

Fordham, Signithia. "Racelessness and Facts in Black Students' School Success: Pragmatic Strategy or Pyrrhic Victory." *Harvard Educational Review* 58, no. 1 (February 1988), pp. 54–84.

Foucault, Michel. *Power/Knowledge*. New York: Random House, 1981.

Fraser, Nancy. *Unruly Practices*. Minneapolis: University of Minnesota Press, 1989.

Giroux, Henry A. "Schooling and the Culture of Positivism." *Educational Theory* 29, no. 4 (1979), pp. 83–97.

Giroux, Henry A. *Theory and Resistance: A Pedagogy for the Opposition*. South Hadley, Mass.: Bergin & Garvey, 1983.

Giroux, Henry A. *Teachers as Intellectuals*. Granby, Mass.: Bergin & Garvey, 1988.

Gouldner, Alvin W. *The Future of the Intellectuals and the Rise of the New Class*. New York: Seabury, 1979.

Greene, Maxine. *Landscapes of Learning*. New York: Teachers College Press, 1978.

Grossberg, Lawrence. "Rocking with Reagan, or the Mainstreaming of Postmodernity." *Cultural Critique* 10 (1988), pp. 123–49.

Habermas, Jurgen. *Legitimation Crisis*. Boston: Beacon, 1975.

Hall, Stuart. "The Great Moving Right Show." In *The Politics of Thatcherism* by Stuart Hall and Martin Jacques, p. 30. London: Lawrence and Wishart, 1983.

Hall, Stuart. "Thatcher's Lessons." *Marxism Today* (March 1989), pp. 20–27.

Hall, Stuart and David Held. "Lefts and Rights." *Marxism Today* (June 1989), pp. 16–23.

Harrington, Michael. *Decade of Decision*. New York: Simon & Schuster, 1980.

Harrington, Michael. *The New American Poverty*. New York: Holt, Rinehart & Winston, 1984.

Hartsock, Nancy. "Foucault on Power: A Theory for Women." In *Feminism/Postmodernism*, ed. Linda J. Nicholson, pp. 157–75. New York: Routledge, 1990.

Hirsch, E. D. *Cultural Literacy*. Boston: Houghton Mifflin, 1987.

Jacoby, Russell. *The Last Intellectuals*. New York: Farrar Straus & Giroux, 1987.

Kaplan, Anne E. *Rocking Around the Clock: Music, Television, Postmodernism and Consumer Culture*. New York: Methuen, 1987.

Katznelson, Ira, and Margaret Weir. *Schooling for All*. New York: Basic Books, 1985.

Kellner, Douglas. "Reading Images Critically Towards a Postmodern Pedagogy." *Journal of Education* 170, no. 3 (1988), pp. 31–52.

Kellner, Douglas. *Critical Theory, Marxism and Modernity*. Baltimore: Johns Hopkins University Press, 1989.

Kirst, Michael W. "Who Should Control the Schools? Reassessing Current Policies." In *Schooling for Tomorrow*, ed. Thomas J. Sergiovanni and John H. Moore, pp. 62–88. Boston: Allyn & Bacon, 1989.

Kliebard, Herbert M. *The Struggle for the American Curriculum, 1893–1958*. Boston: Routledge, 1986.

Kozol, Jonathan. *The Night Is Dark and I Am Far from Home*. Boston: Houghton Mifflin, 1975.

Kuttner, Robert. "The Declining Middle." *Atlantic Monthly* 252, no. 1 (July 1983), pp. 60–72.

Lanier, Judith E., and May W. Sedlak. "Teacher Efficacy and Quality Schooling." In *Schooling for Tomorrow*, ed. Thomas J. Sergiovanni and John H. Moore. Boston: Allyn & Bacon, 1989.

Lasch, Christopher. *The Minimal Self*. New York: Norton, 1984.

Lasch, Christopher. "What's Wrong with the Right." *Tikkun* 1, no. 1 (1986), pp. 23–29.

Leadbetter, Charlie. "Power to the People." *Marxism Today* (October 1988), pp. 14–19.

Lerner, Michael. "A New Paradigm for Liberals: The Primacy of Ethics and Emotions." *Tikkun* 2, no. 1 (1987), pp. 22–28, 132–38.

Lerner, Michael. "The Pro-Flag and Anti-Abortion Pathology." *Tikkun* 4, no. 5 (September/October 1989), pp. 8–9.

Marcuse, Herbert. *One-Dimensional Men*. Boston: Beacon, 1984.

Melman, Seymour. *Profits without Production*. New York: Knopf, 1983.

Meyerson, Harold. "Government as Gesture." *L. A. Weekly* 12, no. 16 (March 23–29, 1990), pp. 59–63.

McLaren, Peter. "Broken Dreams, False Promises, and the Decline of Public Schooling." *Journal of Education* 170, no. 1 (1988), pp. 41–65.

McLaren, Peter. *Life in Schools*. New York: Longman, 1989.

McLaren, Peter. "Critical Pedagogy, Multiculturalism, and the Politics of Risk and Resistance: A Response to Kelly and Portelli." *Journal of Education* 133, no. 3 (1991), p. 38.

Moberg, David. "Choice No Easy Remedy for American School Ills." *In These Times* 13, no. 23 (May 15–21, 1991), p. 3.

Moberg, David. "For Better Education, It's a Choice Combination." *In These Times* 15, no. 24 (May 22–28, 1991), pp. 8–9.

Moberg, David. "Decline and Inequality after the Great U-Turn." *In These Times* (May 27–June 9, 1992), p. 6.

Moore, Suzanne. "Gender, Post-Modern Style." *Marxism Today* (May 1990), p. 91.

Mouffe, Chantal, and Ernest Laclau. *Hegemony and Socialist Strategy.* London: Vergo, 1985.

Mulgan, Geoff. "The Buck Stops Here." *Marxism Today* (September 1990), pp. 22–27.

Niebuhr, Reinhold. *Moral Man, Immoral Society.* New York: Scribners, 1960.

Ogbu, John V. *Minority Education and Caste.* New York: Academic Press, 1978.

Omi, Michael, and Howard Winant. *Racial Formation in the United States.* New York: Routledge, 1986.

Peller, Gary. "Creation, Evolution and the New South." *Tikkun* 2, no. 5 (November/December 1987), pp. 72–76.

Phillips, Kevin. *Post-Conservative America.* New York: Random House, 1982.

Pinar, William, ed. *Curriculum Theorizing: The Reconceptualists.* Berkeley, Calif.: McCutchan, 1975.

Popkewitz, Thomas P. *A Political Sociology of Educational Reform.* New York: Teachers College Press, 1991.

Poster, Mark, ed. *Jean Baudrillard: Selected Writings.* Stanford, Calif.: Stanford University Press, 1988.

Postman, Neil. *Amusing Ourselves to Death.* New York: Viking, 1985.

Purpel, David E. *The Moral and Spiritual Crisis in Education: A Curriculum for Social Justice.* Granby, Mass.: Bergin & Garvey, 1988.

Ravitch, Dave. *The Troubled Crusade.* New York: Basic Books, 1983.

Ravitch, Dave, and Chester E. Finn, Jr. *What Do Our 17-Year-Olds Know?* New York: Harper & Row, 1987.

Ryan, William. *Blaming the Victim.* New York: Vintage, 1976.

Schlafly, Phyllis. "Education, the Family and Traditional Values." In *Education and the American Dream,* ed. Harvey Holtz, Irwin Marcus, Jim Dougherty, Judy Michaels, and Rick Peduzzi, pp. 21–29. Granby, Mass.: Bergin & Garvey, 1989.

Sergiovanni, Thomas J., and John H. Moore, eds. *Schooling for Tomorrow: Directing Reforms to Issues That Count.* Boston: Allyn & Bacon, 1989.

Shapiro, H. Svi. "The Making of Conservative Educational Policy." *Urban Education* 17, no. 2 (July 1982), pp. 233–52.

Shapiro, H. Svi. *Between Capitalism and Democracy: Educational Policy and the Crisis of the Welfare State.* Westport, Conn.: Bergin & Garvey, 1990.

Shor, Ira. *Critical Teaching and Everyday Life.* Chicago: University of Chicago Press, 1987.

Shor, Ira. *Culture Wars: Schools and Society in the Conservative Restoration.* Boston: Routledge, 1986.

Sidel, Ruth. *Women and Children Last.* New York: Viking, 1986.

Sivard, Ruth. *World Military and Social Expenditures.* New York: World Priorities, 1985.

Sizer, Theodore. *Horace's Compromise.* Boston: Houghton Mifflin, 1984.

Sloterdijk, Peter. *Critique of Cynical Reason.* Minneapolis: University of Minnesota Press, 1987.

Smyth, John. "Teachers-as-Intellectuals in a Critical Pedagogy of Schooling." *Education and Society* 5 (1987).

Soelle, Dorothee. *The Window of Vulnerability.* Minneapolis: Fortress Press, 1990.

Spring, Joel. *The Sorting Machine*. New York: McKay, 1976.

Spring, Joel. *American Education: An Introduction to Social and Political Aspects*. New York: Longman, 1985.

Starr, Jerold. "The Great Textbook War." In *Education and the American Dream*, ed. Harvey Holtz, Irwin Marcus, Jim Dougherty, Judy Michaels, and Rick Peduzzi, pp. 96–109. Granby, Mass.: Bergin & Garvey, 1989.

Taylor, Ella. *Prime-Time Families*. Berkeley: University of California Press, 1989.

Thurrow, Lester. "A Surge in Inequality." *Scientific American* 256, no. 5 (May 1987), pp. 30–37.

Toffler, Alvin. *Powershift* (excerpted in *Newsweek*, October 15, 1990, pp. 86–92).

Walker, Pat, ed. *Between Labor and Capital*. Boston: South End Press, 1979.

Welch, Sharon. *Communities of Resistance and Solidarity*. New York: Orbis, 1985.

West, Cornel. *Beyond the Fragments*. Grand Rapids, Mich.: Wm. B. Eerdsman, 1988.

West, Cornel. *The American Evasion of Philosophy*. Madison: University of Wisconsin Press, 1989.

Will, George F. "School Standards Keep Getting Lower." *Greensboro News and Record*, June 10, 1991, p. 12.

Willis, Paul. *Learning to Labor*. Lexington, Mass.: Heath, 1977.

Index

About the Authors

DAVID E. PURPEL is Professor in the Department of Educational Leadership and Cultural Foundations at the University of North Carolina, Greensboro. He is the author of *The Moral and Spiritual Crisis in Education* (Bergin & Garvey, 1988).

SVI SHAPIRO is Professor and Chairman in the Department of Educational Leadership and Cultural Foundations at the University of North Carolina, Greensboro, and the author of *Between Capitalism and Democracy: Educational Policy and the Crisis of the Welfare State* (Bergin & Garvey, 1990).

ISBN 0-89789-416-2

HARDCOVER BAR CODE

Date Due

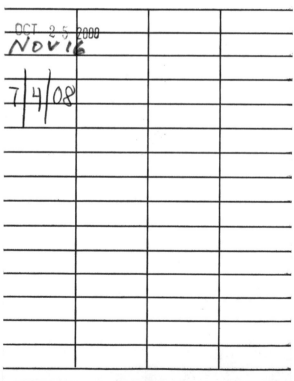

OCT 25 2000 NOV 16			
7/4/08			